Stupid Bankers

The world's worst banking disasters revealed

Paul Kilduff

First published in 2022.

Copyright © Paul Kilduff 2022.

Paul Kilduff has asserted his right under the
Copyright, Designs and Patents Act, 1988, to be
identified as the author of this work.

A CIP catalogue record for this book is available
from the British Library.

Available in paperback, hardcover and eBook.

Paperback ISBN: 979-8-84666-230-8
Hardcover ISBN: 979-8-35186-202-6

Paperback ASIN: B0BB5RQMBX
Hardcover ASIN: B0BF2ZR288
eBook ASIN: B0BDN228V4

ABOUT THE AUTHOR

Paul Kilduff was born in Dublin. He graduated from University College Dublin with a Bachelor of Commerce and later qualified as a Chartered Accountant. He spent six years working with international banks in the City of London and returned to live and work in Dublin. He has worked with HSBC, Bank of Ireland, Bank of America, Barclays and Citibank, and has written four financial thrillers and three non-fiction travel books. Stupid Bankers is his first non-fiction financial book. Search for his books on Google, Amazon or LinkedIn.

Also by Paul Kilduff:

Fiction:
Square Mile
The Dealer
The Frontrunner
The Headhunter

Non-fiction:
Ruinair
Ruinairski
Plane Speaking

For Gerry Kilduff,
a wise banker.
1935-2021.

CONTENTS

'My worry is that the bankers were so arrogant and stupid they might bring us all down.'

Alistair Darling,
Chancellor of the UK Exchequer,
Back from the Brink: 1,000 Days at No 11.

PREFACE

THERE are many smart, intelligent and successful bankers but writing a book about these individuals, or reading such a book, would not be as entertaining or as informative as a book about the most stupid bankers of all time. I have long been fascinated by these latter types of bankers – the ones who act like lemmings desperately in search of a cliff edge.

This book is decades in the making. When Nick Leeson in Singapore sank Barings Bank in 1995, I was an internal auditor with HSBC in London. Whilst auditing the bank's office in Calgary, Canada, I saw The Wall Street Journal headline in the hotel lobby: 'Collapse of Barings - Young Trader's $29 Billion Bet Brings Down a Venerable Firm.'

For the next seven gripping days, the world searched for Leeson in South East Asia. The only thing more enjoyable than a stupid banker, is one on the run from international law enforcement.

I had a personal escape of sorts in the collapse of Barings. Two years prior, I applied for a job in the internal audit department of the prestigious bank. I was interviewed in their Bishopsgate office by an elderly gentleman who wore a three-piece suit, complete with a pocket watch on a gold chain. We sat in a room with polished mahogany tables, dark green carpet and fox hunting paintings on the walls.

Neither of us evidently impressed the other and nothing came of my interview. But if I had been successful in my application, I could have been the internal auditor interviewing Leeson on the floor of SIMEX, and failing to uncover his web of lies and deception.

HSBC dispatched me eastwards on Virgin Atlantic to ensure they did not have a similar black hole in their Singaporean futures broker. Fortunately, they did not. I found nothing of concern in the office, because there was nothing to be found. They didn't even have an error account.

One evening I had a cold beer in Harry's Bar on Boat Quay, where Leeson sometimes drank, and wondered if there was a book to be written about Leeson, but at the time he was the only high-profile case of such banker incompetence.

Later, when writing financial thrillers, I received the following email: 'I read your book 'The Headhunter' with great interest. I thought it was fantastic. My own name is synonymous with part of the banking industry and I have always wanted to expand upon my own piece of literary non-fiction work 'Rogue Trader' but I have had my hands tied until now. I wonder if a collaboration on a book would be of interest to you? Regards, Nick Leeson.'

I didn't believe it was Leeson, but it was indeed the rogue trader himself. Again, I thought there might be a book to be written, this time with Leeson, but we could not envisage the book and nothing came of our correspondence. Fortunately, Leeson was the first in a series of major banking blunders in the globe's financial capitals and this book was born.

There is an innate risk with a trader in a bank who makes a small trading loss, to try to hide that loss, to trade their way to a profit, to double up on their trades, but eventually they usually succeed in digging a bigger hole for themselves.

Some bankers are too clueless to even hold down a job in a bank. After Toshihide Iguchi lost $1.1 billion trading treasury bonds and notes at Daiwa Bank in New York, he admitted: 'In retrospect, I was a complete amateur. I was in the market without grasping the essence of it.'

Kweku Adoboli was out of his depth on a trading desk at UBS in London when he lost £1.4 billion: 'Our book was massive - a tiny mistake could lead to huge losses. We were losing so much money it was mental. We were two kids trying to figure how this could work. We had 30 months of experience between us. I had imposter syndrome every day.'

Joseph Jett went one better at Kidder Peabody in New York. Not content with losing millions of dollars trading treasury bonds and strips, he conjured up $350 million of phantom trading profits, which sadly never existed.

Sadder still is the realisation that it is only the loss-making bankers who become public knowledge. A stupid banker who makes a windfall profit will never appear in the media.

Jérôme Kerviel, who lost €4.9 billion gambling on European stock market futures at Société Générale in Paris, agreed: 'Rogue trading happens all the time, it's just that, if they lose, they quietly get fired. If they win, no one cares. Do you imagine we would be talking here if I made €4.9 billion? Have you ever heard about any rogue trader that has won?'

Far worse are those stupid Chief Executive Officers who lead their banks to strategic destruction. Amongst them are James Cayne at Bear Stearns, Richard Fuld at Lehman Brothers, Fred Goodwin at the Royal Bank of Scotland and Sean FitzPatrick at Anglo Irish Bank.

These stale pale males dominated their organisations for decades in the absence of proper corporate governance, they steered their banks into highly-risky trading and lending activities, they failed to diversify, or to adequately capitalise or fund their banks, and when the financial crisis of 2008 arrived, their rotten banks duly imploded.

There is room too in this book for those stupid bankers who work for equally stupid bank management. Howie Hubler 'lost' $9.4 billion trading at Morgan Stanley in New York and Bruno Iksil 'lost' $6.2 billion trading at J.P. Morgan Chase in London, whilst their management were aware of their trading positions and strategy, yet they failed to halt the bankers. Neither trader was ever prosecuted for any offence.

When John Rusnak lost $690 million trading foreign exchange badly at Allfirst in Baltimore, I was already researching the dirty deeds and odd personas of rogue traders for a financial thriller.

The more I researched about the bankers lives and actions, the more surprised I became. None more so, than when disgraced banker Peter Young of Deutsche Morgan Grenfell arrived for his City of London court appearance wearing a dress, wig, heels, make-up and red lipstick.

Some of what I uncovered in my research was too improbable or fantastical to include in a fictional thriller. No one would believe it could ever happen. I would stretch the bounds of credulity. I concluded that in the world of bankers, fact is often stranger than fiction.

I hope that you the reader agree that the following tales of thirteen particularly stupid bankers supports that informed conclusion.

*

1 – FALSE PROFITS

'I was a formidable foe because I didn't care about winning friends. I wasn't about to accommodate anyone, to compromise my methods or objectives. I knew I had enemies. I also knew they couldn't defeat me. Survival requires supreme confidence. Doubt means weakness. I never doubted myself.'

Joseph Jett,
Kidder, Peabody & Co. Inc.,
New York, April 1994.

JOSEPH Jett, a 36-year-old head government bond trader at Kidder, Peabody & Co. Inc., awoke at 5am in his Lower East Side TriBeCa apartment. The pre-dawn starts were a hazard of his chosen vocation. He was usually at his desk or the gym by 6am. But Monday 18 April 1994 was unlike any other day Jett had experienced in his three years at the U.S. investment bank. On Sunday evening, his manager at Kidder had a letter couriered to his home to advise that his employment was terminated.

The only furniture in his 2,700 square-foot, $3,600 per month co-op loft apartment was a bed, a table for eating and working, and a couch. As was Jett's custom, he turned on the TV set which lay on the floor. It was tuned to CNBC where the host updated market players on overnight geopolitical and macroeconomic news. Suddenly, Jett heard the name of his ex-employer.

He sat on the couch in front of the TV and deduced the news anchor's words came from a carefully written press release issued by the bank's media relations people: 'Kidder, Peabody & Company has announced that it has dismissed its chief government bond trader after it uncovered fraudulent trading apparently intended to inflate the brokerage firm's profits and the trader's 1993 bonus. As a result, Kidder says $350 million in profits it recorded in the last three years never existed.'

Kidder was embarrassing itself and stunning the financial world by claiming that one person had outwitted its controls, yet there was no information on how this had happened. Management was accusing Jett of committing the largest securities scam in U.S. history. He was living the worst nightmare of the late twentieth century – watching his life destroyed real-time on a television network.

He paced about the apartment, looking downtown at the Wall Street skyline. His career had been stellar. After making millions of profits trading bonds for Kidder, last year he won the 'Man of the Year' award at the bank as the firm's top individual contributor and was paid $9.3 million. His bonus was so large it required approval by the board of directors of Kidder's parent company, General Electric Co.

His apartment door buzzer rang unexpectedly after 7am and an excited male voice shouted over the intercom: 'Mr. Jett, we know you're up there, come down and talk to us, it's for your own good.'

Standing by the window, he saw people loitering way below in front of the entrance to his apartment building. They stood in clusters while some of the men had cameras hanging around their necks. An NY1 TV news truck was parked by the sidewalk. The media were hunting the trader.

Jett decided not to hide in his apartment but to descend and face the assembled press pack. He scribbled some words to say to the reporters, but he tore up each version and tossed it into the garbage can. The words sounded verbose and complex. Eventually he had a short script ready to use.

He took the elevator down to the lobby and exited the building, then he stood upright and took in a gulp of air as he walked outside purposefully. No one impeded his way. No one shouted a question. No one thrust a mike in his face. No one clicked a camera shutter. Everyone ignored Jett.

Jett later said: 'That Monday I woke up in a daze. I got dressed in a suit as if I was going to work. When I got downstairs and opened the door, there was a network television crew. And you know what, they let me walk right by. At that point the media didn't know I was black. So, they let me walk right by.' None of the press pack expected a top Wall Street trader to be black.

*

Orlando Joseph Jett could trace his paternal roots back to a plantation slave named Fred Lattimore from Montgomery, Alabama. His own parents, James and Juanita Jett, lived in the deep South during the civil rights movement where their lives were poisoned by racism. When his elder brother, Pizarro, was born in 1955, his father moved the family north of the Mason-Dixon line to escape the South: 'No son of mine is going to grow up here, not even for five minutes.'

Jett was born in 1958 and grew up in Wickliffe, northeast of Cleveland, Ohio. His father was now an accountant at the East Ohio Gas Company and his mother was a science teacher. Jett referred to his parents as Pops and Mops. He had a strict upbringing yet wrote that his father was his mentor, his inspiration and the yardstick against which he measured his life. His father believed that the only hope for African-Americans lay in their economic independence.

Jett recalled watching black and white TV pictures with his father, where Martin Luther King Jr. and a group of calm black men and women walked along a street in Alabama, when they were viciously attacked by baton-wielding police with Alsatian dogs and powerful water hoses. His enraged father jumped up, slammed his fists and his head against the wall, and with tears running down his face repeatedly screamed at the TV images: 'Why don't they fight back?'

Jett senior taught his children to rise early each day, a lesson he learned from his time in the U.S. Army. He said a lot could be done before dawn. The young Jett had a newspaper route at the age of eight which required him and his brother to rise at 4am. His father kept an egg-timer at his bedside and his sons were given no more than three minutes to rise, dress and leave the house. Their father was an ogre.

The parents stressed the value of education and discipline to their three children. Jett said: 'My Dad pulled us out of team sports; he felt it was a trap. If we didn't get good grades, we were punished. When we did something wrong, he'd take a belt to us.'

Jett was an avid reader and a mathematics whiz kid. 'There's a beauty to math's', Jett noted. 'It's logical. It adheres to rules always.'

Not only was Jett somewhat nerdy, but he sometimes went out of his way to challenge other blacks. He said once in ninth grade, he walked onto the basketball court in a park and stole the basketball in the midst of a game. He climbed up on a bench and told the players: 'It's time that we as a people stop making baskets and start making A-grades. We must throw down the basketballs and start picking up our textbooks.' He admitted later on: 'I got beat up.'

Jett's father dissuaded him from majoring in philosophy by showing him the vacancies page in the newspaper and asking his son: 'Show me the job adverts that say 'Philosopher Wanted." Jett attended the Massachusetts Institute of Technology in Cambridge, where he earned a bachelor's and a master's degree in Chemical Engineering in 1984.

He spent two years working at the General Electric plastics division in Albany, New York. At G.E., Jett abandoned his first name, Orlando, in favour of his middle name. 'Orlando would never be called back a job interview', he believed. 'But Joseph would be called back almost immediately.'

Jett had far less responsibility than he wanted at G.E. He decided that the people who were skilled in general management and marketing, rather than the engineers, would be running things in the future. Since he thought technology people would always be order takers, he decided to study for an MBA at the Harvard Graduate School of Business. He disliked the fashionable affirmative action programmes for blacks so much that he refused to identify his race on his application form for Harvard.

Although he intended to return to G.E., Jett was drawn at Harvard to the students in his class who worked in finance on Wall Street: 'They had the drive and the energy.' He got his first taste of trading in a summer internship job at Ford Motor Co., where he helped to manage the company's short-term funds. A career in the staid world of chemical engineering was no longer for him.

When at Harvard, Jett complained about a minority recruiter from the investment bank Shearson Lehman Hutton who visited the college: 'We're always running around trying to find some white person to like us. It doesn't matter. Let them hate. If I have the ability, I will still overcome.'

Wall Street beckoned. After graduating from Harvard in 1987, Jett joined Morgan Stanley as a junior bond trader. But there he alienated colleagues and supervisors by being loud and brash in an effort to blend in with other more voluble traders. After less than two years, he was laid off.

Jett contacted head hunters who said there were jobs on offer but when they met in person, the jobs disappeared. Finding a job was as difficult as a black man trying to hail a cab at night in Manhattan, even if he wore a good suit.

He was unemployed for six months, until he secured a job at First Boston. Here he was careful to present a new persona: 'I felt I simply could not allow a personality. I became very dry. My God, did I become a dry, quiet, dull person.' Former colleagues at First Boston said Jett was dismissed in early 1991, partly for poor trading performance and partly for inflating his work experience from his time at Morgan Stanley. But he said he was let go after the bank discovered he was looking for a job at Kidder.

Jett joined Kidder, Peabody & Co. on Monday, 24 June 1991 at one of their six New York offices, 60 Broad Street. He was aged 33. Kidder was a venerable grand old lady of Wall Street with a proud 130-year history but it was a bank in trouble. Those on the Street referred to it as Kidding Nobody. The insider trading scandal of 1986, involving takeovers, junk bonds and crooks Michael Milken and Ivan Boesky, took a heavy toll on the bank. Kidder's top banker and insider dealing supremo Martin Siegel trashed the bank's reputation. General Electric bought 80 percent of Kidder for $600 million in April 1986. G.E. soon wished it had never dipped its toe into investment banking. G.E. grew tired of the low morals and poor ethics in Kidder. It was known G.E. was looking to unload Kidder if the sale price was right.

Jett began working on Kidder's Zero Coupon Trading Desk at a starting salary of $75,000. He was recruited by, and reported to, Melvin Mullin, who in turn reported to Edward Cerullo, the powerful athletic head of the 750-member fixed income trading team and a 15-year veteran of the firm.

Jett said he developed his strength of character partly from his father and partly from the fact that he was picked on so often when young. To defend himself in his youth, he began to lift weights and do bodybuilding to bulk up. Although only five feet eight inches tall, he was now powerfully built.

One journalist noted that in person, Jett was delicate and otherworldly. His eyes were 'twice as wide as those of most humans and he would fit in perfectly playing an alien crew member on Star Trek.'

Jett didn't like the uncultured life of a trading desk: 'We had a farting contest. I am telling you that bets were made in the office. People would go out searching for the worst things to eat. The reason why Wall Street can be such a great opportunity is that this type of nonsense goes on 50 percent of the time. If anyone spends just half of their time actually working, they'll take off like a rocket.'

He didn't enjoy the social side of work at Kidder. He said people often then asked him: 'Why don't you quit and go work somewhere else?' He didn't move on 'because Kidder was the most bottom-line oriented company. Young traders do not get opportunities like they do at Kidder. So, if that opportunity meant no socialising, I was prepared to do it. I'm a total failure at male bonding.'

Jett became the ultimate outsider, a fierce individualist with few close friends and who drove himself hard. Others noted he sat with an upright, almost military, bearing, and he was very formal and composed in dealing with people as he pursued his own self-interest: 'I was a formidable foe because I didn't care about winning friends. I wasn't about to accommodate anyone, to compromise my methods or objectives. I knew I had enemies. I also knew they couldn't defeat me. Survival requires supreme confidence. Doubt means weakness. I never doubted myself.'

*

By the end of 1991, Jett was in danger of failing again and losing his dream job. During his first five months, he made only $417,000 trading profit for the firm, far less than the modest goal of $1 million per month that Mullin had set for him. Despite a regimen of 12-hour work days and study at home after hours, he received a warning from Mullin that he would have to become more profitable or face dismissal. His bonus for 1991 was $5,000. This meant only thing on Wall Street – Go And Look for Another Job.

Jett was then living in a 400-square-foot, $700-a-month apartment on West 54th Street in Manhattan. To punish himself for his poor work performance, he deprived himself of every home comfort. For a long while, his apartment was furnished only with a bed, a stereo and a weights set. Soon he removed all the furniture and began sleeping on the floor. He was more determined than ever to prove himself.

At Kidder, Jett traded 'stripped' government bonds, which are 30-year U.S. government bonds that have been converted into a series of zero-coupon bonds. Zero-coupon bonds do not earn interest like regular bonds, on which interest is paid semi-annually. With zero-coupon bonds, the interest builds up, or accrues, in the price of the bonds. A zero-coupon bond bought for $900 today may pay $1,000 when it matures. The $100 is the interest that accumulates over the life of the bond. 'Strips' was an acronym of the Federal Reserve's Separate Trading of Registered Interest and Principal of Securities programme.

The 'stripped' U.S. government bonds were created when a bank such as Kidder brought a 30-year government bond to the Federal Reserve and received a series of zero-coupon bonds in return. A firm could request the reverse process at any time and reconstitute, or rebuild, a 30-year bond from the underlying zero-coupon bonds in the same way. The reconstitution of the original bond was called a 'recon.' A 'recon' was once best described as the exchange of four quarters for one dollar.

The markets in the bonds were efficient, in the sense that many market participants traded the bonds, which kept the prices of the 'strips' and the 'recon' close to each other. So, the arbitrage profit to be made in these two types of trading activities was small, and the opportunity to profit was fleeting. It was not expected that any trader trading 'stripped' bonds would ever make much money.

Jett booked his trades on Kidder's Government Trader computer system, which appeared to be a leading edge system, but in reality, it was based on software written in the 1970s. Kidder's system treated a 'recon' exchange of zero-coupon bonds for regular bonds as a sale and a purchase. Although no cash ever changed hands, the Kidder system required the entry of an equivalent 'price' for each sale and purchase. Therein lay the system flaw.

In 1992, Jett's fortunes suddenly improved. He was seen as a hard worker who arrived at the office earlier and stayed later than his co-workers. In the first ten months of 1992, Jett reported trading profits of $28 million and attracted the attention of his managers. Mullin rated Jett's performance as 'outstanding' and doubled his salary to $150,000. At the end of 1992, Mullin gave Jett a $2.1 million bonus. Jett craved recognition, and he tried harder and harder to achieve the performance that would bring it.

Good government bond traders usually had trading profits of $10 million to $30 million a year. But in 1993, Jett's profits began exceeding $10 million a month. It appeared to Melvin, Cerullo and others, that Jett had transformed himself from a mediocre bond trader into a major money machine.

By February 1993, Jett was so successful that Cerullo promoted him to replace Mullin as the head of the banks government bond trading. Jett led a 36-person bond trading operation with desks in New York, Los Angeles, Tokyo and London. He directed bond investments worth over $50 billion, and he personally controlled 25 percent of Kidder's total assets and 12 percent of G.E.'s total assets.

Despite his roles in blue-chip organisations such as G.E. and Kidder, Jett still saw himself as invisible to others who mattered at Kidder. Initially, the notion of a degree of invisibility appealed to him. He spoke often of the lure of Wall Street as a place where he was judged not by the colour of his skin, but by the amount of trading profit he could make: 'The government bond market is exquisitely objective. It cares nothing about a person's race, colour or creed. Trading was the perfect job.'

But he was reminded that this was not always the case. 'It was fascinating', he said, recalling how some visiting Kidder sales people sought to congratulate him after his promotion to the head of the government bond desk. They would walk up to a different colleague to offer their congratulations, rather than to Jett himself. 'It never entered their minds that I could possibly be Joe Jett', he said.

Jett oversaw recruitment efforts for Kidder to become a more diverse workplace, by hiring more women and minorities. But getting women to work on Wall Street was an uphill battle at the time: 'The culture of Wall Street is to try to create a hostile work environment so women don't want to be on the trading floor. Guys on Wall Street really don't read books. They just all have Playboy magazines sitting on their desk to say to women: 'We don't want you here."

Jett stated he was told not to engage in inappropriate office romances with white females: 'I'm not trying to date her', he said of one white colleague, in a typical defence. 'I have no interest in her.' Instead of possibly quitting or suing for discrimination, Jett restricted himself socially: 'When a woman said hello in passing, I responded with a zombielike expression and a mantra: 'Discipline must be maintained!' and I walked away. I refused to have any interaction with white women in the office.'

Kidder honoured its top performers at an annual management conference. In January 1993, Jett attended the event in Disney World, Orlando, Florida, as a member of a task force on recruiting minorities. The experience made him determined to earn a place at the gathering based on his performance, rather than the colour of his skin. 'I did not want to be viewed as an affirmative action case', he said. 'With affirmative action, all of a sudden, the expectation of lower standards was being codified.'

Jett earned trading profits of about $200 million in 1993. His performance earned him an invitation to the annual Disney World conference in January 1994, this time on merit. He accepted the 'Man of the Year' award. People there recalled Jett comparing trading to war. 'I told them a story about my father in the war in Korea', Jett said. 'My dad was a sergeant. His troop was Hispanics, blacks, and rednecks from the deep South. When they landed, they set aside their differences and set about destroying the enemy. What I said was, 'At Kidder, we had to unite and work together.'

As word of his success spread, other traders at Kidder and on Wall Street grew curious about Jett's trades. He declined to speak about his technique for trading 'stripped' bonds in his dealings with fellow traders. It was noted he was executing a high volume of one specific type of transaction.

Jett had entered a series of 'forward recon' trades into Kidder's books. These trades indicated his intention to reconstitute zero-coupon bonds back into regular bonds at dates in the future. While many types of bond market transactions were settled in the future, known as forward trades, there were no forward trades for 'recons.' Yet, Kidder's computer system still accepted Jett's transactions.

*

By early 1994, Jett's trading volume increased so much that the archaic computer systems had difficulty processing all his trades. The technology staff investigated the systems performance issue and were stunned to see the sheer scale of Jett's trades. They noted that very few of Jett's trades ever led to any actual bonds changing hands. If his trades were only rarely consummated, they wondered where had the hundreds of millions in trading profits booked by Jett come from?

One other Kidder bond trader said he was greatly puzzled at the time: 'Since we were not settling any money, my concern was that they were paper trades.' The technology staff worked with accountants, Cerullo and other executives, and all grew increasingly alarmed about Jett's trading.

Jett's monthly reported profits doubled in 1994. Cerullo asked a fixed income accountant to investigate whether Jett was taking unacceptable risks. The accountant discovered $42 billion of bookings in 'forward recons' of bonds, far more than the firm would ever be able to settle.

Subsequent investigation showed that in the first three months of 1994, Jett booked 'forward recon' trades involving $1.76 trillion in principal value. Only $79 billion of those trades were real. The 95 percent of remaining trades - $1.68 trillion - was never consummated or settled in the real world.

They investigated his 'forward recon' trades, thinking at first there was an accounting problem, but they soon concluded that the only likely explanation for the bookings was a fraud committed by Jett. Management now became aware of the inherent implausibility of what Jett said he was doing to generate such unprecedented profits.

They observed that two or three days before a 'forward recon' trade was due to be completed, Jett rolled the trades over to a later date but he kept the profits on the books. One such fake trade was on 17 November 1992, when Jett booked in the system a reconstitution of $200 million of bonds to settle 203 days later, on 8 June 1993. This booking produced an immediate profit in the system of $12 million.

Kidder believed Jett was taking advantage of the difference between how regular bonds and zero-coupon bonds were traded and entered on the firm's books. Regular bonds were quoted in terms of the face value of the bond with the interest earned to date added on at settlement. But with zero-coupon bonds, the interest earned was always factored into the quoted price. Even if the price of a regular bond does not move, the price of a zero-coupon bond rises every day to account for the earned interest accrued daily.

Jett had booked trades to sell bonds in the future, at a higher price, while paying the lower, current price, now. By simply announcing an intention to have two offsetting long and short bond positions, Jett recorded a phoney profit. This price difference and profit should have disappeared on the day in the future that the trade was scheduled to be settled, but Jett postponed the settlement of his phoney trades.

Jett knew that as the future date neared, his fictitious profits would vanish from the books. So, to get the profits back, he booked more and more phoney trades. The trade quantities became so large that he was controlling twice the total amount of some bonds that had been 'stripped.'

The large volume of phoney trades made Kidder initially suspect that Jett must have had help. But later they determined he acted alone and he was able to book the volume of trades, since the computer system was so automated, one trader could book a series of trades with only a few keystrokes.

The banks investigative work showed that while Jett always claimed that his profits came from 'stripping' treasury bonds into individual payments of interest and principal, he did in fact very little 'stripping' and he merely took advantage of the processes in the Kidder accounting system.

Kidder then discovered that Jett's fake trades covered other losses on actual real trades, which they estimated to be about $85 million. Rather than being hugely profitable, Jett was loss-making.

In late March, Cerullo directed Jett to settle or pair off his 'forward recon' trades to remove the positions from the firm's records. Cerullo was devastated when he learned that eliminating the forward positions resulted in a shortfall of over $300 million. Jett's magic profits were no more.

A former Kidder executive later told The New York Times: 'I think Joe was someone who had a tremendous psychological need to be a star trader. It was like a lab rat in a cage. He pushed the lever, and food came out. The rat doesn't give much thought as to why the food came out.'

Early in the week of 11 April, Kidder alerted Jack Welch, Chairman and CEO of G.E., that the Jett trading problem could significantly impact Kidder's bottom line.

On Thursday 14 April, Jett's trading was halted and

he was summoned to a meeting with Cerullo and other executives. Jett denied he had done anything wrong and he offered various, yet unconvincing, explanations. Kidder froze $8 million of assets he held in three personal accounts at the firm. At the end of the meeting, Jett walked out of the Kidder office for the final time. Next day, Kidder froze his Bank One ATM card connected to his Kidder account. Jett found that he couldn't withdraw a cent from any bank.

*

Kidder hired Gary Lynch of New York law firm Davis, Polk & Wardwell, and a former head of enforcement at the Securities & Exchange Commission, to investigate the problem with Jett's trading. When Lynch first arrived, Jett was still employed. Jett did not appear for a scheduled interview with Lynch, so he was then dismissed. Jett said a social engagement kept him from the interview.

Lynch investigated the events and recommended steps to prevent a recurrence. His 90-page report issued in August 1994 blamed a total breakdown in the firm's system of trader supervision, saying Jett's superiors could have detected the fraud if they had scrutinised such basic details as trading and settlement dates.

The report concluded Jett acted alone and deliberately when he faked $350 million of fictitious profits and it said he began faking trades five months after he arrived at Kidder, in November 1991. He booked transactions that generated $32 million in false profits for 1992, $196 million for 1993 and $100 million for the first three months of 1994. Lynch said Jett simply made up trades and marked them down as having made money, but his trades were economic nullities.

Jett never enjoyed a single profitable year or even a single profitable quarter. In 1992, the year that Mullin declared Jett 'one of the best strips' traders in the business' and gave him the $2.1 million bonus, Lynch's report determined that Jett actually lost Kidder $9.5 million in that year. Overall, he lost $85 million. Jett carefully timed the trades that generated phoney profits to cover his real losses.

Lynch said there was 'lax supervision', 'poor judgements' and 'missed opportunities' by those charged with supervising Jett. He was 'provided the opportunity to generate false profits by trading and accounting systems', Lynch wrote. 'But it was his supervisors, however, who allowed Jett that opportunity for over two years because they never understood Jett's daily trading activity or the source of his apparent profitability.' Lynch said that even though Jett's trading activity accounted for more than a quarter of the fixed-income division's total net income in 1993, his two supervisors, Mullin and Cerullo, never bothered to understand where his lucrative profits were coming from.

Kidder's internal auditors blundered too. After auditing Jett's zero-coupon trading desk in 1993, the auditors did not detect any problems, even though they knew Jett was trading in 'forward recons.' Lynch reported the auditors saw that Jett had booked billions of dollars of unusual transactions more than one day ahead, but no one followed up this anomaly, including his managers and the internal auditors.

Cerullo blundered so he resigned from Kidder three months after Jett left, albeit with a $9 million severance package. He stated he continually monitored Jett's performance but that he had to rely on the firm's internal audit reports, which gave no sign of irregularities. In mitigation, he said it was he who first began the firm's investigation into Jett's trades: 'My reputation took a beating, unfairly so. If I need to fall on my sword, fine. I'm not smart enough to comprehend all the bad things that people can do. Joe Jett was a person to whom I had given an opportunity, someone I'd taken a chance on like a dozen other people, all of whom responded to the opportunity.'

Cerullo emphasised that Kidder's accounting and control systems gave a reassuring picture of Jett's trading activity, that ultimately grew to $600 billion of trades per month and involved more than 60,000 fake trades: 'No numbers I saw even came close. Every single bit of evidence, the inventory reports, the P&L statements, the control reports, the risk management reports, was reinforcing.'

G.E. CEO and corporate guru Welch blundered too. In his memoir, Welch regretted not following his practice of personally looking into how one of his employees could become so successful so quickly. He wrote that it is incumbent on a CEO to understand how any one person can make supernormal profits. He wrote too that no one in Kidder was willing to take responsibility for the debacle, with most Kidder executives more concerned about the effect on their bonuses. This convinced Welch that Kidder's culture did not fit well with that of G.E., and it led him to sell Kidder to Paine Webber in October 1994 for $670 million, since in turn consumed by Swiss bank UBS. Welch wrote that on first hearing about the scandal: 'I rushed to the bathroom and my stomach emptied in awful spasms.'

Welch said later there were limits to the effectiveness of any control system: 'When we have 220,000 employees, you can't legislate morality. Obviously, we made a mistake in hiring and obviously the controls were not good enough to stop the clever scheme this fellow put together.' At a later speech at a New York awards ceremony, Welch revealed that his golfing partners had been ruining his putts by asking him, on the green, how Joe Jett was doing?

If anyone in a bank is suddenly making huge unexpected profits, the nature of their activity and profits must be investigated by their superiors immediately to determine if they are genuine. And if management and internal auditors identify something unusual, they are both obliged to follow it up. Jett essentially invented a phoney product which no one else traded and which could not be settled in the market.

Jett's biggest personal blunder was in not transferring his $8 million of personal assets offshore from Kidder in early 1994 and retiring on the first plane to a country which did not have an extradition treaty with the U.S.

*

Jett faced civil charges and fines but he never faced criminal charges or risked jail time. In 1998, an SEC administrative law judge found that even though Jett misled Kidder and pocketed millions of dollars in undeserved bonuses, he could not be penalised for 'securities fraud' because his activities did not involve the sale of 'real' securities. The judge said that just because someone commits a fraud in a securities firm, that is not necessarily securities fraud. Instead, she said he violated the books and records provisions of the securities laws. Jett was fined $200,000 and he was ordered to return $8.2 million in bonuses to Kidder. Jett and the SEC appealed the decision and in March 2004 the SEC finally ruled on the appeal, and concluded that Jett had in fact committed securities fraud.

Jett maintained his innocence but he was up against corporate goliaths in Kidder and G.E. 'After what has been done to me there is no room for truth', he stated. 'They've depicted me as a despicable character. The words have been twisted, and the truth turned merrily on its head. I have to fight because I am innocent', he said. 'I won't let them railroad me.' Jett said the recent years were 'a hellish ordeal.' He used an emotive turn of phrase, saying he was 'lynched on the front page.'

He claimed Kidder knew about his phoney trades but encouraged his trading, in order to boost Kidder's profits and facilitate the sale by G.E. But there was never enough definitive evidence to support his accusation.

Jett seemed to be deluded: 'They accuse me of fraud, but there is so much evidence that I was open and honest and that other people looked at and understood my positions. In order to be good at trading, you have to have a lot of self-confidence. But it has to be backed up by discipline that says that you actually do know what you are doing. I thought that I was doing so well that no one could touch me. I never dreamed of this idea of fraud.'

By 1997, Jett was doing odd jobs, working on construction sites, making deliveries, occasionally investing on others' behalf and acting as his own unpaid paralegal in his legal battle. He recovered some of the $8 million held in his personal accounts at Kidder: 'They had no more right to take my money than they would anyone walking down the street. $4.5 million was returned to me. It took from 1994 to 1998. The best revenge is success.'

His biography appeared in 1999, with the innocent title of: 'Black and White on Wall Street: The Untold Story of the Man Wrongly Accused of Bringing Down Kidder Peabody.' The book was dedicated to his father 'who forged my will.' His lengthy tome revealed a man who was opinionated, arrogant, status-obsessed, contemptuous and lacking any altruism or social conscience. He was above all Machiavellian at Kidder – the end justified the means. Ironically, all that should have made him the ideal Wall Street trader.

In his book, he paints a picture of a driven, hard-working employee who tried to change a staid bond trading department, but who made many enemies and ended up a scapegoat, in part because he was black. Some of the content is ludicrous, such as when he wrote: 'Kidder used a technicality to keep two sets of books – the lower balance sheet we showed to G.E., the higher balance sheet we kept to ourselves.'

Although only one percent of traders on Wall Street were black, Jett never played on this at the time. 'I took pains throughout this entire affair to never mention my race. The very idea of playing your race card - using your race to justify your performance - all those things my father would never allow. Certain weapons indicate weakness rather than strength. The race card is one of them. Even though I was black and my accusers were white, I felt the evidence and the numbers would see me through.'

Jett kept his personal life out of the media until the New York Post reported in 2010 that he was battling his ex-partner Melissa Leonardo, a director at Merrill Lynch, over the custody of their three children. Jett met Leonardo when both were at Kidder. In 1998, they moved in to a $1.1 million house in Princeton Junction, New Jersey. Their 4,000 square foot home was set on one acre in Colt Circle, an upscale cul de sac where every house had a large swimming pool.

Their legal battle was a series of counter-claims, police complaints, protection orders and failed counselling attempts. Leonardo accused Jett of being mentally and sexually abusive and alleged he harassed her at night by shining infrared beams into her eyes. In court documents, Jett said he had lost touch with Leonardo, but he alleged she was still keeping his money which he needed.

Jett ran Jett Capital Management but their website is defunct. He has a personal website where his last blog post was in 2017. He has a Twitter account where he describes himself as: 'Father, CEO, Author, Speaker, Harvard MBA, MIT MS BS, Private Equity, International Corporate Finance, Expert Witness and Reputation Management.'

He has a LinkedIn profile where his achievements from his time at Kidder still include: 'Generated $357 million in profits from proprietary trading in domestic U.S. government strip securities.' Clearly, he remains in denial that his bond trading profits were illusory. It is simply impossible to earn trading profits without settling those trades in the real world – otherwise you are merely trading with yourself.

Jett was interviewed in 2008 by the France News 24 TV channel. He stood outside the New York Stock Exchange building and stated: 'I made over 11 million dollars for myself, personally. It was a fantastic time, being a trader.' He drove the TV crew in a modest Honda saloon to the shared family house in Princeton Junction. Bizarrely, he took them to the 'raw and unfinished' windowless basement and said he was living down there on a part-time basis. The footage showed an old brass bed where he said he slept. 'It's a very spartan existence but it's one that I am most comfortable with', he stated unconvincingly.

Next to the bed was a pile of Iron Mountain bankers boxes which Jett said contained all his legal paperwork for the prior 14 years. He looked around the dark basement: 'This is literally all the SEC can take from me. If they take the bed, I can sleep on the ground. If they take the gym equipment, I can do push-ups on the ground as well. I don't believe they are allowed to take the clothes from my back. So, I have no fear of them. I really don't care.'

If he was trying to show that he was broke, then he failed. He stood before the camera in a good suit with an immaculate white shirt and a neat tie. His broad shoulders showed he still bench-pressed and his huge eyes bulged and popped with white lies and bended truth. He seemed as phoney as his false trading profits.

*

2 – THE KING OF SIMEX

'I'd bought everything the market had to offer. I'd made the market bounce a couple of times, but I'd had the shit kicked out of me all the way down. I was now scared to death. I had to get out of here.'

Nick Leeson,
Baring Futures (Singapore) Pte.,
Singapore, February 1995.

SHORTLY after 2.15pm on Thursday 23 February 1995, when the bell rang for the end of the dealing day on the floor of the Singapore International Monetary Exchange, Nick Leeson, General Manager of Baring Futures, scribbled 'I'm sorry' on a piece of notepaper and left his trading booth. He walked over to the Barings office in Ocean Towers on Collyer Quay, where everything looked strangely normal. His settlement staff sat at their desks handling the usual paperwork and fielding telephone calls from clients, brokers and the London head office, oblivious to his existential unparalleled personal crisis.

By the close of business, Leeson owned 61,000 Nikkei contracts and had lost tens more millions of pounds in a few short hours. SIMEX would soon come looking for another $40 million in margin calls. Every other dealer in Asia knew he had an £11 billion exposure to the Japanese stock market. The press called his huge long position the 'Barings Overhang.' But no one in Barings Singapore or London had worked it out yet.

The next day was Baring's bonus day, when Leeson would receive £450,000. And Saturday was his twenty-eighth birthday. But he was a beaten man. It was time to flee.

Yellow post-it notes from Barings London colleagues were stuck to his computer screen, asking Leeson to call them urgently. He didn't return any of their telephone calls. He lied to colleagues and told them his wife Lisa was ill and he was needed at home. At 4pm, Leeson left the Barings office, saying to no one in particular: 'See you later, I'll be back in a while.'

At Singapore's Changi Airport he and Lisa bought two tickets for the shuttle flight to Kuala Lumpur. That evening the Leeson's checked into the five-star Regent Hotel in KL.

On Friday morning, Leeson faxed a single-page apology and resignation letter to his two Singapore bosses: 'My sincere apologies for the predicament I have left you in. It was neither my intention or aim for this to happen but the pressures, both business and personal, have become too much to bear and after receiving medical advice, have affected my health to the extent that a breakdown is imminent. In light of my actions, I tender my resignation with immediate effect and I will contact you early next week to discuss the best course of action. Apologies, Nick.'

The couple flew next to Kota Kinabalu on the coast of Malaysia and checked in to the Shangri-la Tanjung Aru hotel. Leeson read that Nikkei futures fell only 300 points on the Friday. He believed Barings had sold his position and assumed the bank had survived his departure. But on Monday, he saw a headline in the New Straits Times newspaper: 'British Merchant Bank Collapse.' He whispered to his wife: 'Barings is bust.'

Lisa telephoned her mother to find out what was going on in the UK and learnt her husband was the subject of a House of Commons debate, the Chancellor of the Exchequer had called Leeson a 'rogue trader', the Barings Chairman Peter Baring went on TV to say Barings had lost £600 million, the couple had replaced Prince Charles and Lady Diana on the front pages of the tabloids and Leeson's father had punched a Daily Mirror photographer who had called to his house to ask the whereabouts of his son.

On Tuesday, the Leeson's somehow needed to reach Europe but both daily flights out of Kota Kinabulu to Brunei were fully booked. The pair checked in to a Hyatt hotel under Lisa's maiden name, Sims. Next day, at the Royal Brunei airline ticketing office, they asked for any flight to Europe. Leeson paid cash for two tickets to Frankfurt, via Brunei, Bangkok and Abu Dhabi. The ticketing agent misspelt their surname on the tickets as Lesson. Neither of them corrected her error. Leeson hoped her mistake meant they were less likely to be identified on an aircraft passenger list.

On Wednesday, they left Kota Kinabalu without any challenge from immigration officers. At Brunei Airport, Lisa made a quick reconnaissance of the transit lounge and reported there were no police checking the passports for the BI535 flight to Frankfurt.

Speaking later, Leeson recalled: 'It was bonkers that trip. Lisa goes up first in the hope that she will get through and they will just catch me. You've got this long walk up to the immigration guards. Then he looks at the passport and whatever else and he stamps it. I get on the flight and we go to Brunei. The departure gates have all these TVs above them. My face is on every one of these TVs. I've got the collar up. I've got the hat on. I get on the plane and then they come round and start handing out newspapers. French newspapers, English newspapers - it's all about me. I've got the blanket up over me.'

Leeson hid in seat 43A. The couple endured the overnight Bangkok and Abu Dhabi stopovers, until their Thursday early morning arrival into Frankfurt. Police officers stood at the foot of the aircraft steps. Lisa went first to the exit and the police officer asked her: 'Where's your man?' Leeson stepped forward and advised: 'I'm her man.'

*

The man Nicholas William Leeson was born in Watford, Hertfordshire on 25 February 1967. His father Harry was a self-employed plasterer and his mother Anne was a mental health nurse who died from cancer when Leeson was twenty years old. He spent his early years in a council house in Orbital Crescent in the suburb of Leavesden in Watford, before the Leeson family moved to a council house in Garston, north of Watford.

He attended Kingsway Junior School, Garston and later Parmiter's state school where he left with two A-level passes in English Literature and History. He had to retake his A-level Mathematics in order to achieve a pass. He was a striker on the school soccer team and also played for Abbots Langley FC, and later played for Barings London soccer team. Out of 120 pupils in his year at school, he was selected to be one of the prefects.

Leeson was not destined for university so he set out for a career in finance in the City of London. His first job was in 1985, when as a school-leaver he joined the Lombard Street office of Coutts & Co, the bankers to the Queen. Soon bored there, he joined American investment bank Morgan Stanley in June 1987 to work in their Futures and Options Settlements department, on a salary of £20,000 plus an annual bonus. Many of his friends worked as builders and tradesmen and were impressed at his City career.

Leeson learned how to settle financial transactions and how to move large sums of money. In 1989, he applied for a junior role in the trading team and was offered it, but his boss would not let him leave settlements for three more months. Leeson resigned on the same day. He joined the settlements team of Barings on 10 July 1989. Leeson admits he had never before heard of Barings: 'There was no Barings Bank in Watford.'

Barings was a small but well-known bank in the City,

with a highly respected and glittering 233-year history of the innovative financing of everything from shares to real estate to coffee. It was the Duc de Richelieu who reputedly said in 1817 that there were six great powers in Europe – England, France, Prussia, Austria, Russia and Baring Brothers & Co. The bank funded the construction of the Panama Canal and the purchase of Louisiana from France by the United States of America. In the classic travelogue 'Around the World in Eighty Days' by Jules Verne, Phileas Fogg's bet was guaranteed by a cheque for £20,000 drawn on none other than Barings Bank.

Leeson worked in Futures and Options Settlements in Barings. He volunteered to work on an assignment in Jakarta but all was not what it seemed. Barings did not even have an office in Jakarta and his team worked out of a hotel. The place was a mess since Barings had lost control of the settlement of £100 million worth of local bearer shares.

Leeson spent ten months in a bank vault reconciling share transactions with share certificates. Barings sent out more people to assist in the work and amongst them was Lisa Sims from Kent. Jakarta was alive and the Barings team worked and partied hard. By Christmas 1990, Leeson had resolved 90 percent of the share transactions and was in love.

His success meant that others in Barings asked for his help on settlements. He joined management on several visits to their overseas offices in Europe and Asia. Barings had acquired a seat on the Singapore International Monetary Exchange, or SIMEX, but it was not yet activated. Leeson and others in the bank advised management to activate the seat so that Barings could earn commission revenue on transactions on the regional exchange. Management knew and trusted Leeson and offered him the post of the General Manager, and they instructed him to recruit some local traders and settlements staff.

Ten days after this job offer, Leeson married Lisa Sims on 21 March 1992 at the Church of St. Edmund King and Martyr in Kent. The wedding was followed by a reception at the Brand's Hatch Thistle Hotel. They honeymooned on the Orient Express to Venice and flew to Singapore in April 1992, where they planned to enjoy an expatriate life in the capital city of a tiger economy in Asia. Singapore was squeaky clean with no beggars, no violence, no litter, no graffiti and no chewing gum. It had a highly regulated financial market where authorities believed nothing could go wrong.

The couple moved into an apartment in Angullia View, where Barings paid the monthly rental of S$5,000. Workers mowed the lawns, washed cars and cleaned the grounds and the communal outdoor swimming pool. Their home was near the upscale Orchard Road commercial area with its shopping malls, five-star hotels and fine dining.

While Leeson worked on SIMEX, Lisa went to the gym with other Baring wives, had noodle lunches with the girls and shopped in the malls. The couple rarely went out during the week. They spent time as if they were in the UK. Lisa cooked and they watched cable TV or videos. At weekends Leeson played golf or soccer, the couple shopped, met friends or went to the movies. At other times they took holidays in nearby Malaysia, a one-hour drive away, or in other resorts. Leeson bought a relatively cheap Rolex watch and a modest car. They had the use of the bank boat, called 'Baring Up.'

*

Leeson's Singapore team bought and sold futures contracts on behalf of clients on the Japanese Nikkei 225 index, which is the index of the leading 225 stocks listed on the Tokyo Stock Exchange. Financial futures are derivatives, since they derive their value from the underlying stock market. Bizarrely, futures allow you to sell something you don't own and to buy something you don't want to own. Futures move roughly in tandem with the underlying stock market but they are more volatile and illiquid. Leeson had no authority to trade for the bank and to buy or sell financial futures for the banks own account.

Nikkei 225 futures were traded in Singapore and on the Osaka Exchange in Japan. The two prices should always be the same but sometimes small price differences arose between the two locations. Leeson monitored these price differences and he saw that sometimes he could trade at a better price in Singapore, rather than in Osaka, or vice versa. He was able to make a small intra-day trading profit from these price differences by trading the same product in two different physical locations, known as arbitrage.

Leeson sat at his desk in SIMEX, took calls from clients or other Baring's offices, and passed the orders to his two colleagues on the floor who transacted with another floor trader of another bank. From his seat he could see and smell the money on SIMEX. After six years of pushing settlements paper around, he was now in the midst of the action.

Leeson applied for his license to trade on the floor of SIMEX, he passed the exams in late 1992 and then got to wear a navy and gold striped traders' jacket in the colours of Barings. Every trader received a SIMEX badge with three initials of their own choice to identify themselves. Leeson chose LJS – his wife's initials. Now suddenly, he was both managing the office settlements function and he was able to trade on SIMEX.

All banks make errors and accept it as a cost of doing business. Banks can buy rather than sell, banks can buy or sell the wrong future, or banks can make an error between the price dealt with another bank and the price advised to the client. Barings Singapore office had an error account in their books, numbered 99905. Each month any trader errors were booked to it and the balance was transferred to the London head office.

Barings London management asked Leeson to open another local error account in Singapore since there were too many small entries to review in London. Leeson opened a new error account in Singapore and asked a local Settlements girl to give it a lucky number. She advised that the number eight is a lucky Chinese number, simply because it is a round number with no hard edges. A new error account 88888 was opened.

On Friday 17 July 1992, the SIMEX closing bell rang and there was a big cheer on the floor since the Nikkei index had risen by 400 points. Leeson spent some time alone in the office checking the days transactions. By about 8pm, he realised there was an error.

One of his team had sold 20 contracts but he couldn't find a matching buy transaction. She had sold rather than bought in error. Barings had sold in a rising market and had to make the client good and resolve the error, so they would have to buy back 40 contracts at a higher price. Leeson calculated they had lost £20,000. It was a person's annual salary.

Leeson instructed his staff to book the position to the 88888 account. It was too big a loss to tell London about, he feared for his job, and for the first time since his arrival Leeson told no one in London that he had hidden a loss-making position.

Over the next few months up to the end of 1992, he booked thirty errors to the 88888 account. There were other smaller errors booked to the London error account but only the larger errors were booked to 88888 since these might lead to recriminations for the Singapore floor traders, perhaps even the termination of their employment.

The staff knew if they had a large error, they could ask Leeson to book it to account 88888. It wasn't their money; it wasn't the clients' money; it was the banks money. Their logic was that every bank had an error account – Barings just had two.

Leeson soon faced problems. Firstly, the error account balance was becoming too big to write off against the commission income. Secondly, the number of futures contracts sitting in the error account was becoming too big to hide. Thirdly, SIMEX made a daily margin call on contracts (a call for funds to insure against a party not paying up in the event of a loss) and this included those positions held in the error account. Leeson needed cash.

Each day Leeson received funds from London to cover the margin calls for Baring's clients, and this money was passed on to SIMEX. No cash should be left in Barings books and records. He decided to ask for more cash than he needed, to keep the excess, and hope that no one in London noticed. The first day he faxed the request to London, the extra cash arrived without a question. He was amazed.

Leeson had to find a more creative way to generate more cash to pay the daily margin calls. He realised that if he sold options to banks, he would receive an amount of Japanese yen from the buyers, called the premium. By selling options he knew he was taking an illicit proprietary position for the bank and exposing the bank to risk.

Leeson also began to transact cross-trades in the books of the office. Cross-trades are a way to effect through an exchange a buy and a sell order between two clients belonging to the same broker, and they are perfectly legal. He booked cross trades between his Singapore trading account and other Barings offices in London and Tokyo at high prices, which generated good trading profits. He booked cross trades between his Singapore trading account and the 88888 error account at lower prices. The balance in his trading account was large, profitable and visible but the balance in his error account was even larger, loss making and hidden, because the error account was not included in regular reports sent to the London head office. By December 1993, Leeson had concealed losses of £23 million.

Barings announced annual profits in 1993 of £200 million. The apparent trading profits in Leeson's arbitrage business in Singapore amounted to £10 million. Leeson received an annual bonus in February 1994 of £135,000. He was 27. He and his wife bought a flat in Blackheath, London. His wife said to him: 'It's an insurance policy for when get sacked and we have to go and work back in London as a plasterer and a waitress.'

*

Leeson's great results were noticed back in London. His trading volumes, arbitrage profits and commissions were soaring. He was told the Barings London internal audit team would visit to audit his operation. Two auditors arrived for three weeks. He took them on a tour of the SIMEX trading floor to keep them away from the office, showed them the market chaos, made sure they saw he was very busy and avoided speaking to them.

He received the internal audit report and saw internal audit had missed the evidence staring them in the face. The report made recommendations but nothing that exposed Leeson's activities. The report stated that: 'while the individual controls over Baring Singapore's systems and operations are satisfactory, there is a significant risk that the controls could be overridden by the General Manager. He is the key manager in the front office and the back office and can thus initiate transactions and then ensure they are settled and recorded according to his own instructions.' They had come close to the dire truth.

In September 1994, Leeson's trading in SIMEX Nikkei futures amounted to 7.2 percent of all SIMEX's volume and Barings received an award for 'Trader of the Year.' There was an awards ceremony and dinner to mark the tenth anniversary of SIMEX and none other than the Prime Minister of Singapore gave the keynote speech. Leeson did not attend but his Singapore boss collected their award. Leeson was now known as the 'King of SIMEX.'

Leeson was losing control. He was now in the red to the tune of £170 million. At the financial year end he needed to find more funds to cover his losses. He had received 7.78 billion Japanese yen in all, or about £50 million, from the London office over time to cover option margin payments and he had paid these funds to SIMEX, but he had no corresponding entry on the balance sheet of the Singapore office. He instructed his local settlements staff, who all reported to him, to book fake entries in the office ledger.

He faced huge obstacles. He was expecting an audit from the banks external auditors Coopers & Lybrand. He had yet to create an explanation for the fictitious 7.78 billion Japanese yen booking. He was sending faxes to the London office asking for $10 million of funds each day. SIMEX were sending letters to his Singapore boss asking about the large size of the margin requirements for the 88888 account. And Lisa suffered a miscarriage.

On Wednesday 18 January 1995, real disaster struck. The city of Kobe suffered a major earthquake. The Nikkei 225 stock market held up well at first but a few days later it fell into a major decline. Leeson had to ask London for $40 million in funds but he felt strangely elated at the thought, hoping that London would finally challenge the ever-growing requests for money from head office, but they did not. The funds duly arrived.

The auditor from Coopers and Lybrand Singapore asked for audit documentation for the 7.78 billion Japanese yen booking. So, Leeson invented a fictitious trade and said he had brokered an option trade between a broker in the U.S. named Spears, Leeds & Kellogg, or SLK, and the French bank Banque National de Paris. He said the trade was executed away from SIMEX, known as an OTC trade, or over the counter. An OTC trade takes place outside of an exchange and there are less protections for the two parties.

In his desk drawer Leeson found a letter from SLK on their headed notepaper. He typed up fake option details, cut out a signature of a managing director at SLK from the letter, and soon he had created a trade confirmation. His effort contained the trade details in one typeface and the MD's surname in a different typeface and overall, it looked suspicious, in the event that anyone had examined it carefully. He forged a Barings inter-office memorandum from his London boss, saying his boss had approved the OTC trade.

Barings London management were concerned. How was their trader making so much money doing apparently risk-free intra-day futures arbitrage trading between Singapore and Osaka? Why did Leeson now need $30 million plus daily to be sent from London? Why had Leeson transacted an over the counter option trade with SLK? They sent two managers, Tony Hawes and Tony Railton, to Singapore in February 1995 to investigate.

Leeson did his best to derail his visitors to ensure they didn't find the hole in the balance sheet, now up to about £200 million. When Railton asked about the SLK trade, Leeson told him that Coopers & Lybrand had all the paper work. Leeson even took the pair for a game of tennis, such was his desire to keep the visitors away from the office.

His losses mounted so he decided to double down.

If he bought 1,000 Nikkei futures contracts expecting the market to go up, and instead the market fell, on the next day he sold 2,000 Nikkei futures contracts. These trades were gigantic and were all booked to the 88888 account. He no longer held a view of the market. This was pure gambling.

Monday 20 February 1995 was the first day of his last week in the Singapore office. Nikkei futures for March delivery began the week priced at about 18,400. Monday and Tuesday were quiet trading days. On Wednesday the futures price fell to 18,000.

Thursday was as bad. The Nikkei futures contract price fell from 18,000 to 17,600. For every 100 points fall in the price of the Nikkei futures, Leeson lost another £20 million. He walked around the booths on the SIMEX floor in a complete daze, knowing he was done trading and it was time to run. He wrote later: 'I'd bought everything the market had to offer. I made the market bounce a couple of times, but I'd had the shit kicked out of me all the way down. I was now scared to death. I had to get out of here.'

Railton appeared in the office and wanted to meet immediately to discuss what he called 'a hole in the Singapore office balance sheet.' Leeson said Lisa had called him and she was unwell and he had to go home first. Railton suggested having the meeting on the Saturday. Leeson shook his head and advised that Saturday was his birthday, but said a meeting on the Sunday would be fine. Leeson knew he would never attend the meeting.

*

The total damage inflicted on Barings by Leeson amounted to £869 million, and with only £360 million of share capital, the bank was insolvent and bust as early as the weekend of his flight to Kota Kinabalu. Barings was sold to Dutch bank ING for £1, with ING providing an additional amount of £660 million of new capital for the bank.

The Guardian ran a cartoon showing two beggars sitting on a London pavement with a cap on the ground with some coins. One beggar says: '7 pence more and I can buy Barings.'

Barings collapse was a case of a young, inexperienced and dishonest trader working at a bank which was run by remote incompetent superficial management. At the time, Leeson was 28. He didn't even pass A-level mathematics first time around. Leeson had never trained as a trader and never sat beside another trader to learn the trading job.

Leeson admitted as much in a 2019 interview with a Singapore expatriate website: 'When things started going wrong for me in Singapore, I was 25 years of age. I thought I could cope and perceived asking for help as a sign of weakness. I was wrong on both counts. I couldn't cope and asking for help and advice is a sign that you want to do things correctly.' Barings management had sent a boy out to Singapore to do a man's job.

Management failed spectacularly in Barings. Managers need to manage. As Leeson said: 'The only good thing about hiding losses from these people was that it was so easy. They were always too busy and too self-important, and were always on the telephone. They had the attention span of a gnat. There were too many chiefs who would chat about it at arm's length but never go any further. They never dared to ask me any basic questions, since they were afraid of looking stupid about not understanding futures and options.'

Management failed to ensure the segregation of duties between the front-office (sales and trading) and the back-office (payments, settlements, risk management, finance and compliance). An internal bank memorandum written by management in March 1992, one week before Leeson arrived in Singapore, stated that Barings were 'in danger of setting up a structure which will subsequently prove disastrous . . . and that if the Singapore office is involved with SIMEX, then Nick Leeson should be responsible for the operations side.' This intention to keep Leeson away from trading in the Singapore operation was soon forgotten.

Leeson had four bosses. He reported to Simon Jones in Singapore who was the regional operations manager for Barings South East Asia. He reported to Mike Killian in Tokyo who was the head of global futures and options sales. He reported to both Mary Walz and Ron Baker who led the Financial Products group in London. Four bosses are three too many.

The one local boss Leeson had in the same office was not even located on the same floor. Leeson and his team worked on floor 14 of the Ocean Towers building in Singapore while his local manager Simon Jones worked on floor 24. Leeson stated Jones never walked down to see him. Leeson made the effort to go up to see Jones sometimes but said they only ever talked about football, and rarely about his work. This arrangement suited Leeson perfectly. It was a case of out of sight, out of mind.

The bosses failed to control Leeson. Every trader has a trading mandate which specifies what the trader can and cannot do. Leeson was not allowed to hold any overnight positions, but he did so. He was not allowed to broker OTC option trades with SLK, but he did so. Management took no action to discipline him for his unauthorised actions.

The amazingly easy profits which Leeson said he generated were a warning sign. In banking, one must always consider the risk/return ratio. There is no return unless you take risk, and the bigger the return you make then the bigger the risk you are taking.

Another old adage is true in banking, as it is in life. Follow the money. If someone manages a treasury funding team in a London head office and they receive ever increasing daily requests for funding from an overseas office, it is incumbent on them to understand why these funds are required and when will they receive the funds back?

Banking blunders are as likely to occur in faraway branch offices as in head office. If Leeson had been based in the London head office, senior management could have ensured that he attended 1-1 meetings with them and could have grilled him at his desk on his trading.

Leeson enjoyed a 7-hour time difference with London management who thus only had a few hours in the day in which to try to reach him by telephone or by facsimile machine, in the days before emails and video calls. He could safely decline any telephone call.

Barings internal audit department did not cover themselves in glory. Internal auditors are not specifically trained to find fraud and they do not expect to find fraud on every audit. They are often described as watchdogs guarding the company's assets, rather than being blood hounds trying to sniff out a fraud. But when a fraud is large, endemic and perpetrated for years, the expectation on the internal auditor grows ever larger.

The most important part of the internal audit report was the recommendation entitled 'Back Office Controls' which correctly stated there was a concentration of responsibilities in the role of the general manager and this represented an excessive concentration of powers. Management had agreed to make the necessary changes but when calamity occurred eight months later, Leeson was still performing both of the roles. When internal audit makes recommendations, they must ensure they are actioned to their full satisfaction.

Every great banking blunder deserves a post-mortem report penned by the regulators, who arrive like soldiers on the battle field after the battle is over, their function being to bayonet the wounded. The Bank of England published a report which concluded that all the losses were incurred by reasons of unauthorised and concealed trading activities in Singapore, that the true positions were not noticed earlier due to a serious failure of controls and managerial confusion in Barings and that the true position had not been detected by the external auditors, supervisors or regulators of Barings.

*

Hoechst Prison in the Frankfurt suburbs was

Leeson's home for nine months. He learnt to exist alone in a small space, rather than bounding about the expansive SIMEX floor, and learnt to live without a telephone by his side 24/7. He played table tennis with other criminals and read a Tom Clancy paperback 'Without Remorse' until he discovered the library. He walked in circles in the prison yard for one hour a day. Lisa visited as often as she could afford the flights.

Leeson declined voluntary extradition to Singapore. He hoped that the Serious Fraud Office in London would look to extradite him home, so that he could serve time in a UK jail. His case was based on the fact that his actions had led to the collapse of a British bank headquartered in London. But the SFO viewed his crimes as being committed in Singapore. When a German court announced that it had accepted the Singaporean extradition request, Leeson said he would voluntarily return to Singapore. He met the eager media at Changi Airport, walking between two police officers, with his hands in his pockets, grinning like a school boy caught with his hands in the sweets jar.

He plead guilty to deceiving the auditors of Barings and was sentenced to six and a half years to be served in the Tanah Merah prison. There was no trial so the evidence accumulated by the Singaporean authorities was never presented in public. Leeson said of prison life: 'I was the only white guy in there. You're locked up in a cell for 23 hours a day with two other people. You wake up at 6am in the morning and it's a hundred degrees outside. You get three books a month. So, there's not much to occupy your mind.'

Leeson was diagnosed with cancer in jail in Singapore and had an operation to remove parts of his intestine and colon. He was released early after four years on health and good behaviour grounds in July 1999 and flew to the UK. He correctly described himself: 'I am the most unemployable man in the world. I want to get on with the job of rebuilding my life. I am not proud of my activities as a trader with Baring's Bank. I was foolish and very much regret what happened. I am looking forward to the ordinary things.'

He wrote his biography in jail, or rather a ghost writer Edward Whitley wrote it on his behalf. His literary agent sold the book to Little, Brown & Co. for £450,000. 'Rogue Trader' was published in February 1996, one year after Leeson fled Singapore.

In his book, Leeson takes the opportunity to expose Barings inner failings and screw-ups, with particular emphasis on the incompetency and negligence of management, and the annual expense account junkets to Hong Kong, London and New York where strategy and team building sessions turned into alcoholic binges, food fights and parties with geisha girls. He doesn't hold back when describing one of his bosses as an 'arrogant bastard', and the settlements girl who made the first trading error as a 'stupid cow.'

Leeson ends his book with the ludicrous assertion that as he sits in his humid Changi prison cell, he is the envy of the wretched Barings management who have their freedom, while he has come clean, done the fraud, been caught and is serving the time.

He resides near Barna, Galway, in the west of Ireland. After a divorce from Lisa, he married a Galway beautician named Leona in 2013, whom he met in a night club in Watford.

Leeson wrote two other books, called 'Back from the

Brink – Coping with Stress' and 'Don't Panic – Understanding Personal Debt.' He participated in the UK's Celebrity Big Brother in 2018 where he finished in a credible fourth place. He is an after-dinner and conference speaker where he talks about banking fraud and risk management.

He operates a website called Bull and Bear Capital Ltd, offering tips on investments and trading. Subscribers pay €200 to receive monthly trading updates. He sells signed copies of his book for €20 and signed Barings Futures SIMEX traders jackets for €200.

In 2018, Leeson gave an interview to the Financial News London website: 'People often ask me: 'have you shown enough remorse'? I tell them I don't know what enough remorse is, I don't know what it looks like, and the judge certainly didn't say I had to do 20 years of remorse. But I know I've shown enough.'

He concluded: 'If people disagree, that's okay as I never really try to affect opinion. I know I went through a long period of being sorry and then decided I had to pick myself up and move on, otherwise you might as well shoot yourself in the head and be done with it. I'm sorry for what I did but I'm not going to walk around with my head hung in shame for the rest of my life and so anybody expecting that will be disappointed.'

*

3 – THE CONFESSION

'I didn't set out to rob a bank. At the same time, I was not strong enough to admit my mistake. In hindsight, yes, I could have stopped myself along the way. I wish that someone else would have stopped it for me.'

Toshihide Iguchi,
Daiwa Bank Ltd.,
New York, July 1995.

ON 17 July 1995, Toshihide Iguchi, a 44-year-old Executive Vice President and U.S. government bond trader at Daiwa Bank's New York branch sat at his desk on the 31st floor of the downtown World Financial Centre and admired the view. Way below, the Hudson River flowed into the Upper New York Bay and the orange Staten Island ferries cruised back and forth past the Statue of Liberty. Iguchi looked at his wrist watch again. He was anxiously awaiting the arrival of the afternoon FedEx courier.

At 4pm the bank mail clerk telephoned Iguchi to say FedEx had arrived. Iguchi handed a large sealed envelope to the courier, addressed to Mr. Fujita, the Chief Executive Officer of Daiwa Bank in Tokyo. Inside was a 30-page typed letter, written in Japanese. Iguchi's mammoth letter was all of eleven years in the making.

His letter began as follows: 'Dear Mr. Fujita. I am Toshihide Iguchi of the New York branch. What's written here is my honest confession. When I consider the extent of harm this may bring to the bank, I curse the extraordinary situation in which an employee can cause such enormous damage, and regret that I happened to be in the middle of it.'

Iguchi had suffered years of anguish as he wrestled with whether to confess. He began writing his letter eight years earlier at a low point in his life, during a bad divorce. He had wasted a large part of his life. He had also wasted a large amount of dollars.

The letter explained his situation: 'I have amassed a loss of approximately $1.1 billion by trading U.S. treasury securities without authorisation. I covered it by selling treasury bonds and notes that we are holding for our clients.'

Iguchi believed it was the right time to come clean. When his two sons were younger, he did not wish to disappointment them publicly as a father. Now his sons, Ben, a 16-year-old in high school and Ryan, an 18-year-old freshman in college, were mature enough to deal with the fallout.

The events had taken a great toll on his personal life. Tired of his neglect and long hours spent at work hiding his nefarious activities, his wife Vicki left Iguchi and was awarded custody of their two sons. Iguchi continued his sorry tale: 'The distortion of my dual life finally created a crack in the relationship with my wife, and she asked for a divorce. For the last 11 years, I have been alone in the darkness, shivering with fear.'

The mail clerk told Iguchi it took four days for mail to reach Tokyo. Iguchi carried on with his life in the meantime. He went to work, taking the commuter train to Hoboken terminal and catching the ferry from 14th Street across the river to the financial district in Lower Manhattan. He told other bond traders on Wall Street he would soon be moving on from Daiwa, so his forthcoming absence would not spark concern.

He rechecked ten cardboard boxes stored in the office, which contained 30,000 trade confirmations, account statements and books and records to support his giant loss. Fifteen operations clerks working for Iguchi had unknowingly processed all the trades.

Then early one morning at home, his bedside telephone rang and woke him. The head of international operations in Daiwa was on the line with other senior management.

'This is Yasui from Tokyo. We waited until now so we wouldn't bother you in the middle of the night. I've read the letter you sent to Mr. Fujita.'

'I am very sorry for causing such a problem', Iguchi apologised.

'Well, it's over', said Yasui. 'I can see from your letter how hard this has been for you, but forget the past and let's figure out what we should do.'

Iguchi replied: 'We need to buy back the treasury bonds that are missing from the clients' accounts. Once that is done the New York branch will be made whole.'

Yasui was not convinced: 'A billion dollars. Where do we get the money?'

'As a proprietary investment of the head office. We should find the money in Japan and swap it into dollars', Iguchi suggested. 'What should I do now? Am I fired?' he asked.

'No', Yasui replied. 'We are planning to report this incident to the Japanese Ministry of Finance after our semi-annual earnings report is released in November. Can you continue hiding it until then?'

Iguchi was stunned. The most senior executives in Daiwa were asking him to hide the loss for another four months. He stumbled out a reply: 'I think so.'

The call concluded with the Tokyo executives saying they would travel to New York. Iguchi's mind was racing about where all this might lead. He thought perhaps the management could make the loss magically disappear, or that they wanted to take credit for discovering his major crime. He wondered if they had leverage with the Japanese Ministry of Finance, or if they had a devious plan to bury the loss, and to bury him alongside. His banking career was destroyed but his managers faced personal disaster too, since they bore responsibility for overseeing his trading activities for years. For the next eight weeks, Daiwa stalled and failed to inform the U.S. authorities of the fraud.

Saturday 23 September was like any other weekend. Iguchi was watching TV when the doorbell rang. He opened the door to find three men in suits on his front porch. One of them introduced himself as a Special

Agent with the Federal Bureau of Investigation.

The FBI drove Iguchi to an Embassy Suites motel near Morristown. Iguchi was read his rights and told he didn't have to say anything and he could ask for a lawyer, but Iguchi agreed to waive his rights and to speak. An assistant U.S. attorney asked Iguchi questions.

The lead FBI agent showed Iguchi a copy of his letter. Iguchi now greatly regretted writing the letter. He had incriminated himself and wished he had first consulted with a lawyer, because no good lawyer would have let him write such a damning letter.

Iguchi now realised the bank he worked for had turned him in and the senior executives whom he had trusted had given his name and address to the FBI. He began to wish he had instead shredded the evidence in the ten boxes and taken a holiday to Japan.

The FBI agent advised Iguchi he was arresting him since he had admitted to committing a federal crime. That night the FBI raided the Daiwa office and took away about 100 cardboard boxes of evidence.

Iguchi was taken to a holding room in the high-rise Metropolitan Correctional Centre in Lower Manhattan. The lead Special Agent was an expert in financial fraud and computer crime and he led the questioning. The case was the biggest banking scandal ever perpetrated in the U.S. so the FBI wanted to know everything about Iguchi's life.

*

Toshihide Isamu Iguchi was born on 10 March 1951 in Himeji, Japan. Himeji is one hours drive west of

Kobe, the scene of the 1995 earthquake. The family comprised his father Isamu, his mother Tsuneko, his older sister Kazuyo and older brother Akio.

Iguchi's father's family was too poor to send his father to a high school so he had started work at the age of 12. His father had few prospects without an education. He fought in the war and when he returned home in 1945, he opened a grocery shop, with long hours. He studied English and worked later for an exporter, where he was posted overseas often.

The young Iguchi did not see his father for a year or more at a time. He received monthly post cards from his father to say that all was well, plus an occasional telephone call. Iguchi attended the Kobe Municipal Fukiai High School. In his younger days in Japan, he never gave others the impression of being any kind of future trading buccaneer.

Iguchi arrived in New York in 1969, to spend time with his father who was posted to work there for a Japanese corporation which exported clocks and radios. His father was living alone since it was considered too expensive for Japanese executives to bring their families to the U.S. Iguchi was happy living in Japan and he had a girlfriend. He did not wish to visit the U.S. and had to be told by his parents to travel. He only went on the basis he could return to Japan after six months spent in the U.S.

But so enthused was he with American life, Iguchi decided to go to college and enrolled in the obscure Missouri State College, in Springfield, in 1970. He was one of only 54 foreigners in a student body of 12,000. His college days were not very exciting. He joined the gymnastic club and played the guitar, but he did become a cheerleader in college.

With his owlish glasses and baby-face, he had a studious demeanour. 'He was a little shy', recalled his mathematics professor, who remembered Iguchi as 'an A and B student and a courteous young man' who was active in the campus international students group. 'He was a good student, a personable chap, and clever, too', he added.

Whilst studying, Iguchi worked part time as a salesman at a Chevrolet dealership, selling cars and trucks to farmers, but he struggled in the role and later did other odd jobs. He received a Bachelor of Arts degree in Psychology with a minor in Modern Art in 1975.

He shed his Japanese roots and became a naturalised United States citizen. At college, he met an American girl named Vicki from St. Louis and soon they were married. The couple rented an apartment in Queens, and Iguchi went looking for his first proper job.

He entered banking by chance. His father's corporation had a long-standing business relationship with Daiwa Bank so his father secured him an interview there in January 1976. Iguchi junior was hired as an institutional securities custody officer and he performed this role for eight years. The job involved recording purchases and sales of bonds and notes for the bank and for its customers, and updating custody records. Daiwa held its bonds at a third-party custodian bank, Bankers Trust of New York. He worked in the Daiwa office on Broadway, two blocks north of the New York Stock Exchange, from 8am to 9pm.

Iguchi was now a Japanese salaryman. The Japanese government was broke, and everyone knew they had to work, work, work and save. After experiencing economic devastation in the war, a secure lifetime job was a godsend. Working for a bank was the second best job to have, second only to working for the Japanese government.

Iguchi would be employed by one company for all his working life, he would be expected to be polite, he would receive pay rises and promotions provided he made no horrendous mistakes and he was guaranteed a pension for life at retirement age.

Iguchi's wife took a job as an editor with the United Nations. Their first son Ben was born in 1977. The Iguchi's moved to a two-bedroomed house in Lincoln Park, New Jersey. Everything looked good for the burgeoning family.

*

Iguchi was promoted in 1984 from custody operations to managing a team engaged in short-term interest rate trading in U.S. government issued bonds and notes. His job was to buy and sell treasury bonds and treasury notes on a proprietary basis using the banks cash and to make trading profits at the expense of other market participants. Essentially, he was betting on the future direction of U.S. interest rates, which required a good degree of expertise. He had a maximum position limit of $10 million, which he would go on to well exceed.

His main problem was he wasn't very good at the job. He admitted: 'In retrospect, I was a complete amateur. I was in the market without grasping the essence of it.' Within six months he lost $200,000 trading treasury notes but concealed this loss to protect his reputation and job. He continued trading to try to recover the loss but it worsened.

One day in 1989, he made a huge bet and took a one billion dollar short position in U.S. treasury bonds, selling what he did not own, hoping for the price to fall. But the price steadily moved up in the days that followed. He sold more and more each day, leading to a short $3 billion position. He sat hunched at his desk, looking at the green Reuters screens in horror. Every point increase in the bond price was a $30 million loss. By the end of the trade, he lost $200 million.

His other problem was that because the branch office was small and lightly resourced, Iguchi kept his back-office role when he moved to the front-office role. He was now doing two different jobs for one salary. He was able to both trade, and move, bonds.

Despite knowing little about bond trading, Iguchi managed to perform the job. He slowly became well-known on Wall Street, if only because of the long number of years he participated in the bond market. He bought treasury bonds and notes from brokers and sold them on to other banks and to Daiwa customers. While not a player on the Street, Iguchi occasionally moved the bond market with purchases of up to $500 million a day.

He was known to some as 'Toshi' or 'Tom' but he earned the trading nickname of 'Mr. 52', because he had the unusual habit of buying bonds in lots of $52 million when others would buy in round sum amounts such as $50 million or $100 million. Iguchi struck most brokers and traders as being a hard-working and modest banker. A few traders later confessed they had wondered about

Mr. 52 sometimes as they had detected an increasing recklessness in his trading. 'Some of us thought he was a bit of a loose cannon', said one trader. Other traders said Mr. 52 was often worryingly abrupt and aggressive, or could be aloof.

Iguchi embodied the Japanese work ethic of extreme conscientiousness and long working hours. It was taken as a positive sign by bosses that Iguchi never took more than two or three days holidays at a time, preferring to stay at his trading desk at the bank. But later officials put a different interpretation on Iguchi's reluctance to be away from work.

As a locally hired employee in New York, Iguchi was not rotated between different work responsibilities, in the way the expatriates sent over from Japan were moved internally. Iguchi performed well enough that he was promoted to the rank of a Senior Vice President in 1991, and to the rank of an Executive Vice President in 1995.

Iguchi was a quiet man who never drank alcohol. He wore cheap suits and did not socialise with colleagues. His main passion was golf, and he was a regular star player in Daiwa's in-house golf championships. The divorced Iguchi gained custody of his teenage sons and the threesome lived in a spacious but unspectacular home in the comfortable New Jersey suburb of Kinnelon, Morris County, 30 miles northwest of New York City.

Iguchi bought a Colonial-style home for $330,000 in 1991, taking out a mortgage of $247,500, according to the local property records. The house had a Japanese-style rock garden and pond out front, with large goldfish and a comical ceramic raccoon sporting a jaunty hat, plus a basketball hoop for practice. Their home telephone answering machine had a recorded message in Japanese and English.

Iguchi had a lifelong interest in home building and renovation work, garden landscaping, and raising koi fish. He was known as an excellent cook of authentic Japanese cuisine, he was an avid fan of 1960s and 1970s folk music and he enjoyed playing his acoustic guitar and singing the folk songs he knew so well. He was known by friends as a straight shooter, he was sincere, and he lived his life his own way, never compromising on his principles or ideals. His friends said he enjoyed having philosophical conversations.

Few in the neighbourhood knew much about the Iguchi household. After his arrest, his family members and others expressed astonishment over the trading allegations. 'I don't think there's any way he could do something like that', his son Ben told the media.

'I've never seen him, and we live right across the street', said a Kinnelon neighbour. 'I've seen the kids playing basketball, but that's it. No one knew him. He just came and went. Even during the summer, when everyone around would have a picnic or a family gathering, they wouldn't. They were reclusive.'

A government bond trader for a Wall Street firm told TIME magazine: 'This went on undetected for 11 years? Come on, who's kidding whom? It's a joke.'

Mr. Yasui, the Daiwa executive, gave his personal view of Iguchi to the press: 'We had great expectations for him, and so he felt obliged to keep going instead of coming clean.'

'We really believed in him', Mr. Fujita, Daiwa's CEO, said at a news conference at the bank's headquarters.

'He created a system where he was in charge of everything.'

*

The motive for his fraud was to cover up the large losses he incurred because of his repeated bad bets on future interest rate movements over the 11-year period from 1984. Iguchi had to do something drastic to protect his reputation, his job and his lifestyle. 'So, I sold our customers' securities held in the bank's custody account', he admitted.

He decided to steal bonds held in Daiwa's custody account at Bankers Trust. Some of the bonds in the account 053110 belonged to Daiwa itself and some belonged to its customers. He sold the latter bonds in the market and used the proceeds to cover what he had lost in his trading. The bank's customers never knew, because Iguchi in his back-office role moved bonds between different customer accounts to honour their holdings.

Iguchi retained full control over the back-office settlements department where the trades were booked and the accounts were updated. He adjusted the accounts before anyone else saw them, leaving out the illicit trades and including profits on his bond dealing that were fictitious. The sales tickets for each bond purchase or sale also came to him for his approval. 'People that were working there were all loyal to me because I was their boss. Basically, I had the back and front office under my control', he told CNBC.

In the meantime, the value of Daiwa's custody account at Bankers Trust was being gradually eroded.

The monthly account statements from Bankers Trust, showing the correct state of the account, would come first to Iguchi in the mail. He would destroy these and using official Bankers Trust headed stationery which he had acquired, he forged new custody statements showing bond balances that were inflated in value: 'At the beginning I was typing the balance statements all by myself', Iguchi wrote. 'But since it was so time-consuming around 1991, I started to use a word processor.'

A statement of Daiwa's account at Banker's Trust showed assets of $4.6 billion. But when Daiwa went directly to Bankers Trust to verify the account balance, the real value of the assets held was only $3.5 billion. It was by calculating the difference that the U.S. authorities charged him with trading away $1.1 billion.

Iguchi said his managers at the New York branch were so inept he was able to make unauthorised bond deals within their earshot. Japanese executives in the branch spoke barely any English and knew little about trading. Iguchi said he regularly made $100 million unauthorised bond trades in English on the telephone beside his bosses.

'To trade a hundred million dollars in U.S. bonds that were not authorised by a branch manager sitting just a few meters away in his office requires unusually bold nerves', he once boasted. 'I was sometimes frightened by my own surprisingly strong nerves. I traded the same bonds for 11 years. It was pretty simple for management to understand. I had several managers over me who should have understood. But the New York branch depended on me so heavily for profits. We were producing more than half of their profits. They wanted to keep their eyes closed and they didn't want to know anything.'

Later he admitted to embezzling money to provide for his family, if Daiwa discovered his crimes. 'I realised I had reached a point of no return', he said. He personally pocketed $570,000, to buy a cottage in Pennsylvania. By 1995, he was earning $200,000 per year.

In 1985, his wife asked for a divorce, and so he revealed his plight at work to her in a futile bid to keep her, but she left with their two teenage sons. Iguchi fell into a deep depression. He drew up a will for his children and sent it to a priest, who convinced him that suicide was a cowardly way of escaping from reality.

He said he amazingly passed 179 different regulatory, internal and external audits in the long period of his fraud, all of which should have uncovered his illicit activities. In 1991, the Daiwa securities custody department moved to the World Financial Centre, and the move came with a new trading room. This was risky because the Daiwa office was approved by the New York State Banking Department for use as a custody operations centre only, and no bond trading was permitted.

In 1992, the Federal Reserve Bank sent an inspector to examine the downtown Daiwa office for two days. Four employees, led by Iguchi, doing the unauthorised trading moved to another Daiwa office in midtown. Cardboard boxes were piled up in the unauthorised dealing room downtown to make it look like a spare storage room, and the lights turned off. The bank inspector, who Daiwa staff believed was under the influence of alcohol, left the office after fifteen minutes and he never saw through the deception.

In 1993, on legal advice, Daiwa voluntarily confessed to misleading the Federal Reserve Bank and assured the regulator it was not concealing any impropriety. The Fed conducted another investigation of the operation of the downtown office but found nothing unusual. Daiwa received a toothless reprimand for their deceit from the Fed.

Later, regular Fed inspections were entrusted to a part-time inspector who was a college student in her early 20's with little knowledge of bond trading. She often finished her inspections in 20 minutes. The Japanese Ministry of Finance inspectors were no more thorough, when in 1994, they concluded a two-day inspection tour in about one hour and then headed off to Las Vegas, Nevada, for a short holiday before returning to Japan.

But it may have been action by the Federal Reserve Bank that led Iguchi to determine the game was up. After noting that he had responsibility for both front-office trading and back-office operations, the Fed ordered that Iguchi be assigned to one or the other role, but not both. In October 1993, Iguchi moved back to operations and gave up his bond trading, although he still exerted some influence over the dealing activity.

He endured until he decided it was time to give up and to mail his confession letter to Tokyo: 'Personally, after 11 years of fruitless effort to recover the losses, my life was simply filled with fear, guilt and deception', Iguchi admitted. Daiwa belatedly informed the Fed on 15 September 1995 about the fraud and announced its loss to the public on 25 September. Daiwa fired Iguchi on 26 September.

Iguchi had finally given up, not because he was about to be caught, but because he might never be caught and he might have to endure his life of fraud indefinitely. But every case of rogue trading comes to an end, one way or the other. He chose to end it.

*

Iguchi blundered like others before him and others after him. Having suffered a small trading loss, he believed it was best to bury it and trade away to make the money back. Sadly, he just dug a bigger hole for himself which eventually would cave in on him.

Everyone compared Iguchi to Leeson, but while Leeson was engaged in the complex business of derivatives dealing, Iguchi did his deed in the simple and less intellectual realm of the bond market. As the old adage on Wall Street goes – 'What's the difference between a bond and a bond trader?' Answer – 'The bond eventually matures.'

Daiwa came through their blunders largely unscathed. Unlike Barings, Daiwa had ample resources to withstand the huge trading loss. Daiwa at the time was the world's 13th largest bank, while Barings was ranked only 474th. Daiwa announced thirty of its top executives would suffer pay cuts of 30 percent for six months and would forego annual bonuses as a collective and public penance for what was allowed to happen.

The bank did not have the most basic of internal controls in place. They allowed one man to manage the front office and the back office for years in a flagrant abuse of adequate segregation of duties. No one supervised Iguchi's trading activity and the local expatriate managers knew nothing about bond trading and didn't even speak adequate English. The Daiwa internal audit function was nowhere to be seen for years. Hiding a team of four unauthorised bond traders from regulators by moving them uptown is beyond belief.

It is disgraceful that Daiwa allowed two months to pass after receiving the confession letter from Iguchi before passing on the information to the banking authorities in New York and Tokyo. Under U.S. guidelines, a bank is obliged to report any discrepancies to the authorities without delay. In the two-month intervening period, Daiwa used the time wisely. They sold $500 million of their own preferred stock and $336 million worth of real estate in Tokyo, Osaka and Hiroshima to soften the impact of the $1.1 billion loss.

When they first learned of the scandal, the reaction of Daiwa management spoke volumes. Telling Iguchi to keep quiet and asking him to continue the fraud for several more months while management figured out a plan, underlined the rotten ethical culture in Daiwa.

The detail of holiday taking at Daiwa was seized upon by those who struggled to understand how one man managed to sustain his subterfuge for so long. Under Federal Reserve guidelines for U.S. securities firms, every employee was obliged to take one break of two consecutive weeks a year, precisely to ensure that somebody else gets to be familiar with what that person is doing. In any large American financial institution, alarm bells are always sounded by any employee not taking the normal amounts of leave.

Ultimately, Daiwa received large penalties from the U.S. regulators. The bank pleaded guilty to 16 fraud charges, all of its 19 branch offices in the U.S. were shut and the staff lost their jobs, the bank was expelled from the U.S. and it agreed to pay a $340 million fine. The bankers fell on their samurais. CEO Fujita and Yasui left Daiwa.

The powerful Japanese Ministry of Finance were not happy about being left in the dark. One Daiwa executive stated about bank regulation in Japan: 'The Japanese banking regulators want to know everything. They want to know what size your underwear is.'

The regulators blundered badly. Their various reviews of Daiwa Bank were amateurish, brief, cursory, under-resourced and negligent. The regulators failed to follow up on the many clues indicating something was drastically wrong at the Daiwa New York branch. Iguchi was correct when he prophetically wrote in his letter: 'I can clearly say on the basis of the experience I gained from the Federal Reserve Bank inspection the year before last, that there is zero possibility that this case would be found out in the U.S.'

*

In his first Federal District Court appearance in late September 1995, a diminutive shuffling Iguchi stood in handcuffs, looking nothing like a Wall Street trader. He offered no plea, as he pledged to assist the FBI in its investigations. Iguchi's lawyer depicted Iguchi as being a victim. After making an initial, modest loss of $200,000, he was spurred on only by the Japanese cultural tradition of saving face and protecting his honour.

Iguchi pleaded guilty to six counts of financial fraud,

embezzlement and conspiracy in connection with the losses and the resulting cover-up. Iguchi asked the federal judge for leniency, saying: 'I no longer have any fear or guilt, because I finally did the right thing.'

The harmless non-violent white-collar criminal awaiting sentence was held without bail in Manhattan's Metropolitan Correction Centre. Afraid of what other inmates would do to him for cooperating with the FBI, Iguchi requested solitary confinement and spent 15 months in a small cell, in the same wing as hard-core hoodlums and Mafia Goodfellas. Iguchi became friends with a bank robber: 'Bank robbing is much like trading - you have to do your research, set up a viable strategy with a clear exit plan, and execute it.'

He spoke of life at the MCC jail: 'We were locked in the cell for 23 hours a day. One hour a day we could come out. In front of the cell there was a corridor about 20 feet long and you could walk along there. That is what we called recreation. Only one person could come out. We had to be separated. You had eight people in that one section. We took turns coming out. You could see other prisoners through a small glass window in the door. In the MCC, the moment you stepped out of your cell, you were in handcuffs. To go to the shower, you had to wear them. They locked you in, and you put your hands through a slot in the door so they could unlock the handcuffs. It was like being an animal.'

During time in the solitary cell in the oppressive jail, Iguchi began to write his first book. He said rather dramatically he sharpened his pencils on the cell window frame as he filled several pages of prison stationery each day for months: 'I thought that it would be my social responsibility to reveal the truth about the case, which left a huge stain in Japanese financial history. I can now perhaps feel redeemed that my suffering was not all in vain.'

His book 'The Confession' was published in 1997 and recounts the U.S. and Japanese authorities useless inspections and the cover-up of the losses by Daiwa. The book was published in Japanese and it became a number one bestseller in Japan.

In January 1997, a judge sentenced Iguchi to four years in prison and ordered him to pay $2.6 million for concealing $1.1 billion in losses. The judge said he was imposing the stiff sentence and financial penalties to deter others from committing similar crimes of 'historic dimensions and potentially world-shattering implications.'

Iguchi was moved to the relatively comfortable Allenwood Federal Prison Camp, a minimum-security facility in Pennsylvania. There the normally media-shy Iguchi gave an interview to TIME magazine. He also made the cover of TIME, but for all the wrong reasons: 'I understand that I have to pay a price. But this is not a crime that I set out to commit. I didn't set out to rob a bank. At the same time, I was not strong enough to admit my mistake. In hindsight, yes, I could have stopped myself along the way. I wish that someone else would have stopped it for me.'

He was asked if he believed he was a criminal but he wasn't sure: 'To me, it was only a violation of internal rules. I think all traders have a tendency to fall into the same trap. You always have a way of recovering the loss. As long as that possibility is there, you either admit your loss and lose face and your job, or you wait a little, a month or two months or however long it takes. No one ever goes into the market thinking he is going to lose money. The only reason you do it is because you already have a loss and you don't want to show it. You want to try to recover the loss.'

He was asked if he could pay the $2.6 million court fine: 'I have no money, period. I have zero. I forfeited everything I own: the house, the cars, everything.'

Iguchi had been in prison without bail since his arrest and was only required to serve only 26 more months of incarceration. In March 1999, he was released from Allenwood.

In 2000, Iguchi moved to Atlanta, Georgia, where he faced the problem of all ex-rogue traders – how to earn a living after a public disgrace. He began a new life as a writer, and he authored seven books in the fiction and non-fiction genres. His biography written in prison was published in English in 2014 as 'My Billion Dollar Education - Inside the Mind of a Rogue Trader.'

The book includes photographs from Iguchi's life, as a mop-haired cheerleader in college, as a baffled banker in his first year in the Daiwa custody department of two people and as a spectacled bond trader sitting at the desk where he typed his letter of confession, with the Statue of Liberty in the background. He wrote a private and personal dedication inside the book: 'To Edward M. Stroz – Without his compassion for humanity and dedication to fairness, I would not be here to write this book.'

Iguchi told CNBC TV Asia when promoting his updated book: 'I never profited a penny from this. That's the difference between a rogue trader and a swindler - they are trying to enrich themselves. Rogue traders aren't doing this to enrich themselves, they are trying to get their jobs back. Once you've stepped in to rogue trading, it's like quicksand.'

In the interview, Iguchi demonstrated he was impervious to reality. He said he was not a 'bad apple', which he is. He said it was the fault of the 'banks corporate culture', which it was not. He seemed to be living in a parallel world, perhaps on planet Iguchi.

Iguchi returned to Kobe in 2007 and started an English language academy. He wrote press articles and spoke at conferences and events on the subject of rogue traders.

Iguchi, aged 68, died peacefully, from cancer, in Naples, Florida on 6 April 2019. He was survived by his new wife of five years, Roma Maria Testa. Tributes were posted to his online obituary. One read as follows: 'I knew Toshi when we met in the 1990s while he was going through a difficult time at Daiwa Bank. I worked for the U.S. government at the time, but I tried to take a 'care-for-the-person' approach to my work with Toshi. He was always a gentleman and was cooperative. He also was honest about difficult circumstances in a way that you rarely see in people. We lost touch over the years but every once in a while, I would get an email. He also cited me in the book he wrote, which I found deeply touching and a source of pride to this day.'

The tribute was from FBI Special Agent Edward M. Stroz who had arrested Iguchi on 23 September 1995, and to whom Iguchi dedicated the book of his life as a banker.

*

4 – SEX IN THE CITY

'When things are going well, everyone in the bank turns a blind eye. There weren't any internal controls. Control is boring, my colleagues agreed.'

**Peter Young,
Deutsche Morgan Grenfell,
London, September 1996.**

ON 10 November 1998, the trial of Peter Young, a 40-year-old former director of Deutsche Morgan Grenfell began at the City of London Magistrates Court, EC4. He was charged, along with another banker and two London stockbrokers, with conspiracy to defraud Deutsche Bank, the owners of Morgan Grenfell Asset Management, between August 1994 and October 1996. Observers waiting outside the court at the entrance to Bank underground station to catch a glimpse of Young were in for a shock, as a black London cab pulled up by the kerb and the rear door opened to reveal the accused.

Young gracefully alighted from the cab, wearing a light brown sweater with a pattern of violet and blue pansies over a white dress with a floral print. He had a shoulder-length dark bob, wore make-up, lipstick and beige shoes with two-inch heels and carried a coral blue raffia-weave handbag. Inside the court room, Young told the surprised judge that he now called himself Elizabeth, or Beth, after the name of the daughter of one of his friends.

Some immediately speculated that Young was planning a 'Klinger' type defence, named after the glamorous cross-dressing corporal Maxwell Q. Klinger who tried everything to be sent home from the U.S. Mobile Army Surgical Hospital in Korea, in the 'MASH' hit TV series of the 1970s. Others said it might herald an 'Ernest Saunders' type defence, named after the former Guinness CEO who was sentenced to five years imprisonment, but was released after 10 months, believed to be suffering from a sudden mental illness, which he soon miraculously recovered from.

Until a few months earlier, the six-foot tall Young lived in his family home in Sycamore Close, Amersham, Buckinghamshire, in the Chiltern Hills, 25 miles northwest of London, so the sudden turn of events was unexpected. He was previously married to a university friend, but had recently separated from his second wife and their two sons.

Young married his second wife, Harmanna, in 1991. She was the daughter of a Dutch farmer, had graduated from the University of Leeds, and had formerly worked as a sociologist at York University. With their two children, George aged three, and Henry aged two, the well-off couple lived in a £450,000 five-bedroom detached red-bricked house, set in large gardens behind high hedges in a private cul de sac of fourteen houses. Their affluent picture book family life viewed from the outside appeared to be idyllic.

But Young's 44-year-old wife, using her maiden name of van Dalen, confirmed their marriage ended because of her husband's cross-dressing habit which developed in recent years. 'Like any normal couple with two young children it was hard work but we had a good marriage', she said, but the marriage broke down when her husband wanted to wear women's clothes more often. 'It's been a problem for some time', she advised.

After six years of marriage, his behaviour became erratic. She said he had left the family home because he could no longer control the urge to dress as a woman and described how his appearance had slowly changed over the past eighteen months: 'He started growing his hair long, plucking his eyebrows and waxing his body hair. He needs some help.'

Ms. van Dalen insisted her husband's transformation was not a fake or a ploy, adding that he had talked before about having a sex-change operation. She told the Daily Telegraph that her sons were 'generally unaware of the situation.' She filed for a divorce and was relying on state benefit payments to support her two children. She did not accompany her former husband for any of his City of London court appearances, but she did not believe Young was guilty of a crime: 'I certainly think that over-enthusiasm is a more appropriate description than dishonesty. I do not think my husband is dishonest in any way.'

Their neighbours spoke about the man who wanted to be a woman. 'I never saw him dressed as a woman or in anything unusual', said their next-door neighbour. 'They were just like any other family on the street.' Another neighbour a few doors away told the press: 'Who would have thought it? It's remarkable because I remember him coming up and down the road with his boys. It's actually all rather sad.' Another remembered seeing Young visiting the local zoo with his children: 'He was dressed as a man.'

Young appeared in court alongside fellow accused Deutsche Morgan Grenfell fund manager Stewart Armer, and two former stockbrokers from a London stockbroking firm called Fiba Nordic Securities, named Erik Langaker and Jan Helge Johnsen. All four faced similar charges. Young's lawyer told the court his client was suffering from stress and City magistrates agreed to his application for his current address to remain secret.

Young was sent for trial by the magistrates on charges of conspiracy to defraud and alleged breaches of Section 47 (1) of the Financial Services Act 1986, and he was bailed to return to court. He surrendered his passport and agreed not to leave the UK. Young and his lawyers refused to talk about his newfound fashion sense during the brief court appearance and they did not immediately reveal their planned defence to the charges.

Young and his defence team left the court only to encounter the assembled paparazzi who could not believe their good fortune at an opportunity to photograph a top banker in drag. There was shouting of 'Move to the side' and 'Out of the way, there's a pregnant woman here.' The latter referred to a woman in Young's legal team. There was pushing and shoving as Young and his team barged their way into a black cab. They sped away as some members of the press exclaimed: 'Calm down, fucking hell.' A baffled pedestrian asked: 'What's going on there?' A voice answered: 'Some guy in drag.'

Sub-editors in Fleet Street excelled with their choice headlines, which included: 'City banker dresses up for his day in court' and 'Banker drags himself into court.'

It was later luridly revealed Young had tried to perform his own sex-change operation three times, and he nearly died as he tried to castrate himself after hearing voices telling him he was a woman trapped inside a male body.

Shortly after his alleged crimes came to light, a civil court declared Young mentally unfit to manage his personal affairs, based on a confidential psychiatric evaluation. His brother Robert, who accompanied Young to his court appearances, became his legal guardian.

Under UK law, people who commit crimes while insane can avoid going to prison. If convicted, Young, Peter or Elizabeth, faced up to seven years in prison. But if he was ruled to be mentally ill by the court, he could be sent to a more comfortable prison if convicted, or he could end up with no conviction at all. Was he really mad?

*

Peter William Young was born in 1958 in Guildford, the historic county town of Surrey, located 30 miles southwest of London. In his younger years he was described as a near genius. He graduated from Oxford

University with a 2.1 degree in Mathematics.

He trained first as an actuary and started his working life at Equity & Law, a major life assurance company. He joined a fund manager, Mercury Asset Management in 1990, who were owned by Merrill Lynch & Co., before joining Morgan Grenfell Asset Management in 1992 in London, who themselves had recently been acquired by Deutsche Bank AG.

In May 1994, Young assumed investment management responsibilities for two Morgan Grenfell investment funds; the £800 million MG European Capital Growth Trust and the £450 million MG European Capital Growth Fund. He earned £500,000 a year managing the two funds, whose combined valuation at their peak reached £1.4 billion.

Young made good returns on speculative investments in unlisted stocks, and he continued to ramp up the level of risk in his investment funds to maintain his winning run. In 1996, he delivered a lecture on his investment strategy at the Royal Albert Hall, outlining some of the secrets of his success to an audience of high-earning bankers.

He was named the 'Fund Manager of the Year' by the Investment Week magazine, and took the top two places with his two funds in a competition with other banks in 1995. The funds he ran at Morgan Grenfell were seen as such strong performers that many high-flying City of London colleagues invested their own money in his funds. The more the fund performance grew and outpaced its peers, the more money flowed into the funds.

Former colleagues and acquaintances recall Young as a quiet, intellectual banker and a family man whose conventional dark work suits were anything but flashy. Behind the facade of success was a man described as 'intellectually arrogant', who felt constrained by the rules and regulations designed to protect investors.

A colleague from his time at Mercury told The Wall Street Journal that Young showed little interest in material possessions. He seemed to wear the same suit every day and had a handful of ties. 'He was interested in the intellectual stimulation of the job', she said. Another fund manager who knew Young opined: 'He was very quiet and gentle.'

The Guardian reported that one broker who flew to Norway with Young, said Young had little conversation and 'the only time he came alive' was when talking about Scandinavian companies. On the return flight, Young read a copy of Scientific American rather than talk to the broker. The broker described Young as being 'seriously strange.'

Young found himself working at Morgan Grenfell during a period of huge change. In the 1990s, AAA-rated Deutsche Bank, the largest financial institution in Germany and a giant of German commercial life, headquartered on the river Main in Frankfurt, made a headlong dash to create a global investment banking powerhouse. They threw money at anything that moved in the world of finance on their international acquisition binge.

Wielding an apparently inexhaustible wallet of deutschmarks, Deutsche Bank acquired the City of London's Morgan Grenfell & Co. for £975 million in 1989. The Morgan Grenfell acquisition included Morgan Grenfell Asset Management, a small but solid institutional franchise that managed £9 billion of investments at the time of purchase. It also had some retail funds. The acquisition brought new assets and people.

In building up world-class typical investment banking capabilities such as sales, trading, underwriting and advisory work, the bank had assembled a disparate asset management operation that spanned 21 countries, employed 8,000 people and managed $979 billion of investments. But their problems were only beginning. Next, the bank had to transform the sprawling, seemingly random empire into a single cohesive, money-making business. They also had to maintain a pristine internal control and risk environment in the bank.

Deutsche Bank senior management paid less attention to the fund management part of the bank. The collective view was that asset management was low on Deutsche's priority list. Ideally, asset management is supposed to counterbalance cyclical trading and investment banking revenues and to boost cross-selling opportunities to global clients. It usually delivered a reliable stream of earnings, which is calculated as a percentage of the value of the funds under management. Until 1999, Deutsche Asset Management did not attempt to operate as a single global entity. In the meantime, Morgan Grenfell stuck to seemingly boring low risk fund management in the UK.

But on 2 September 1996, Morgan Grenfell suspended all dealings in its top-performing European Capital Growth Trust, the European Capital Growth Fund and the Europa Fund. The bank made a short statement to the London Stock Exchange announcing that the three funds had been frozen due to 'irregularities' in the funds, and they were pending an investigation by the bank and the Investment Management Regulatory Organisation.

Young still ran two of the funds referenced in the announcement to the LSE. Stewart Armer was the investment manager of the third fund, the Europa Fund. Armer was then suspended along with Young, following the discovery of a suspected breach of personal account dealing rules at Morgan Grenfell. These rules are in place to ensure bank staff do not have a conflict between share dealing for their investment funds and share dealing which they conduct for their personal account. A Deutsche Bank spokesman in Frankfurt said neither Young or Armer had committed any obvious breach of banking regulations: 'But both were hovering on the brink of a grey area', he advised.

Morgan Grenfell identified that the value of the three funds was overestimated. The bank took out full-page press advertisements and sent out letters to the 90,000 small investors to assure them they would not suffer any loss. Trading in the funds was halted for three days and only resumed after Deutsche Bank paid £200 million to buy some of the questionable stocks held in the funds, so as to bring the funds into compliance with UK regulations.

As investors learned more about the irregularities, some began panic-selling their fund holdings. A compensation scheme costing £180 million was set up for the small investors invested in the funds. The final bill for Deutsche Bank reached almost £400 million.

The bank issued an injunction against Young, seeking to determine whether he was personally linked to some of the companies held in his investment fund's stock portfolio. Young's personal assets were frozen as a result of the same injunction. The bank called in expert auditors from Ernst & Young and lawyers from Slaughter & May to assist.

Rolf Breuer, a director of Deutsche Bank, told the media: 'Young is more like rotten fruit on a healthy tree. We saw off the bad apple.' Breuer said he was 'ashamed' at the revelations. The otherwise confident Michael Dobson, the boss of the Morgan Grenfell, was visibly dismayed that the banks internal controls had been so lax. Dobson said there was no evidence that Young, whom the bank had referred to a doctor, acted for personal gain.

Investment management in the UK was governed by the regulations of the Investment Management Regulatory Organisation. The regulations were in place to protect investors and to ensure the orderly operation of the fund management and unit trust industry. Investigations into the irregularities were progressed by IMRO. The UK's Serious Fraud Office, which was responsible for investigating major corporate fraud cases, liaised with IMRO.

On 27 September, the Serious Fraud Office launched its own investigation as fraud office accountants and lawyers, accompanied by City of London police armed with a search warrant, raided Young's Amersham family home and confiscated documents.

Young was fired for gross misconduct and five other Morgan Grenfell employees were also dismissed. The Guardian reported Young's sacking, along with a photograph of the Young family standing behind a wooden garden gate in front of their home. Young wore a shirt and tie and smiled at the camera from behind large spectacles. Next to him was his son George, and then his wife Harmanna, who held son Henry in her arms. All four stared back at the photographer, likely aware their lives had irrevocably changed.

*

In the weeks that followed his firing, it emerged Young had been buying securities in dozens of little-known unquoted private companies located in the far-flung corners of the world, in direct contravention of IMRO regulations. His so-called top performing funds were riddled with dud securities and the stellar performance of his two funds was a sham.

One IMRO rule required that investment funds can invest no more than ten percent of the fund in unquoted stocks. Most investment managers buy quoted stocks which are listed on a recognised stock exchange. This usually means it is easier to buy or sell the stocks, the daily trading volumes can be easily determined so that their liquidity can be ascertained, and the stocks can be fairly valued, based on the last traded price or on the current bid and offer prices quoted on the exchange. Listing a stock on a stock exchange also means there is reliable publicly available company financial information, since there are minimum information threshold requirements in order to obtain the listing. All this helps to protect investors money.

But Young had stuffed his investment funds with obscure stocks that were of uncertain value because they were unquoted and not traded on a recognised stock exchange. He invested in speculative high-technology stocks, many of which were in Scandinavia or the U.S. The bank found that up to 35 percent of his funds were invested in illiquid unlisted stocks, way above IMRO's required maximum ceiling of 10 percent. Young had been ordered in April to reduce this to five percent but he did not do so.

A second IMRO rule barred funds from holding any more than ten percent of a single company. This is to ensure that the funds do not exercise undue control over the investee company. To circumvent this rule, Young set up thirteen unlisted shell holding companies behind brass name plates in the tiny Grand Duchy of Luxembourg. Young had only been in his job as a fund manager for a year before he formed the first shell company in July 1995.

Young would buy a ten percent shareholding of a company, and then use a shell company which he owned, to buy another ten percent shareholding, thereby owning 20 percent of the same company through two different investment methods. In this manner, he found an easy convenient way to get around the IMRO maximum ten percent shareholding rule.

Young's shell companies had neither a front door, a telephone connection, nor staff. They only existed in the commercial register of Luxembourg. Number 5, Boulevard Royale was the headquarters of all the companies, and it was known as an address for such dubious corporate constructs. The grand names of the holding companies suggested large corporations. In fact, the names were made up or often derived from Scandinavian place names, such as Horten or Katrineholm.

The shell companies traded as Société Anonyme

(S.A.) corporations where at least two shareholders are required under Luxembourg law. Interman Services Limited, based in Tortola in the British Virgin Islands, held one share in each company. The other share was held by the Luxembourg Corporation Company S.A., whose two parent companies were also based in the British Virgin Islands.

The shell companies had two directors - Ariane Slinger, the managing director of the Luxembourg Corporation Company S.A. and a notary named Gérard Lecuit. Young soon created a network of cross-shareholdings which were impossible for others to decipher.

There was often a significant difference between the subscribed paid up capital and the maximum authorised capital, a peculiarity of Luxembourg law, so capital increases can be carried out almost informally, and they are not made public. Only when the maximum authorised capital is exceeded, is an entry made in the commercial register. Young liked this secrecy.

In one of his shell companies, Scandi Technology, Young initially registered it with capital of $45,000. Only a short time later, the company magically had assets of $7 million. Young made extensive use of capital increases between two shell companies, as he moved big blocks of shares back and forth, inflating the perceived value of both shell companies.

As well as conjuring up apparently big profits, he could also conceal losses. He mainly bought junk shares of mostly tiny companies. When companies succeed, great returns are possible. However, only a few of these companies ever made profits or paid dividends.

The privacy of the shell companies was an advantage

for some of his investments. Young bought a large shareholding in a UK company called British Biotech. He exceeded the regulatory ten percent shareholding limit and therefore hid the shares in two shell companies, named Medtech and Oralmed. The Oxford-based company was developing an anti-cancer drug called Marimastat that might eventually stop metastases, but it had never made any profits.

Some of Young's money flowed into an American company named Solv-Ex Corporation. This New Mexico company was working on a process to extract oil from tar sands. Young hid the purchases in two shell companies, named Sandvest Petroleum and Alulux Mining. Young's investment fund secretly owned 12.4 percent of this unlisted company's stock. But the investment in Solv-Ex was the riskiest of all his investments. When it later emerged that the company's plant and technology were fake, the shares plunged in value.

The Solv-Ex investment led to Young's discovery and downfall. Morgan Grenfell and IMRO became aware that Solv-Ex had come under Federal Bureau of Investigation scrutiny for possible U.S. securities violations. The company was suspected of links to the Mafia and was among the companies mentioned in a BusinessWeek article entitled: 'The Mob on Wall Street' which suggested that Mafia crime gang members were infiltrating securities firms and manipulating the trading and pricing of some stocks.

Despite the adverse news and a massive sell-off of Solv-Ex stock, Young went ahead with plans to buy more of the company shares. Morgan Grenfell investigated and found that Young's investment funds owned many unlisted shares. One of the companies in his investment fund, Russ Oil & Technology, turned out to be personally owned by Young.

A little-known British stockbroking firm called Fiba Nordic Securities Ltd. became entangled in the investigation. Fiba Nordic, which was set up in 1994, was alleged to have bought many of the unlisted shares for the funds. Fiba Nordic had also valued some of the shares. Young and the two staff at Fiba Nordic were alleged to have colluded to overstate the value of the unlisted shares, leading to Young's apparent success.

The game was finally up on Saturday, 31 August, when Young stood before a hastily convened meeting of colleagues at the banks offices, and told them he could not continue, he was suffering from stress or some mental illness, and he needed to resign.

*

In December 2000, Young went on trial on fraud charges at Southwark Crown Court. True to form, he arrived for the court wearing a scarlet blouse and matching tight skirt, black stockings and black high heel shoes, with a neat bobbed hairstyle and immaculately applied make-up.

A month earlier in November, at an initial hearing in the matter of R v. Central Criminal Court, ex parte Peter William Young, a first jury had been dismissed by the judge after being unable to reach a decision about whether Young was fit to stand trial. Now in December, a second jury was being asked to reconsider and decide the same case.

The Crown Prosecution Service case was that the

four accused conspired to siphon off more than £250 million from three Morgan Grenfell funds into secret stakes in high-risk businesses, and they used an elaborate network of shell companies in Luxembourg, tied together through a complex web of cross-shareholdings, as a smokescreen to hide their fraud.

The CPS team claimed Young broke investment rules in an attempt to win six-figure annual bonuses and to gain promotion at work, and also claimed Young used some dividends from stocks in the investment funds to buy his family home in Amersham.

The Serious Fraud Office representatives challenged the assertion of the defence lawyers that Young was unfit to stand trial in that no mental health problems had been noticed before the fraud was discovered. Initially, Young's appearances in public as a woman were greeted skeptically. The QC, prosecuting for the SFO, said Young had lied about his share dealings and had told an earlier 'fitness to plea' hearing that he was capable of standing trial: 'Peter Young may be vulnerable and confused about his gender, but he was in a jam and for the first time starts to talk about being mad. It was only just before the balloon went up in September 1996 that he said anything about a mental illness.'

The QC for the defence told the jury that the pace of work had driven a star fund manager into a cycle of mental instability, culminating in life-threatening self-inflicted injuries, and Young was now dealing with mental illness: 'He has gone from being a man of the highest intellectual achievement to living the life of a mental patient. Now he sits at home staring at the ceiling unless instructed by his mother or brother to get up and perform some menial task. Some people fake mental illness to get out of a sentence. Others win release from a mental hospital and go on to kill themselves or other people. Peter Young harmed himself in the most bizarre circumstances because he was severely unwell.'

The decline began long before any suspicions were aroused at work. Early examples of Young's eccentricity cited included him buying thirty jars of pickled gherkins on a single trip to the supermarket. Newspapers had reported that Young kept condoms in his office and often spent time in dark rooms at work muttering to himself.

Graphic descriptions of his attempts to complete his transformation to a woman were given in court. The jury heard that his desire to change sex led to him inflicting appalling injuries on himself which eventually led to him losing a testicle. The most recent incident had nearly led to his death from a severe infection. He variously used a craft knife, a length of fishing line and a pair of scissors in repeated attempts to castrate himself. He told psychiatrists that he heard two voices - one male, the other a woman called Sarah - telling him to become a woman.

The jury of six men and six women decided unanimously that Young was 'under such disability of mind' that he was unfit to stand trial. The jury had found that he had schizophrenia, and that the 1964 Insanity Act pertained. He was declared unfit to plead.

Young showed no emotion when he was dismissed and he left court on that day, wearing a cerise top, grey flecked skirt and high-heeled shoes, and carrying a purple shoulder bag. The lanky Young, wearing lipstick of the same colour as his top, paused on the steps of the court for photographers for an instant, before disappearing into another black cab. He was now a free man, but he was accompanied everywhere by a nurse.

The related cases against Young's three fellow defendants also fell apart. A judge first threw out the charges filed against Stewart Armer, the Morgan Grenfell colleague, due to a lack of evidence. The SFO had seized nine months of taped telephone conversations between the defendants, which were recorded as a matter of routine by the Morgan Grenfell internal telephone taping system. One telephone call revealed what prosecution described as 'cynical laughter' from Armer, after Young recounted some of the lies he had told to fellow Morgan Grenfell staff to conceal the investment fraud.

The prosecution said the tapes revealed Armer and Young were plotting to conceal the fraud: 'The important thing is that you know what the lies are, so you do not contradict them', Young was heard on tape telling his colleague. 'Yes', Armer replied.

After it became clear that the network of shell companies was coming under scrutiny, the telephone calls revealed the other defendant, Erik Langaker, trying to calm Young's nerves. 'We've cleaned up our office for all files related to Luxembourg, all were sent off to storage', he said to Young. 'I'm prepared for the guys coming in with the black bags.'

Referring to the telephone calls between the Morgan Grenfell managers, the judge said: 'Armer does not emerge from them in a favourable light. It is clear that Armer did not report to senior management what Young was doing. On the contrary, he seemed to find

Young's reprehensible conduct a source of amusement. On the other hand, there is no rational basis upon which the jury could convict him of a wider conspiracy.'

In January 2002, another suspect in the investigation was found not guilty. Fiba Nordic Securities stockbroker Langaker walked free from Kingston Crown Court after a jury acquitted him and he took an immediate flight back to his native Norway at the end of the series of trials that were estimated to have cost the UK taxpayer up to £10 million. Langaker told reporters he was 'more than happy' with the verdict. 'I don't feel a hero in any way', he admitted. 'But I have paid now with five and a half years of my life.'

Langaker's junior assistant, Jan Helge Johnsen, also faced similar fraud charges, but he did not face trial after being diagnosed with a case of terminal leukemia.

Despite all the losses in court, the SFO was still determined to hold a 'trial of the facts' relating to Young's role in the fraud. The SFO said it was legally obliged to continue with such proceedings against Young under the Criminal Procedure (Insanity) Act 1964.

Their 'trial of the facts' was held in June 2003 and Young was found by a jury to have orchestrated a complex fraud on the investors in his two investment funds. By a majority of 11 to one, the jury found that Young had planned to steal more than £350,000 from a fund under his management using a 'golden bond' investment he designed in secret to deceive his bosses. Young was not present at the Old Bailey for the nine-day hearing.

The judge ordered medical reports be prepared before he decided what action to take in relation to

Young. The three options available were a guardianship order, a treatment supervision order or an absolute discharge. Young was granted the latter.

*

Young's mistake was to depart from the prudent regulatory requirements of investment management and direct his investments into small illiquid unquoted companies of dubious pedigree, and then to collude to overstate share prices and inflate the value of his funds to make himself appear more successful than his law-abiding peers. It is not a blunder. It is an outright fraud perpetrated on his 90,000 small investors.

Deutsche Bank blundered by having an inadequate system of monitoring of the stocks held in their investment funds to ensure they complied with IMRO rules. Soon after the Young incident arose, their London CEO and Head of Compliance left the bank.

Deutsche Bank announced a belated overhaul of its system of internal controls in Morgan Grenfell. Senior bankers from Deutsche Bank admitted to a breakdown of controls and supervision. A Deutsche Bank board member told the German newspaper Handelsblatt, 'We are pushing for substantial improvements in internal controls.' The scandal damaged the Morgan Grenfell brand name and Deutsche Bank discontinued the use of the name in 1999.

In April 1997, Morgan Grenfell was fined £2 million by IMRO and paid an additional £1 million in legal costs. IMRO said Morgan Grenfell was too slow to realise what was happening and too slow to act once it figured things out: 'The mismanagement of these funds has caused unnecessary concern to an enormous number of investors', said IMRO. 'Morgan Grenfell executives ignored warnings about problems in the funds, failed to take prompt action when the problems were confirmed and were slow to let regulators know what was going on. Morgan Grenfell failed to supervise the managers of the funds despite their repeated attempts to exploit perceived loopholes in the IMRO regulations.'

The Serious Fraud Office blundered badly along the way, and not only because of the huge final legal costs. The three adverse court verdicts cast serious doubt on whether the SFO was right to pursue charges against peripheral figures in the wider conspiracy after it became clear that Young would never appear in the dock. The SFO continued to insist that it had been obliged to pursue a 'trial of the facts' under the law.

Counsel for the SFO told the Young jury that one of the reasons the case was still being pursued was to 'protect the system from abuse' and to discourage others from 'putting on a sham.' A spokesman for the SFO said afterwards of their wasted efforts: 'There was a variance in opinion about Peter Young's mental health. In the interests of the public, the only course open to us was to challenge his claim to be unfit to stand trial.'

*

Young, his lawyers, family and doctors refused all press interviews until Young granted a rare interview to the German magazine Der Spiegel in November 1996. Deutsche Bank had run into a series of well-publicised disasters in Germany, and the magazine welcomed the chance to engage in a bout of German banker bashing.

Young gave a frank interview to the reporter whilst sitting with his wife in the kitchen of their Amersham home. His wife said her husband was honest and always enjoyed his job at Morgan Grenfell. The 30 jars of pickled gherkins were mentioned. His wife said: 'So what? Everyone can be confused.'

Young, wearing a plaid shirt and blue jeans, was unconcerned at the furore: 'The investors knew that they were buying risky funds. People believe in gurus. As long as there is success, they don't want to face reality in order not to destroy their illusions.'

He said his bosses weren't interested in the details: 'When things are going well, everyone in the bank turns a blind eye. In the long run', Young said, 'I'll be right.'

Young said he created the Luxembourg shell companies in order to hide his investments from his competitors who were trying to steal his best investment ideas. He said the structures had 'a number of tax advantages' which boosted fund performance.

Young protested his innocence and denied he had enriched himself. He said he didn't hide anything from his superiors, not even the complex network of his Luxembourg shell companies. He said nobody at the bank was interested in what he was doing. 'There weren't any internal controls', Young said, smiling. He said the culture at his investment bank was based on trust: 'Control is boring, my colleagues agreed.'

An unemployed Young was not worried about the future. He had earned good salaries and bonuses for several years. He believed he would probably never get a job as a fund manager again: 'Maybe that's why I should do something completely different.'

Young, under a first name of either Peter, Elizabeth or Beth, disappeared from public view after legal proceedings concluded. There is no auto-biography or book about him, there are no other interviews nor filmed records. Online searches produce nothing of note in the past two decades. There is not even a page about Young on Wikipedia.

His former wife Ms. van Dalen has an inactive profile on Facebook. Her last post was in August 2019, when she posted a photograph of herself taken at the age of 20, where she added a telling comment: '20 years old. Just before I got married. Oh my, I wish I could turn the clock back and make different decisions.'

Young's long-suffering wife gave an interview to the Buckinghamshire Free Press in 2000. She still lived in their home in Amersham and said the familial situation and the lurid events were particularly hard on her two young sons: 'The children did not really know what was going on and even now they don't understand everything. They just know that their daddy does not live here anymore. They know that he is sick.'

Ms. van Dalen, who did not work, was finding it difficult to maintain the house in the cul de sac: 'I don't know what to do with the house. I will just stay here and see what happens. I don't want to move but this house is too big for me. I will have to wait and see what happens. I'm just carrying on with my life and trying to let the children go on with their lives. You never expect your husband to suddenly start dressing in pink dresses.'

*

5 – A PILLAR OF THE COMMUNITY

'Bad news rarely gets better with age. If you mess something up, just tell somebody about it and you won't get fired for it. You are going to get fired for hiding a mistake. I am a little sensitive to that obviously.'

**John Rusnak,
Allfirst Financial Inc.,
Baltimore, February 2002.**

IN early February 2002, John Rusnak, a foreign exchange trader at Allfirst bank in downtown Baltimore, Maryland, had not been seen for several days. The disappearance of Rusnak was unsurprising. His ultimate employer, Allied Irish Banks in Ireland, revealed on 6 February that its small U.S. subsidiary had suffered a suspected fraud of almost $700 million. AIB learnt that management at its American subsidiary

Allfirst had uncovered the losses in its foreign exchange trading department.

Rusnak, 37, a church going father-of-two, was one of only two foreign exchange traders working at Allfirst's headquarters. He stood accused of hiding the huge losses for several years by creating fictitious foreign exchange trades. AIB called in the Federal Bureau of Investigation when Rusnak failed to turn up for work at Allfirst on Monday morning.

In December 2001 and January 2002, management at Allfirst discovered fake trading records and grew worried at the scale of Rusnak's foreign exchange trading. He was finally rumbled in late January when staff at Allfirst identified suspicious confirmations on his trades and learnt of his $25 billion of foreign exchange trading in December.

Rusnak was described by AIB management as 'a pillar of the community', but he was no financial high-flier. He had a salary of $112,000, a low salary by then American foreign exchange trader standards. He bought his home for $217,500. He drove a red Chevrolet Tahoe and owned a Labrador called Barney. Rusnak was among middle-ranking personnel in Allfirst, headquartered in a 22-storey building at 25 South Charles Street, Baltimore.

He volunteered at a not-for-profit ceramic arts centre, Baltimore Clayworks, and was on the board of the Catholic School of the Shrine of the Sacred Heart. He attended church and had an image of respectability in the community. He lived with his wife Linda and their children Katie and Alex, on the 6000 block of Smith Avenue in Mount Washington, a historic suburb of Baltimore. Their wood-built, four-storey Victorian clapboard mansion was perched on a hillside and it reeked of solid, honest American values. A hammock hung from a tree in the garden and two children's scooters lay idle.

Suddenly, the narrow streets of the upper-middle class enclave were full of media. The parish school shut in case reporters tried to approach Rusnak's children. The Irish RTE TV network said Rusnak was not at his home when they called at the residence set back from the road amongst conifer and pine trees. The reporter said he lived in 'an enormous house in a leafy suburb.' Some took the Irish AIB angle and referred to Rusnak as a 'Brogue Trader.' Rusnak was all American, not Irish, and had never been to Ireland.

His wife told reporters that her husband was not home and she asked them to leave 'a private area.' Standing near a handmade greeting card in the hallway celebrating their tenth wedding anniversary, Linda Rusnak refused to talk to the media. 'I know you're just doing your job', she said. 'But my job is to protect my family. I have nothing to say.'

The BBC referred to the clean-cut Rusnak as 'Mr. Middle America.' One neighbour told a BBC reporter: 'He seems like a really cool guy. His kids are cool. I'm shocked.' Another neighbour said Rusnak was a low-key family man who would borrow DIY tools from him when he was renovating his home. 'He never looked to be someone with huge amounts of cash or anything. This isn't a really close neighbourhood, but I think you would know if someone had that much cash.'

The family babysitter lived in the house opposite and told the Irish Independent Rusnak was 'a nice, fairly busy man. They seemed a very law-abiding family. This is not the kind of thing that happens to this kind of family.' She said that earlier her sister had been interviewed by the FBI about the missing trader.

Rusnak's lawyer denied that he was on the run: 'My client is not a fugitive. He's never been in any trouble in his life.' His lawyer said he was in contact with Rusnak and he denied that Rusnak had stolen any money. 'If they're claiming that he stole money, that won't pan out', he said. 'There are no charges. There is no warrant.'

AIB Chairman Michael Buckley spoke at a packed press conference in Dublin on Wednesday 6 February about his trader: 'He has never given anybody any reason to believe from his performance and his job until now that he was an unusual individual in any way. It's a very heavy blow to the bank. He wasn't a star trader. He wasn't earning massive bonuses or anything like that. This was a complex and a very determined fraud. An investigation identified one trader as being at the centre of this and last weekend, as the net was closing in on the trader, he went missing and did not turn up to work on Monday morning.'

Buckley said that hearing of the huge losses was like a bereavement of a family member: 'It was a bit like hearing that my brother had died in a car accident.' A reporter at the press conference asked him where Rusnak was? 'He legged it', advised Buckley.

A diminutive and harassed looking Susan Keating, CEO of Allfirst, stated: 'Until Monday he was an employee of good standing, he performed well over the years, he was a solid performer and he was considered an upstanding member of the community.'

Rusnak was not on the run. He had spent the recent days at a nearby hotel with his family, and he also spent some time meeting with his new lawyer. He returned home and he met voluntarily with the FBI and federal prosecutors. He handed over his laptop and passport to the FBI and assured them he would not flee the jurisdiction.

For five years, Rusnak had lived a frantic double life. He was an upstanding church-going, school board-serving family man in part of his life but during his working hours at Allfirst he behaved like an arrogant, abusive worker, who bullied those who dared to question him as he hid his heavy losses. How had a pillar of the community gone bad?

*

John Michael Rusnak was born on 30 October 1964 in eastern Pennsylvania, across the Delaware River from Trenton, New Jersey. He grew up in a working-class suburb of Philadelphia called Bristol Township. His father Emil was a steel worker and his mother Angelina registered death certificates for the state.

At Harry S. Truman high school, he was academically strong. He attended Bucknell University in Pennsylvania from 1982 to 1986 where he made the Dean's list twice, and he obtained a Bachelor's Degree in Economics and Computer Science.

His first job was in 1986 when he joined First Fidelity Bank in Philadelphia as a foreign exchange trader and he later worked in the same role at Chemical Bank (later to become J.P. Morgan Chase) in New York from 1988 to 1993. He reportedly left New York City because he didn't like the intense pressure and stress of working on Wall Street.

AIB, based in Dublin, acquired the First National Bank of Maryland in 1988 and renamed it Allfirst Financial Inc. Allfirst had 260 branches and 6,000 staff and was among the 50 largest banks in the U.S. In 1993, AIB and Allfirst agreed on a change of strategy for foreign exchange at the bank. Management decided to begin proprietary foreign exchange trading, using their own capital to earn trading profits for the bank.

The bank searched for two new traders. Rusnak applied for one role. He told Allfirst management in his job interview that he could consistently make more money by running a large option book hedged in the cash markets, by buying options when they were cheap and selling them when they were expensive. Rusnak joined Allfirst in July 1993.

Rusnak worked from a cubicle on the 12th floor of Allfirst's city-centre tower, with a number of screens constantly tuned to Bloomberg and Reuters financial news. He bet millions of the bank's money every day on the foreign exchange markets. Usually dressed in a business-casual style of button-down shirt and chino trousers, he would come to work around 7am and leave in the late afternoon, doing 100 trades or more a day. The other participants in the foreign exchange market referred to him as Johnny Ruz.

Rusnak gained a reputation for being quick and hard-working, and was 'a bit cocky', as one acquaintance later put it to the media, 'but he was a regular guy to go to a football game with or to have a pint.' He played golf off an 18 handicap. He socialised in a bar named Peters Pour House on Water Street near to the Allfirst headquarters.

Rusnak showed himself to be an inveterate gambler

when he was invited along with other traders from rival banks to the 2000 Super Bowl game in the Georgia Dome. In a complicated play based on the number of points scored by players with the highest and lowest shirt numbers, he gambled thousands of dollars with the other traders.

Rusnak's compensation comprised a salary plus a bonus of 30 percent of any net trading profits he generated in excess of five times his salary. During his five years of foreign exchange trading at Allfirst, Rusnak earned $859,000, including $433,000 in bonuses

For 1997, he received a salary of $102,000 and no bonus. For 1998, he received a salary of $104,000 and a bonus of $128,102. By 2001, Rusnak's salary rose to $112,000 and he was due to receive his 2001 bonus of $220,456 on 8 February 2002, four days after Allfirst discovered his fraud. That final bonus was never paid.

*

Rusnak engaged in three types of foreign exchange (fx) transactions. He traded spot fx which involves the exchange of two currencies within a two-day time frame at a fixed, agreed-upon exchange rate. The spot fx rate is moving constantly 24/7, but not by much on a daily basis, although the size of each trade can run into millions so that even a one percent adverse fx rate move can hurt a bank. Traders in banks generally trade the currencies of the major G10 world economies, which are more liquid and less volatile.

Rusnak also traded forward fx which is an exchange of two currencies that have a settlement date of more than two days after the trade date, typically within a few weeks or months after the trade date. The difference between the spot fx rate and the forward fx rate reflects the difference in interest rates between the two different currencies.

Finally, Rusnak traded fx options which involve buying or selling an opportunity to enter into a future fx spot trade at an agreed-upon exchange rate, known as the strike price. The buyer of an fx option can exercise the terms of the agreement to exchange currency at an agreed-upon price at a future date known as the expiration date. Fx options allow holders of the options to limit their exposure to changes in the underlying fx rates.

Rusnak's job was simple. He used telephone, email, and electronic communication systems to negotiate with traders, brokers, and sales representatives from other banks and financial institutions to agree an fx transaction. After Rusnak and the other counterparty had agreed the exact terms of the fx trade, he was responsible for entering the details of each trade into the two Allfirst bank computer systems, which were called Opics and Devon.

The Opics and Devon systems produced profit and loss statements for the bank's treasury traders, including Rusnak. In addition to calculating Rusnak's trading profit, bank staff compared Rusnak's profits or losses daily to his month-to-date stop loss limit, which was set at $200,000 in January 2002. His stop loss limit was the maximum amount he could lose in one month before he was required to cease trading for the rest of the month.

The bank imposed a value at risk ('VaR') limit on his trading activities, which was $1.55 million in January

2002. VaR is a statistical measure used to estimate the maximum loss that might be suffered in a single trading day, and is calculated in a complex way using historical market data, but ultimately it is a simple concept. By giving Rusnak a VaR limit of $1.55 million, management were stating their opinion that he could lose that amount in one day and they would accept that level of loss without undue concern.

Rusnak thought the time was right for a recovery in the Japanese yen. He believed the yen would increase in value against the U.S. dollar. With these expectations, a trader normally would buy forward contracts to secure yen now for a cheaper price than the future price, while hedging the position with some options to limit the downside risk.

But Rusnak executed simple trades in the fx spot and forward markets. He did not adhere to the lofty and prudent goals outlined in his Allfirst job interview and he did not reduce his risk by buying fx options to limit his downside. His made good money until a series of policy changes in Asia led to a crisis in Asian markets and prompted a terminal slide in the value of the yen and other Asian currencies. Rusnak was forced to take big losses.

By the end of 1997, Rusnak had lost $29 million. He didn't disclose this blunder to anyone. Instead, he tried to earn the money back by trading. He knew the internal controls at Allfirst were weaker than those he had seen at Chemical Bank and began to hide his losses using fake fx options. These options made it look like he was reducing the risk on his forward positions and they created a fake asset to hide his worsening losses.

Each day, Rusnak entered two fictitious offsetting

option trades into the banks systems. The options had the same premium, they were for the same amounts of currencies and used the same strike price but the expiry dates on the options were different. One had a near date, one had a far date. The near option in the pair would expire immediately and it was worthless, but the far option had a value at a future date.

The premium on each pair of options was the same so the two option trades had a net cash movement of zero, meaning Rusnak did not have to ask the Allfirst treasury department to pay or receive any funds, which might have led to discovery. Rusnak could roll over the options as they expired into new fake longer dated options but had to devise new and better ways to hide his frightening trading losses.

*

By the end of 1998, with $41 million lost, Rusnak convinced Allfirst that a prime brokerage account would allow him to make higher profits from his currency trading operation. A prime broker is useful since once a trade is executed, the prime broker takes care of the less exciting back-office settlement paper work for a small fee per trade.

Rusnak used three prime brokerage accounts with Citibank, Bank of America and Merrill Lynch, to conceal the details of his daily trading activity. The best thing for Rusnak about using a prime broker was that all the settlement monies were rolled up into one net monthly settlement amount, and this reduced the transparency others had to the details of his trading activity.

The prime brokerage accounts permitted Rusnak to enter into fx spot transactions without having to enter individual transactions into the computer systems of Allfirst, and without the back office confirming and settling each transaction. These tasks were instead performed by the prime broker. Rusnak entered fictitious prime brokerage summary transactions into the Allfirst computer systems and amended them as needed.

Rusnak next increased the size of his trades by using an fx contract called a historical rate rollover, known as an HRR. This is a method to extend an fx trade in the event that a settlement of the trade would create a loss for the contract holder. The HRR process is frowned upon in the fx market, and it is rare, but it is not illegal. This allowed Rusnak to postpone realizing his losses, whilst still betting on the yen. Rusnak's loss totaled $89 million by the end of 1999.

The process of confirming Rusnak's fx option trades was done by telephone, faxes, and electronic communication systems with staff in the back offices of the other institution. Allfirst was a small regional bank so the trade confirmation process was entirely manual. Allfirst back-office staff received incoming faxes and if not received, they would chase the other party by telephone.

Rusnak circumvented the confirmation process by creating fictitious faxes from the counterparties of his equally fictitious fx option trades. He used his personal computer to create the trade confirmations. His work PC was discovered to have a folder in his personal directory called 'fake docs.' This incriminating folder contained the logos and letter heads of various banks in

Tokyo and Singapore. Rusnak used the images to construct fake confirmation documents on his PC, which he passed on to bank staff.

Rusnak next convinced the Allfirst back-office staff that it was not necessary to confirm certain foreign exchange option trades. He argued vociferously that since the pairs of option trades netted to zero, they did not need to be confirmed.

By supposedly trading with banks in Tokyo and Singapore, which made sense for yen trades, he also presented the back-office staff with a dilemma. If they wished to check trades and telephone banks in Asia from Baltimore, the Allfirst back-office staff would need to be at work in the early hours of the morning.

Rusnak had next to deceive the external auditors. In January 2001, he was asked by the bank's auditors Price Waterhouse Coopers for a confirmation of a fictitious Asian option trade. So, he rented a mailbox at Mail Boxes Etc. at Suite 162, 2472 Broadway, New York, to receive mail in the name of a Mr. David Russell, a name he invented. Rusnak provided the Allfirst back-office staff with the name of Russell, and a fictitious bank trading counterparty, RBCDS FX, at the address of the mailbox he had rented.

The mailbox provider sent Rusnak the letter from the auditors asking Russell to confirm the option contract. Rusnak signed the false confirmation of this fictitious trade and mailed this confirmation back to PwC. He made sure his reply had a New York post mark and he only used the rented mailbox on one occasion.

Rusnak needed cash to cover his increasing losses. He began to sell genuine yearlong yen / U.S. dollar option contracts to five bank counterparties. One example was in February 2001, when for a premium of $125 million cash, Rusnak sold a put option that gave Citibank the right to sell yen to him at a strike price of 77.37 yen to the dollar. The exchange rate at the time was 116 yen to the dollar so the option would definitely be exercised by Citibank unless some disastrous event sent the yen plummeting. The option was therefore really a high interest cash loan to Rusnak. As well as the $125 million from Citibank, he received $75 million from Bank of America, $25 million from Deutsche Bank, $25 million from Merrill Lynch and $50 million from the Bank of New York.

Rusnak then developed a technique to manipulate VaR reports. He recorded false 'holdover' fx transactions, which are transactions entered into after a certain late hour towards the end of each trading day. Rusnak sent a spreadsheet to the bank risk management team daily and he included his late 'holdover' transactions. But these transactions were not real and they reduced his trading exposure and his daily VaR total.

By the end of 2000, Rusnak's losses had risen to $301 million. In June 2001, Allfirst promoted Rusnak to the rank of a managing director. On 11 September 2001, New York was attacked from the air. Rusnak thought the U.S. dollar would collapse, so he bought huge amounts of Japanese yen, hoping to yield profits spectacular enough to wipe out his losses. But the U.S. dollar stubbornly climbed against the recession-hit Japanese currency. His losses soared to $674 million by the end of 2001.

In December 2001, the Allfirst treasury back-office manager happened to look over the shoulder of one of his employees and saw that there were two trade documents for Asian fx option trades that Rusnak had executed that did not have attached trade confirmations. The employee stated that any Asian option trades that netted to zero did not need to be confirmed. The manager told the employee that all trades had to have a confirmation.

At the same time the Treasurer of Allfirst noted that Rusnak's trading volume was increasing despite his requests to reduce his trading. The Treasurer decided to act. On 28 January 2002, the Treasurer announced at a meeting that Rusnak's positions were being closed down. Rusnak's manager said that he expected Rusnak to quit his job.

On Wednesday 30 January, after the back-office manager heard that Rusnak's positions were being closed, he checked with an employee to see if Rusnak was doing any trading. He was amazed to learn that Rusnak had traded a small number of fx options. The manager noticed once again that no trade confirmations were attached. In all the back-office staff found 12 unconfirmed option trades. The manager ordered the employee to call the Asian counterparties for confirmations that night. The counterparties contacted by the employee informed him that they either did not recognise the fx options or that they did not trade such fx options.

On Thursday 31 January, the back-office manager called Rusnak into his office and told him that the back-office was having trouble confirming his Asian fx option trades. Rusnak said he would call the broker who handled the option trades and obtain the confirmations.

On Friday 1 February, Rusnak left twelve paper trade

confirmations on a back-office employee's desk. The back-office staff reviewed the confirmations and concluded that the confirmations looked bogus. All had indeed come from Rusnak's 'fake docs' folder on his PC. The back-office manager met with Rusnak and his manager and decided that the suspect option trades would have to be confirmed instead by telephone.

Rusnak became very angry and stated he was making money for the bank, and that if the back-office continued to question his activities, they would drive him to quit his job. He left to take a walk outside. Rusnak returned ten minutes later and apologised for having walked out and said that he would do whatever he could to help confirm the trades.

The Asian markets were now closed and the telephone calls could not be made until Sunday night. Rusnak promised to call the Allfirst back-office employee by 9pm to give the employee the telephone number for the broker who arranged the option trades.

Rusnak left the office for the last time and took some personal belongings with him in a cardboard box. He drove his family to a nearby Maryland hotel where his children played in the hotel pool as he told his wife of his trading activities of the prior five years. His shocked wife said her support was conditional on him being honest and telling federal prosecutors everything.

Saturday passed uneventfully. On Sunday 3 February, and not having heard from Rusnak, the employee telephoned Rusnak at his home around noon. There was no reply. The back-office employee stayed at the office until two o'clock in the morning, trying in vain both to reach Rusnak and to confirm the option trades with the Asian counterparties.

On Monday 4 February, Rusnak failed to appear for work. His manager and the back-office manager reported the bogus transactions to Allfirst's Treasurer. The Treasurer and Rusnak's manager drove to Rusnak's home in an effort to find their trader. There was no one at home at the house on the 6000 block of Smith Avenue in Mount Washington.

It took time for management to exclude the fictitious trades from the bank systems and then to rerun their value at risk exposure reports. The shocking loss was revealed. At 3.30pm Allfirst notified AIB of an 'emergency situation.' AIB dispatched senior treasury management from Dublin to Baltimore on the first flight on Tuesday. 'We couldn't get our head around the fact that it was so big', said one stunned AIB executive.

*

Rusnak's biggest blunder was the first time he made a loss trading yen / U.S. dollar and decided to hide the loss through nefarious means. A small loss inevitably becomes a large loss over time, and his was ultimately huge. He told the Irish Times: 'Once faced with that loss, my attitude, ego, mentality at the time said, 'I can make it back and I am smart enough, I have the resources and I have got people around me so I will just grow the business and trade more and try to make it back. That is like throwing bad money after good, it never works out so well. That's what I did. It just snowballed. It got to a point where I was so numb to it that I would say that the majority of the money was lost in the last nine months when I was completely without any reason.'

Bank management blundered. Allfirst's decision to open a foreign exchange trading department with two staff was wrong. They could have used the foreign exchange expertise of AIB's head office in Dublin. Trading departments benefit from scale and expertise and large banks centralise fx trading in teams in the big money centres. A two person trading team in Baltimore has no advantage in the highly competitive, sophisticated fx market. Like much in banking, the saying 'Go Large or Go Home' applies.

Allfirst management, particularly the bank Treasurer, was not experienced in foreign exchange trading and did not adequately supervise his activities. It was not as if they had hundreds of fx traders to supervise. They had two. A knowledgeable supervisor would have seen that option trades expiring on the same day they were purchased were odd. The size of Rusnak's positions and trading volume warranted much closer scrutiny.

Allfirst had installed Travel Bloomberg software so that Rusnak could trade from home and while he was on vacation on his laptop. This was a direct violation of U.S. law which required that traders take 10 consecutive days off from trading every year. Preventing a rogue trader from trading often offers the greatest chance of discovery.

Management ignored issues raised by back-office staff ranging from problems with confirming trades, suspicious trade confirmations and problems with Rusnak's aggressive personality. Back-office staff gave up raising red flags on his trading practices, because they received so much push back from Rusnak and had so little support from management.

Their confirmation process was amateurish and

risky. Large banks at the time used the Crossmar Matching System, supplied by Citibank, to confirm fx option trades. This system confirmed trades instantaneously when both traders entered their trades into the Crossmar system. Instead of using this system, Allfirst used insecure telephone and fax communications.

CEO Buckley kept his job: 'I do not see it as having any impact on my own position. The nature of this fraud was very complex. We have a very adequate series of checks and balances, in the same way that a house has a very good alarm system. But someone who is determined and very expert and, in a position, to overcome that system can do it.' This is of course utter baloney. There was no adequate series of checks and balances. If there was, Rusnak would not have survived five years of trading at Allfirst.

Internal audit at AIB blundered. They had a team of expert treasury auditors in the Dublin head office who regularly audited the treasury functions in Dublin and London but they had no mandate to visit the Baltimore office of Allfirst. AIB and Allfirst management preferred a light touch approach to monitoring the U.S. subsidiary. Internal audit tried to include Allfirst treasury in their scope but they were rebuffed and they did not persevere to ensure sufficient internal audit coverage.

AIB asked the Promontory Financial Group of Washington DC to investigate the affair. Their 57-page report was compiled by Eugene Ludwig, a former lead U.S. banking regulator. The report, produced in March 2002, portrayed a bank with weak risk management and poor controls that allowed Rusnak to alter records and hide losses.

Ludwig opined in an interview about the fraud: 'The company's been mugged, and the mugger was Rusnak.' Rusnak did not cooperate with the Ludwig investigators.

The Ludwig report outlined the blunders in its conclusions. Rusnak manipulated the weak control environment in Allfirst's treasury department. His trading activities did not receive the scrutiny that they deserved. His telephone line at work was not recorded.

The Ludwig report said Rusnak was regarded by some fellow employees as 'strong and confident.' Some others reported him to be hard working and a good family man. At the same time, many at Allfirst, particularly in the back office, found him to be 'arrogant and abusive.' While his manager criticised Rusnak for his conduct toward the back office, the same manager also tolerated abusive and disruptive conduct by Rusnak and he praised Rusnak in his performance evaluations, including his teamwork and interpersonal skills.

As for his reputation in the market, the report stated Rusnak became one of the biggest proprietary fx traders in the U.S. The other banks and brokers heavily entertained him, with meals and travel. Bank of America took him to the U.S. Open golf tournament at Pebble Beach in 2000. Another bank took him to Las Vegas, and another bank took him and his wife for a holiday in Italy. Lehman Brothers took him to the 2001 Super Bowl in Tampa, Florida. On the February 2002 weekend when he went missing from his home, he should have been at another Super Bowl to watch New England play St Louis. His flashy junkets, or indeed his ability to go anywhere, were now gone for some time.

*

Rusnak was charged with bank fraud, and false entry in bank records. He had concealed from officers of Allfirst a trading loss of the exact amount of $691,204,113.

Rusnak plead guilty to one criminal charge of bank fraud. 'I am very sorry for what I have done', he said apologetically inside the federal courthouse. 'I accept full responsibility for my actions. I am going to accept the sentence without any bitterness, and try to make restitution and hope that it will lead me to some redemption later in life.'

In January 2003, he was sentenced to seven years in prison and began his sentence at Fort Dix prison in New Jersey, where he underwent treatment for alcohol, substance abuse and gambling addictions. In all, Rusnak served his time in seven prisons, in Virginia, West Virginia and Ohio. Inside, he taught personal finance to other inmates.

Rusnak told the Irish Times that he was a novelty as inmates sought him out: 'A guy who has committed a white-collar crime is like a celebrity in jail mainly because people want to figure out how they can commit that crime when they get out. People were fairly friendly. They had a lot of time on their hands.'

Rusnak concluded that prison itself wasn't as horrible as people might think. He wasn't worried about survival, but instead he spent time reflecting on what he'd done wrong and trying to put together a better plan for his life afterward. 'The punishment in doing time was the deprivation of contact with your family. It's just extremely boring. So, that's what you do when you have five and a half years in prison. You make plans.'

Faith had been a big part of Rusnak's life but it became more important in prison. When he was at the federal prison in Hazelton, West Virginia, the highest security prison in which he served time, he spent three months, 23 hours a day in a six-by-10-foot cell with only a bible and a sudoku puzzle book to occupy him. There he rediscovered God.

Rusnak was released early, with his sentence reduced for good behaviour and for participating in drug and alcohol education programmes. Upon his release, he started paying back $1,000 a month for the five years of his probation. He can never work for a bank again without permission from the federal government.

Rusnak chose to remain living in Baltimore. His wife stuck by him: She was glad that she knew what was going on with me. I wasn't speaking with her or the kids or anybody really then, and I think she thought that I hated her and wanted to divorce.'

In 2011, Rusnak started work in a local ZIPS dry cleaning business. Some in the dry-cleaning franchise joked they wanted to call the business 'Rusnak's Laundering Clothes & Money.' By 2014, Rusnak managed four ZIPS outlets in the Baltimore area, with 60 staff, many of whom were recovering addicts or felons.

In 2014, Rusnak gave an interview to the Irish Times where he said he went into the laundry business with the hope of helping others. The company's wider mission was to give people a second chance, whether they were returning from incarceration or from drug and alcohol rehabilitation or had been thrown out of school or out of their home.

He said he insisted his staff were up-front in his new business: 'The biggest thing that we tell everybody is transparency. If you screw something up, nobody gets fired from their mistakes so just tell somebody as soon as possible. Bad news rarely gets better with age. If you mess something up, just tell somebody about it and you won't get fired for it. You are going to get fired for hiding a mistake. I am a little sensitive to that obviously.'

'I still struggle with some of the same sin and temptation. I'd love to build a thousand of these laundry stores and make a million dollars', he added. 'I still think about that. My primary motivation now is to return money to investors and then also to create these second chances for guys. Unfortunately, God is still working on me.'

Rusnak told Irish RTE radio in 2014 he believed there will be more frauds like the one he was involved in as long as the bonus culture among traders continues: 'As long as financial markets are set up in a way, they're paying young men large bonuses to produce profits, there's always going to be people pushing the edges.'

In 2014, Rusnak gave an interview to Inc. Magazine entitled 'Coping with Failure', and said his inability to own up to his failures led to far more failures. He said he now looks for that same quality, humility, in the people he employs in his work. 'There's strength in humility. It's not a weakness', he said. 'Learning to apologise is a massive skill. I wish I'd figured this out as a kid.'

He said the original trading losses didn't tear his life apart; it was the cover-up that did that. He said he learned to reveal the challenges in his life and business, quickly and honestly. 'You learn to keep everything out in the open, not to be scared to tell people you don't know things, or to say your business isn't doing as well as you hoped.'

At the core of his failures, Rusnak said, was a desire for things he couldn't have. He tried now to practice restraint, and encouraged others to do so as well. 'It's not just about what I want. It's what my want leads to', Rusnak said. 'For example, I may want to make a lot of money, but not if doing so leads to my going back to prison.'

He stated he had learned to accept the slow pace of a steady process, as with the ups and downs of any business venture: 'For me, we're on God's timetable, not mine.'

John Rusnak, as once described by AIB, has again become a pillar of the community.

*

6 – THE SUBPRIME VILLAIN

'We have a view that, this time, we can help.'

Howie Hubler,
Morgan Stanley,
New York, October 2007.

IN early July 2007, Howie Hubler, a 37-year-old bond trader and head of the Global Proprietary Credit Group at U.S. investment bank Morgan Stanley, sat at his desk on the 10th floor of the bank's Times Square headquarters and dialed into a conference call, along with other executives at the bank. Deutsche Bank traders and management were already on the conference line. Both investment banks knew the U.S. subprime mortgage market was rapidly collapsing and Deutsche had shocking news for Hubler.

Greg Lippmann, the global head of asset-backed

securities trading at Deutsche, opened the call. Six months earlier, Hubler had sold $4 billion of credit default swaps to Lippmann. Deutsche had paid Hubler 28 basis points in two separate $2 billion deals in December 2006 and January 2007. A basis point is one hundredth of a percentage point and it is used to exactly price large trades. Lippmann now advised Hubler that their big trade had moved in favour of Deutsche.

Lippmann said the related AAA-rated collateralised debt obligation bonds, or CDOs, secured on home mortgages, that everyone had assumed to be riskless were now worth only 70 cents on the dollar. He added therefore that Morgan Stanley owed Deutsche $1.2 billion. Instead of Morgan Stanley receiving small cash premiums from Deutsche, it was time for Morgan Stanley to pay a sum to Deutsche: 'Dude, you owe us one point two billion.'

Hubler was incredulous and refused to believe that this could be the case, and that he could owe Lippmann such a huge amount of money. The loss was so enormous that it was beyond belief. As well as the $4 billion of credit default swaps sold to Deutsche, Hubler had sold $12 billion more of identical swaps to Goldman Sachs and other banks. If all $16 billion of his trade was in the same sorry state, the losses would be catastrophic.

Hubler and others from Morgan Stanley insisted that their in-house valuation model showed the bonds to be worth 95 cents on the dollar. A valuation model can tell what something was worth yesterday or may be worth tomorrow but the only way to know what something is really worth is to try to sell some of it in the market to someone else. But Lippmann disagreed with the

Morgan Stanley view: 'Dude, fuck your model.'

Lippmann tested Hubler's disbelief by asking whether Morgan Stanley wanted to sell the related CDOs back at seventy cents on the dollar, and buy more at seventy-seven cents. 'I'll make you a market. They are seventy, seventy-seven. You have three choices. You can sell them back to me at seventy. You can buy some more at seventy-seven. Or you can give me my one point two billion dollars', demanded an irate Lippmann.

Hubler didn't take up his offer of the trade since he knew the related CDO bonds were no longer as good as he had thought. He continued to insist to his own management on not taking any loss, since he believed that the related CDOs were still worth 95 cents on the dollar. But Lippman wanted his money and he wanted it to be paid by wire transfer by the end of the same working day.

In the event of such a pricing disagreement, Morgan Stanley or Deutsche could take the matter to a panel of Wall Street banks who would independently and objectively evaluate how much the CDOs were worth, and that price would become binding for both banks. The fact that neither bank took this step underlined the level of confusion and misunderstanding which prevailed on Wall Street at the time. Deutsche particularly did not trust that the other banks would agree how rotten the CDOs had become, since then all banks would face the same problem valuing their own CDO positions. Eventually, Hubler's superiors relented and they wired Deutsche $600 million as a compromise.

In the following months, the related collateralised debt obligation bonds continued to fall in value and Deutsche repeatedly offered Morgan Stanley chances to exit the worsening credit default swap trade. When Lippmann held the first conference call with Hubler and others, he offered Hubler the chance to exit the $4 billion trade at a loss of only $1.2 billion, but by the second time Lippmann called Hubler, the exit price had risen to $1.5 billion.

Hubler still disagreed about the price and he refused to exit the trade. In retrospect, he had misunderstood his own trade. He didn't realise how bad the CDOs had become.

Deutsche fared much better, being on the other side of the worst bond trade in history. Lippmann prospered greatly. He received $47 million personally from Deutsche: 'I don't have any particular allegiance to Deutsche Bank', he stated. 'I just work there.'

But it was the end for Hubler. Morgan Stanley finally admitted defeat and exited the bad trade in the autumn of 2007, at a price of seven cents on the dollar, costing Hubler his job. He disappeared on vacation leave for a few weeks in October and never returned.

In November, Morgan Stanley announced a loss of $3.7 billion dollars on the credit default swap trades. In December, the bank announced a further loss of $5.7 billion on the trades. The total loss of $9.4 billion on Hubler's bond trades was the single largest trading loss in the history of Wall Street.

*

Howard Leroy Hubler III was born on 20 September 1969 and was raised in Boonton, Morris County, New Jersey. His mother was named Judi and Hubler has a sister, Tracy. His father was Howard Jr. or Howard II, who worked first as a teacher and guidance counsellor, before becoming a real estate broker. He worked with the real estate firm Coldwell Banker Realty, in their Mountain Lakes, New Jersey office.

His father later said of his son's infamy on Wall Street: 'I only know him as a good person. And I'm sure he'll come out on top, basically, because of who he is. But it's hard to analyse his world.' His father spoke about his own father, Howard I. 'The other guy was the toughest of the three. He died at 97, and I never got a word in.'

Howard, or Howie, attended Boonton High School and Montclair State College. He was a college football player and was known for his large and tough physique, his stubbornness and loudness, and his aggression. The 1989 college football roster shows that Hubler weighed in at 215 pounds, and was a six foot one inch tall linebacker wearing the number 49 shirt.

Hubler joined Morgan Stanley as a bond trader in the late 1990s. The pre-eminent global financial services firm, founded in 1935, was a market leader in securities, investment management and credit services, with more than 50,000 staff located in 700 offices in 28 countries by 2007. It was known for its traditional investment banking prowess, advising companies on mergers and acquisitions, trading for its clients, and raising capital but it dived headlong into risky proprietary trading in the boom years of the early 2000s.

Hubler's job in the fixed income division was easy. Trading bonds is a relatively simple process, and in time he specialised in trading asset-backed bonds, which are bonds secured on other assets such as receivables or loans. Employees on his trading desk passed slower days by betting on the number of chicken nuggets a junior trader could eat in one hour.

At work, Hubler largely refused help from others and preferred to do things his own way. He was seen as an acquired taste, still as tough as on the football field, and was once characterised as being 'the type to react to any intellectual criticism of his trades by telling the critic to get the hell out of his face.' Hubler kept a quote at his desk from ice hockey player Wayne Gretzky which read: '100% of the shots you don't take don't go in.'

In December 2002, Morgan Stanley announced the appointment of 124 new Managing Directors in the bank. One of them was Howard L. Hubler. There were 983 MD's at the bank and Hubler had made it to the top two percent of the banks worldwide employees.

Hubler's boss was Neal Shear, a former commodities trader who in turn reported to Zoe Cruz, the head of the institutional securities group and Co-President of the bank. Shear's division made so much of the firm's money annually, sometimes earning him a bigger bonus than Cruz, that some believed Shear was hoping to leapfrog Cruz to run Morgan Stanley someday.

But Cruz was no pushover, having started at the bottom, trading on the banks foreign exchange desk and steadily rising through the senior ranks. She reported directly to the Chairman and CEO John Mack and was considered as Mack's successor in waiting. She was the most senior female leader in the bank and in 2006, Forbes magazine named her No.16 on its list of the 100 most powerful women in the world. Cruz was not so popular with the alpha-males at the bank, who referred to her as 'Cruz Missile.'

Both Mack and Cruz had a healthy appetite for risk,

so they went in search of 'alpha', being those outsized investment returns that surpass market indices, such as the newer more complex products called mortgage-backed securities. It made sense for Hubler to be the banks point person for these type of asset-backed securities. Those in investment banking coin their own acronyms to make the industry largely unintelligible to others. Consequently, collateralised debt obligations are known as CDOs. They are small loans packaged together into a larger size, which will default if the underlying loans default.

Hubler lived at Somerset Drive, Rumson, a borough of Monmouth County, New Jersey, with his wife Maria and family. Their home was due south of Manhattan. He took a 60 minute New York Waterway ferry from Belford Docks across Lower New York Bay to Manhattan and a connecting midtown shuttle to the banks H.Q. at 1585 Broadway.

His 6,876 square foot home was built in 1932 on a four-acre estate. It had five bedrooms, ten bathrooms, a pool, spa, gym, cabana, plunge pool, tennis court and a three-car garage. The home had a wine room, a basement movie room, and a second laundry room, in case the first laundry room was found to be inadequate for the occupants needs.

Hubler paid $4.65 million for his home in October 2006, at the very peak of the housing bubble. According to a later online Zillow listing, the home disappointingly sold for $2.635 million in August 2020, having been originally listed for sale at $4.5 million. His home was another investment where Hubler came off second best.

*

Hubler's bond trading team had purchased credit default swaps on bonds as far back as 2003, to cover, or hedge, themselves in case the prices of the many bonds they held fell. Since the bank originated and packaged loans into bonds which they went on to sell, they always had an inventory of bonds, and they needed to protect the value of the inventory in between origination and ultimate sale.

A credit default swap is a financial derivative that works like an insurance policy. It represents protection. The buyer makes payments until maturity, and the seller must pay off a third-party debt to the buyer if the third-party defaults on its loan. A buyer of a credit default swap bets the lender will default, while the seller hopes there will be no default. Credit default swaps can be used to hedge default risk for those who own bonds, or they can be used as a way to speculate on the creditworthiness of other parties.

Home loans had been given to many people in the U.S. who should have never received a loan. There are apocryphal examples of illegal alien Mexican strawberry pickers working on Californian fruit farms who were given large 100 percent mortgages to buy homes. These borrowers took out their loans at higher rates of interest because they had a higher likelihood of defaulting on the loan. They had below prime risk, or subprime, loans.

Hubler saw the packaging and sale of these dubious mortgage bonds up close in the bank. He grew increasingly suspect about the poor quality of the bonds, and wanted to find a way to bet against them. He was bearish, but not bearish enough to realise he needed to bet against all subprime mortgage bonds, and not just the worst of the bonds.

In 2003, Morgan Stanley invented the credit default swap on mortgage-backed bonds. In 2004, Hubler placed a bearish bet against the U.S. real estate bubble when he bought $2 billion in credit default swaps on risky B-rated mortgages from bank customers, betting there would be defaults.

Hubler was very confident the credit default swap trade would be profitable. As soon as at least four percent of the mortgages in the related CDOs defaulted, he would make a full $2 billion profit from the credit default swaps. It was a sure-thing one-way bet because mortgages usually suffered a four percent default rate, even in times of economic prosperity.

By late 2004, Hubler was one of Morgan Stanley's biggest earners because, unlike most others, he was taking positions against the subprime mortgage market. Hubler's team correctly wagered that the subprime mortgage market was weak and it would become weaker, and his insight continued to pay off handsomely during 2006.

Incredibly, Morgan Stanley bond traders were still hypocritically selling worthless B-rated mortgage bonds to investors, such as German Landesbanks and pension funds, but at the same time, Hubler was betting on those same bonds to fail via the swap trades.

By April 2006, Hubler and his team of eight traders were generating an estimated 20 percent of all Morgan Stanley's profits. The team were aiming to make $1 billion in profits in 2006. For the bank leadership, Hubler's profits were a godsend. Hubler was paid tens of millions annually by the bank but he wanted hundreds of millions. The bank soon became afraid that Hubler would leave to start his own hedge fund.

The Global Proprietary Credit Group was formed in April 2006. With it, Morgan Stanley gave Hubler his own proprietary trading group where he could keep a slice of the profits generated. He became a mini-hedge fund within the bank, with fifty staff. Cruz approved the new group which was designed to profit from a bear mortgage market. The ultimate management plan was that Morgan Stanley would spin off Hubler's trading unit into a separate entity and sell it. Hubler and his team would keep 50 percent of the new entity.

Hubler staffed his team with the best of the best from Morgan Stanley. Bond traders queued up to join the GPCG. Hubler relocated his group from the 2nd floor to a new location on the 10th floor. The 2nd floor was crammed with bond sales and other traders and the physical separation would ensure there was no conflict of interest between customer activity on the 2nd floor and the firms proprietary activity on the 10th floor.

Unfortunately for Hubler, Armageddon in the mortgage industry took too long to arrive. Hubler had bought insurance and everyone who buys insurance pays premiums. He was paying out over $200 million annually in premiums on the credit default swaps he had bought until the defaults began, and these outflows reduced his annual profits. As the bubble continued from 2005 to 2006 and onwards, maintaining his bet became very expensive. To solve this negative cash flow problem, Hubler decided to sell credit default swaps on less risky AAA-rated mortgage bonds, where he would receive the cash premiums.

Insuring something that's less risky is less lucrative, so he had to sell a multiple of the amount of credit default swaps that he had initially bought. The inflated ratings on the bonds worked against him. The AAA-rated bonds he had sold were rated higher, so the cash premiums they generated were lower. It always costs less to insure a safer asset.

Hubler needed to sell ten times the amount of credit default swaps he had bought to even out the premium cash flows. He entered into a $16 billion trade in late 2006, assuming he was selling insurance against higher quality AAA-rated bonds, that no one would ever use. But his risk exposure was essentially the same as owing $16 billion of AAA-rated mortgage bonds.

A mortgage bond was like a pyramid with different levels of loan quality. At the top were the high quality loans, then came the lower quality loans and lastly were the lowest quality loans. As long as the majority of all the loans, say 80 percent, was of high quality, then the mortgage bond received an AAA-rating. But even an AAA-rated mortgage bond included some low quality loans and if these loans defaulted then the mortgage bond lost value. A credit default swap on these same bonds worked quite differently. It only took a small percentage of the loans to default for the bond to be in default and then the credit default swap kicked in. The credit default swap is worth either nothing or it's worth 100 percent. There is no in-between. It is an all or nothing trade.

Hubler's swap strategy was now a more complex trade that involved 'shorting' (betting against) low quality subprime B mortgages while taking a 'long' position (betting) on the high quality AAA mortgages that most analysts considered to be very stable. Hubler did not seem aware that the AAA-rated bonds were not as safe as he thought.

An analogy of Hubler's complex trading position at the end of 2006 is as follows. Imagine seeing an old house built on quicksand, which you expect to fall in value, so you sell it short. This is a good trade and you make money. This represents Hubler's $2 billion credit default swap trade. But soon you begin to worry you are too pessimistic about all houses. You see a nice new house next door to the old house and decide to buy that nice new house, to give you some less risky exposure. This represents Hubler's $16 billion credit default swap trade. But both houses, no matter how old or new they are, are built on the same quicksand and both will be wiped out as soon as the foundations collapse into the dirt. When Armageddon does arrive, you will make a $2 billion profit and a $16 billion loss. Your only chance to reduce the $14 billion net loss is to sell the nice new house built on the quicksand fast, to someone else who is more gullible than you are.

In the midst of his trading, Hubler argued with Morgan Stanley management about when the bank would spin-off his unit and allow him to own 50 percent, and about the $25 million bonus he received for 2006, so that it would be larger in 2007.

*

Revenues in Cruz's division rose in 2006, earning her $30 million. CEO Mack was becoming more public about Cruz leading the bank. At the shareholders meeting in April 2007, Mack noted that the company's 'all-time highs in revenues, in income, and in earnings per share' were 'in large part due to Zoe Cruz and the institutional securities group, which manage a tremendous amount of risk in a very smart and disciplined way.'

In the first quarter of 2007, the bank earned $1 billion by shorting subprime mortgages, because of Hubler's successful trading strategy. But even as Hubler and Cruz were riding high, the events that would bring about their downfall were already in motion.

In April 2007, New Century, the U.S.'s largest subprime lender, filed for bankruptcy. As the housing market grew more precarious in 2007, Hubler argued with Cruz about his trades and said that any losses on subprime loans would not be severe.

In May, Cruz ordered the banks chief risk officer, Tom Daula, to run 'stress tests' on Hubler's positions by calculating the potential losses in the most extreme negative market scenarios. This is performed by a bank using complicated mathematical modelling. For 10 days, the risk management team performed an analysis of the portfolio of the Global Proprietary Credit Group and were horrified at what they found in the trading books.

Hubler's trades were stress tested by the risk management team for scenarios in which subprime mortgage pools experienced moderate losses, but nothing higher than a six percent default rate, which was the highest rate of default faced in recent history. They found that the portfolio would be fine at a six percent default rate but that a ten percent default rate would trash the trade and lead to a $2.7 billion loss. Hubler argued with the banks risk management team on this assessment. When his team were asked what would happen if the worst scenario occurred, they said: 'That state of the world cannot happen.'

The risk team found Hubler to be confused. He

somehow believed he was still betting against the subprime mortgage market, but if it collapsed, he would be destroyed.

Hubler and GPCG were offended that the tough questions were even asked. 'It was more than a little weird. There was a lot of angst about it. It was sort of viewed as, these folks don't know what they're talking about. If losses go to ten percent there will be, like, a million homeless people', said one other trader at GPCG. No one yet knew it, but Hubler's chosen subprime mortgage pools would reach default rates of 40 percent.

Cruz was at her vacation home in Aspen, Colorado, for the Fourth of July weekend when Daula called her to say he had concluded Hubler's trades could lose Morgan Stanley up to $2.7 billion, but he said he considered that an unlikely scenario. Cruz told Daula: 'I don't care what your view of probability is. Cut the position.' The risk was too high to bear. But Daula later denied that Cruz advised him to cut the position.

Irrespective of who told who and when, if Cruz did tell others to cut the position, she never followed up to ensure such action was taken. Some in Morgan Stanley said when a boss in the bank gave an instruction, you did it, but when Cruz gave the instruction, a negotiation would ensue.

By the summer, a team of Hubler's managers took over the management of the position. Many of those executives wanted to sell, but some were reluctant to record a big loss. Hubler and others frantically looked for a good price to sell in the stricken market.

In August, Cruz told the banks board of directors: 'We're going to be the best house in a deteriorating neighbourhood', meaning Morgan Stanley would outperform the other big banks in the mortgage crisis. But no one in management, neither Cruz or CEO Mack, understood how bad things were as the subprime market continued to fall apart.

Hubler managed to sell $1 billion in subprime CDOs to Mizuho Financial Group, the trading arm of Japan's second largest bank. UBS bought another $3 billion in ailing CDOs. He also managed to unload another $1 billion to other smaller banks, making $5 billion in all. The buyers should have known better. Hubler was not the most foolish person on Wall Street. Some traders hung on to their CDOs even longer than he did.

As the market imploded in late 2007, Hubler's early bearish bets paid off handsomely. Unfortunately, the 'safer' assets were decimated, and a potential $2 billion profit became a catastrophic loss. The final loss was the outlay of $16 billion, less the $5 billion which was unloaded, less the $2 billion profit, giving a net loss of $9 billion plus.

By the end of 2007, the bank had lost $37 billion through subprime mortgage bond and derivatives trading. Mack called the result: 'embarrassing for me, for our firm.'

Hubler left Morgan Stanley in late 2007. He was not fired but he was allowed to resign gracefully, safe from the fallout that resulted because of his bad trading decisions. After he was forced out, executives considered trying to seize back some of his compensation, including the $25 million bonus before the trading blow up, but he kept all of his deferred compensation because he was not fired. He reportedly left the bank with $10 million in back pay.

The Wall Street Journal reported in 2010: 'On his way out the door, Hubler checked to make sure he would be allowed to keep all the shares previously awarded to him. The company felt it had no choice because Hubler hadn't broken any rules or deceived the higher-ups about his strategy.' When his big bet ended up costing the bank an enormous amount of money, the subprime villain was long gone from his desk.

*

In its ranking of the Top 10 Biggest Trading Losses in History, TIME magazine ranked Hubler in pole position. Hubler made his bets in what turned out to be a disastrous way. As part of the complex array of trades, he bet against the lower B slices of subprime mortgage CDOs and bought the supposedly safer AAA top slices. The income from the top slices offset the cost of betting against the lower slices. But when the market collapsed, the top slices simply didn't hold their value.

Hubler's mistake arose because he was too clever. Like some other traders at the time, he had correctly predicted trouble ahead for the U.S. housing market and placed bets on the default of the riskiest types of subprime mortgage bonds. But his trading desk took things one stage further, funding the trade through an even bigger wager that the top-rated slices of the same mortgage debt would remain intact. Hubler wrongly believed that not all subprime mortgage pools are created equal, when they were all equally bad.

Hubler blundered as his crisis unfolded. He argued with other banks, such as Deutsche, on the other side of the CDO trades. He argued with the result of the risk management review which warned him how much he could lose in the event of a serious market fall. He argued with his managers, and with Cruz, about the optimal course of action. He failed to offload the dud trades on other less astute banks quickly enough. All these arguments and delays ultimately cost Morgan Stanley much more as the disputes caused them to remain in the bad trades longer. His bank took almost the largest possible loss.

Hubler has never been accused of a crime or charged with an offence. Some might say he made management aware of exactly what he did. Others might say he is a rogue trader. But the GPCG was never a rogue operation. Cruz and others approved its formation, they knew the risk he was running, they told Hubler to cut the position but he failed to do so.

The risk management team at the bank missed the early warning signs. They viewed AAA-rated CDOs as being like other AAA-rated debt, such as U.S. government bonds and believed they were risk free. They used complex Value at Risk calculations to measure risk yet none of their daily VaR monitoring and reporting showed problems until they were requested by Cruz to perform a review of the specific portfolio of the GPCG.

CEO Mack blundered badly. The trading game had grown too complex for even the bosses of Wall Street banks to understand. Losses on U.S. subprime-related assets would eventually exceed $1.75 trillion. There is no evidence that Mack ever had even one 1-1 meeting with Hubler to learn about his trades. Everything went through Cruz.

In a conference call with his shareholders on 19

December 2007, Mack revealed that he had little understanding of what his bond department had been up to. On the call, Mack tried to explain to investors how the bank suffered the loss of $9.4 billion. He fielded tough questions about what had gone wrong but had a difficult time explaining himself, because he had never fully understood what was happening, even when it was happening, and he knew little more after it had happened. Some of the recorded telephone call went as follows:

Goldman Sachs (GS) analyst: 'Help us understand how this could happen, that you could take this large of a loss. I would imagine that you guys have position limits and risk limits. It bewilders me to think that you guys could have one desk that could lose $8 billion.'

Mack: 'That's a wrong question.'

GS: 'Excuse me?'

Mack: 'When these guys stress loss the scenario on putting on this position, they did not envision that we could have this degree of default.'

GS: 'Okay. I am surprised that your VaR stayed stable in the quarter given this level of loss. Can you help me understand why your VaR didn't increase dramatically?'

Mack: 'I am very happy to get back to you on that when we have been out of this, because I can't answer that at the moment.'

Mack wrote in his annual letter to Morgan Stanley shareholders in February 2008: 'The write down that Morgan Stanley announced at year end in our mortgage-related business was the result of an error in judgment made by a small team in one area of fixed income and a failure to manage that risk appropriately. It was deeply disappointing to me - as I know it was to all of our shareholders.' This was all Mack wrote in explanation.

A CEO of a bank like Morgan Stanley, which was so involved in the subprime mortgage market, must make every effort to be fully appraised of the bank's core activities. The bank announced it was exiting the riskiest types of proprietary trading, and it closed all but one of its proprietary trading desks. Mack offered to resign, but the board of directors decided to keep him. He declined to accept an annual bonus for 2007.

Cruz appeared to retain Mack's confidence. In November 2007, the New York Times reported that she was still Mack's leading choice to next lead the company. But on 29 November, Mack asked her to a meeting in his office. Cruz took in the view of Central Park that she thought would one day be hers. Her destiny as CEO seemed inevitable, perhaps imminent. 'I've lost confidence in you', Mack told Cruz. 'I want you to resign.'

This came as a shock for Cruz. Only one week earlier, Cruz and her husband had dined with Mack and his wife at a fine Italian Manhattan restaurant, San Pietro, on East 54th Street. After the ten-minute meeting with Mack, Cruz left the building and never went back.

Morgan Stanley reported Cruz was leaving the firm as a 'retirement' after twenty-five years of loyal service. The earlier article in the New York Times had led others in the bank to tell Mack that Cruz was not the right choice as the next CEO. Her fate was sealed. Some of the alpha-males joked it was worth the $9.4 billion loss to be rid of Cruz.

Bizarrely, Hubler's loss was a blessing in disguise

because it exposed flaws in the firm's risk management systems and controls at an early stage, and it came a year before other banks such as Bear Stearns and Lehman Brothers discovered that poor internal control over asset quality and liquidity can be fatal. Morgan Stanley tightened its controls and raised additional capital in time before the U.S. financial crisis deepened in 2008.

The bank received a $9 billion investment in a cash for stock swap with the Japanese Bank of Tokyo-Mitsubishi UFJ, which acted as a buffer against any future unexpected trading losses. The payment was supposed to be wired electronically, which is how most large banking payments are made, but because it was made on an emergency basis on Columbus Day, when banks in the U.S. are closed, the Japanese bank wrote a physical cheque. It remains the largest cheque ever written and it was photographed for posterity.

*

Hubler maintained his anonymity for three years. His name was never mentioned in any Morgan Stanley press release and it did not appear in any news media. It was only when U.S. author Michael Lewis published 'The Big Short' in 2010, that Hubler was outed as a villain. The book tells the story of three individual-led institutions that took the bet that the subprime market was bound to fail, significantly before the rest of the financial world realised that there was a giant problem. Chapter nine was dedicated to Hubler's exploits.

Lewis went on the U.S. TV news programme '60 Minutes' to promote his book. Half-way through the programme, a mug shot of a half-grinning banker in a pinstriped suit filled the TV screen, probably one taken for work purposes. It is the only known publicly available photograph of Hubler. With a thick neck, big head, neat hair and chubby face, and a mouth turned upwards, Hubler smiled out unknowingly at the millions of viewers.

Lewis said the banker had lost Morgan Stanley: 'somewhere between $7 billion and $12 billion in the space of six to eight months, more than any single trader has ever lost in the history of Wall Street. And no one knows his name.' They did now.

Lewis stated Hubler did not understand the forces at work in his own market: 'He was supposed to be the smart guy, so what were the dumb guys doing?'

'What happened to Howie Hubler?' asked the programme host.

'He was allowed to resign from Morgan Stanley and he takes with him millions of dollars in back pay', Lewis answered. 'Tens of millions of dollars in back pay, that was all hushed up basically.'

After his departure from Morgan Stanley, Hubler retired early behind an unlisted telephone number for a quiet life in Rumson, New Jersey but it didn't take long for him to re-emerge. In an office in a converted church building near his home, Hubler returned to the mortgage business. He founded the Loan Value Group LLC in 2008 with some former Morgan Stanley colleagues, to advise those mortgage lenders whose borrowers were threatening to walk away from homes that were worth less than what was owed on them.

It was a start-up designed for the times in that it aimed to help both lenders and home owners, as the company offered incentives to prevent the struggling homeowners from defaulting. The borrowers were promised a large cash reward if they kept making their mortgage payments, and Hubler's firm collected fees from lenders that signed up for the service.

Hubler was trying to move on quietly. His name did not appear on the Loan Value Group company website. Neither did his contact details such as an address, a telephone number or an email address. He did not court publicity or grant interviews, but in this instance he gave an interview to The Wall Street Journal to publicise his new company.

Asked about his trading loss at Morgan Stanley, Hubler did not cooperate and replied: 'I'd rather focus on the Loan Value Group.' He said he was 'comfortably confident' that the new product was working as designed and it would become widely accepted in time. However, his business venture did not endure and it shuttered in 2014.

The irony of a former Wall Street mortgage bond trader who lost $9.4 billion giving advice to lenders and home owners on mortgages was not lost on the journalist. When asked as to whether he was best person to advise others on mortgages, Hubler would only say, 'We have a view that, this time, we can help.'

*

7 – THE OUTSIDER

'To invest €150 million, it only takes a second. For €1 billion, you need four seconds. Things go so quickly with computers that you lose any sense of the amounts involved. The wheel continues to spin faster and faster. It's insane.'

Jérôme Kerviel,
Société Générale,
Paris, January 2008.

IN late January 2008, there was sudden panic and fear on major world stock markets. On Monday 21 January, the London stock market fell by 5.5 percent, the biggest one day fall since the 9/11 terrorist attacks on New York. Japan dived six percent. The U.S. markets fell too. The crisis was fueled by the sale of billions of euros of futures on European market indices, driving prices down and making traders suspicious that something was wrong.

None of the traders knew that the tumultuous events of the week could be traced directly to a lone French trader at Société Générale's head office in Paris, who had been secretly betting €50 billion of the bank's money. Now SocGen had to quickly sell his positions of €30 billion of futures in the EuroStoxx 50 pan-European stock index, €18 billion of Frankfurt DAX futures and €2 billion of London FTSE 100 futures.

On 24 January, SocGen announced a €4.9 billion trading loss, after they had unwound the futures positions in the market over the prior three days. The bank accused one of its traders of taking unauthorised positions. They said he began creating fictitious trades in 2006. SocGen filed a lawsuit against 'a 31-year-old person' for creating fraudulent documents, using forged documents and attacking the banks computer systems.

SocGen's CEO Daniel Bouton said he did not know the whereabouts of the trader, but he added: 'If he escapes, he will be found, there is no doubt about that.' He compared the trader to a lone 'arsonist' who 'creates an accidental fire which destroys a large factory at an industrial plant.' He said the trader kept one step ahead of his managers by manipulating fictitious trades and evading bank controls like 'a mutating virus.' The trader had 'an extraordinary talent for concealment and knew all the internal controls of the bank.'

Jérôme Kerviel was breakfasting at his brother's house in Paris when SocGen made the announcement. Kerviel was surprised - he didn't think his long futures position in European stock market indices was more than twenty-five or thirty billion euros.

He was also surprised by the CEO's comments about the trader being missing, because Kerviel was nearby and in regular telephone contact with the bank's doctor. He had only left his apartment to avoid the press which he expected to shortly descend on his home. His world changed forever: 'That day was a nightmare I could not wake up from.'

Kerviel's actions decimated SocGen's annual financial results. In 2006, the bank posted a net income of €5.22 billion, but in 2007 restated net income slumped to €0.95 billion. The bank's share price tumbled and CEO Bouton resigned three months later.

Opinion was initially divided on Kerviel's perceived guilt. Some saw him as a mathematical whizz-kid and computer genius who had successfully managed to hack his way into complex bank computer systems to hide his nefarious activities for years from lax management at one of Europe's biggest banks. Others who knew him saw a mediocre former middle-office staffer who could not solely be responsible for such trading losses. He was seen by some in France as a flambeur (a 'high roller') or a joueur (a 'gambler').

After his work ID photograph from SocGen appeared in newspapers and online, strangers approached him in public, seeking an autograph and offering encouragement. A retail website launched a pink 'Jérôme Kerviel's girlfriend' cotton top, along with t-shirts offering slogans such as 'Jérôme Kerviel is a genius' and 'I bet on Jérôme Kerviel.'

Kerviel was not particularly well paid for a financial trader in a large European bank. In 2006, he earned a salary of €74,000, and received a bonus of €60,000. He rented a €2,000 per month apartment in a nineteenth century building in the upmarket western Neuilly-sur-Seine suburb of Paris, within easy walking distance of the SocGen head office.

The media soon descended to speak to neighbours, one of whom said: 'He used to leave early in the morning and come home late at night. He was a busy young man. We hardly ever see him. He's always at work.' Now they knew why.

Another neighbour said: 'He is very handsome and well-mannered. I didn't know him all that well, but we used to say hello on the stairs. He loved to pet my corgi. But he didn't talk, he climbed the stairs four at a time and disappeared.'

So many media arrived that a friend posted a notice on the front door of the apartment: 'Don't search here. He has been seeking refuge elsewhere, probably for some time now.'

Kerviel stayed at his brothers place for one week and then arrived at a financial police unit in southeast Paris on 26 January, to face the consequences. He handed over his expired passport, theoretically confining him within France, and was arrested by police.

Kerviel gave an interview at his lawyer's office: 'The bank has tried to make out I'm solely responsible for what happened. I accept my share of responsibility, but I will not be made a scapegoat for Société Générale. I never had any personal ambition in this affair. The aim was to earn money for the bank. You lose your sense of the sums involved when you are in this kind of work. It's disembodied. You get a bit carried away. I never thought of running away from the law.' He dismissed press reports casting him as mentally unstable: 'I am neither suicidal nor depressed.'

*

Jérôme Kerviel was born on 11 January 1977 in the small Breton commune of Pont-l'Abbé, in Brittany, on a peninsula on the western edge of France, 300 miles from Paris. It is a pretty yet windswept medieval coastal village lying on a river estuary.

His parents were of modest means. His father Charles was a self-employed metalwork teacher who died suddenly from lung cancer in 2006, and his mother Marie-Jose was a retired hairdresser who sold her hair salon soon after her husband died.

Kerviel's brother, Olivier, was six years older and also later worked in the finance sector in Paris. Young Jérôme was a diligent pupil at school. The brothers attributed their interest in the markets and finance to a school teacher who knew the basics of economics and markets. The close-knit family had a simple life and were practicing Roman Catholics.

The press arrived at the Kerviel family home, a well-kept single-storey stone cottage with a tidy garden and a white picket fence, next door to a small foundry where his father had worked. A neighbour told reporters: 'They are an honest, working-class family. I have only good things to say about them. My heart goes out to his mother. She worked hard to provide for her sons, and then this bomb explodes to ruin the final years of her life.'

Some people said the only thing that marked Kerviel out as a boy was his obesity. By the age of 13, he was so heavy that he was forced to give up all ball sports. He continued to put on weight, and by 1995, aged 18, though not tall, he weighed 16 stone. A judo class photograph from those days shows Kerviel self-consciously dwarfing his teammates, with greasy hair and a bad complexion. He was rarely seen with a girlfriend. But much later his judo teacher met Kerviel, aged 21, on a beach, and could barely believe his eyes. Kerviel had a six-pack build and was sunbathing beside a beautiful, bikini-clad girl. He seemed transformed and ready to take on the world.

A local lady confirmed her surprise to reporters: 'I can't believe it's little Jérôme who lived just down the road. I've known him since he was a baby. It's a great tragedy, I'm sure he didn't do it on purpose. I'm sure he tried to make it right. His father died less than a year ago and about the same time he was dropped by his woman.' Kerviel was married for two years but separated from his wife before his world at SocGen collapsed.

'He was your ideal son-in-law', said one lady at his mother's former hair salon, who remembered Jérôme helping his mother out on Saturdays at her salon. His aunt said his mother travelled to Paris when the scandal broke because her son 'wasn't doing well.'

The Curriculum Vitae of the man allegedly responsible for one of the biggest banking blunders in history was soon circulated online amongst bankers and media. Outside of banking, Kerviel listed eight years of experience in judo. He held a green belt and was qualified to teach children judo. He listed sailing as a hobby and spoke fluent English.

Not listed on his CV was his interest in local politics. In 2001, Kerviel stood for Nicolas Sarkozy's Centre-Right UMP party in the municipal town elections in Pont l'Abbe, but he was unsuccessful. The deputy mayor campaigned with him but said his reserved and shy nature inhibited his electioneering style. 'He would put pamphlets in letterboxes, but unlike the real politicians, he wouldn't always knock on the doors', he observed.

A teenage friend from the commune said the young Kerviel was ambitious and focused: 'I knew him when he was 18. He wasn't like others, chasing girls. He wasn't into alcohol. He would spend hours swotting up about economics. I don't think he was after money. He certainly wasn't into flashy things or fast cars and designer clothes.' A bank colleague revealed that Kerviel, who he confirmed he had recently split from a partner, was 'more interested in liberal economics than finding a new girlfriend.'

Kerviel attended the University of Nantes where he graduated with a Bachelor's Degree in Finance in 1999. During his final year, he worked as an intern at the local office of SocGen, where his manager encouraged him to continue his studies and to apply there for a full-time job. He graduated from the Lumière University in Lyon in 2000 with a Masters in Finance, specializing in the organisation and control of financial markets.

One of Kerviel's former lecturers at Lyon University stated later that Kerviel 'was a student just like the others, a young man, and he didn't distinguish himself from the others.' He added: 'He is a student with whom we had no problems, who was completely a totally normal student, very hard-working and with very good results.' Another academic said of his now infamous student: 'If he is a genius, we didn't spot it.'

*

Founded in 1864 by Napoleon III, Société Générale pour Favoriser le Dévelopement du Commerce et de l'Industrie en France is known as Société Générale, or SocGen. By 2000, SocGen, once a cautious unexciting domestic French bank had grown onto the world stage, and had 150,000 employees working in eighty-two countries globally.

Kerviel joined the middle-office operations team of SocGen in August 2000. He was located in the open-plan, sixth-floor dealing room of the Alicante building, one of two 550-foot tall steel and glass skyscrapers which serve as SocGen's Paris headquarters.

Middle-office staff support the front-office staff, they book trades, handle queries from the back-office or from market counterparties, and monitor daily trading profits. A good job in the middle-office can be a stepping stone to a better job in the front-office, and the middle-office is a good place to work to learn how to process a market trade.

His first job was typing other people's trades into the banks computer systems. His CV stated he performed 'Process Automation', which is the optimal way to book many trades. Kerviel stated in his CV that his professional ambition was to 'reach a position as a retail listed derivative products trader, managing a volatility and Delta One book.'

In August 2002, his dream almost came true when he was promoted to a Traders Assistant on the Delta One trading desk. In March 2004, he was promoted to a Trader on the same desk. But he feared his untypical rural working-class background might be a handicap in his new front-office role. 'I had realised during my first meeting, in 2005, that I was not as well regarded as the others, owing to my education and my personal and professional background', he explained later. 'Because, you see, I didn't go straight to the front lines. I went through the middle-office, and I was the only one who did.'

Delta, the fourth letter of the Greek alphabet, refers to the rate of change. Delta One products are derivatives with a delta of one, or very close to one, meaning that for a given change in the price of the underlying asset there is expected to be an almost identical change in the price of the derivative. Kerviel's job was to arbitrage differences between the price of cash equities and equity derivatives. The eight-member Delta One trading team which Kerviel belonged to had a maximum trading limit of €125 million.

His colleagues on the trading floor observed he was shy, reserved and quiet. 'He spoke very little, answering questions with nothing more than a yes or a no', said one banker. They referred to him as 'JK.' One colleague at SocGen's head office told the media: 'We often told him that he looked just like Tom Cruise. Like Tom Cruise, he's not particularly tall but he has a presence. He's also clean cut and generally very presentable.'

SocGen's trading arm was expanding fast. 'The atmosphere was seriously aggressive', Kerviel later told the Financial Times. He was determined to keep up with the traders from the better schools: 'I would get to the bank before 7am and often times only leave it around 10pm. It was stress and adrenaline and a passion for the job that allowed me to make it through it all. Oftentimes, I wouldn't even go outside to get something to eat. For me, it was a passion. At the time,

I found this virtual life completely normal; the only thing I paid attention to was the ups and downs of securities on my computer. Whenever I did go out, it was only with my co-workers from the trading room.'

Kerviel noted he could undertake unauthorised trading on the Delta One trading desk. If a trade was intra-day (one opened and closed in the same day), it was not reported as a position on the bank's end of day records. He began taking intra-day positions. If the trade was held overnight, he learnt how to enter a false offsetting trade to mask the unauthorised overnight position. He was now able to hide his unauthorised trades: 'I only had to make sure that, when evening came, it looked like the trading limits had been observed.'

Kerviel knew it took back-office staff about two days to confirm a trade externally so he routinely cancelled and rebooked his trades before the 2-day period expired. He continuously rolled forward his trades, cancelling old trades and rebooking new trades.

The first big money Kerviel made for the bank was on 7 July 2005. At the time, he traded in German equities and German DAX index futures. He sold short €10 million of the shares of the German insurer Allianz, hoping their share price would fall and he could buy them back cheaper. That day London was hit by a terror attack. Insurance company shares fell. Kerviel made an instant trading profit of €500,000.

He told the Financial Times: 'The boss came up to me and said, 'Great job, Jérôme', which made me feel good. But then five seconds later I look at the TV and see the blood and the dead bodies in London. It was hard to take in. But my bosses said, 'Forget your feelings, you know, leave your feelings outside the trading floor.'

Kerviel liked their praise: 'I wanted that pat on the back, like anybody. Their first reaction was satisfaction, naturally, although they told me to avoid such positions, because I could just as easily have lost.'

He knew what he had done with the large trade was wrong: 'As a trader with only six months on the job, I wasn't supposed to take those kinds of positions. Still, right after that, my boss praised me and increased my freedom to make speculative deals from €2 million up to €5 million. That is typical for the contradictory world of the trading room. Risk limits were exceeded on a daily basis. The bosses knew that, but there were never any admonishments.'

He made €4 million for SocGen in 2005, and made €11 million in 2006: 'It was exciting to win more and more. The boss comes over and says, 'Jérôme, you are a cash machine.''

He was now considered to be one of SocGen's best traders. 'It gave a good image of our activity', he later told a court-appointed psychologist. 'It made money for the bank. It proved that my models were good, and it repaid the trust that had been placed in me.'

*

In 2007, the global financial crisis loomed. Kerviel expected that world stock markets would fall so he took a short position on the German stock market index. He bet big on the DAX: 'In July 2007, the market had its first panic attack, and I was able to pull out with a gain of €500 million. Still, I was convinced that the markets would continue to fall, so I got back in with €30 billion. From dawn till dusk, I would stare at the screen, trading enormous amounts, hardly getting any sleep and making €1.5 billion in profits for the bank before the year was up. Almost every day, I declared mind-boggling results.'

Kerviel knew that if he declared a profit of €1.5 billion to management, they would investigate his trading and would find his large hidden positions. On New Year's Eve 2007, sitting alone at his desk on an empty trading floor, Kerviel created eight fictitious loss-making forward contracts to reduce his profit. A forward contract is a customised future-dated trade between two banks conducted away from a recognised stock exchange. Kerviel is likely unique amongst the stupid bankers in that he hid his profits, as well as his losses.

For 2007, he declared an annual trading profit of only €43 million and he expected to receive a €300,000 annual bonus. 'At this point, no one was complaining', he said. 'I told myself that Société Générale would never fire someone who was generating this much cash.'

Shortly afterwards, the SocGen back-office staff asked Kerviel about the market counterparty for the eight forward contracts. He had entered the name of Baader Bank, a small German brokerage, as the counterparty in the banks systems. When asked for more details, Kerviel told the back-office staff it was a mistake and he would rebook the trades correctly. On 9 January, Kerviel told the back-office staff he had cancelled the trades.

By early 2008, he had a €50 billion long position as he bet markets would rise. 'I was confident, even though I was losing money, because I had always been right before.' But by now he had lost control due to the scale of his trading and his deception: 'It was just numbers on a screen. I was not even thinking in terms of money, just numbers of contracts. I had thousands, hundreds of thousands. The whole story is completely crazy. It was stupid. The atmosphere on the trading floor is completely unusual.'

The start of 2008 did not go well. The first five days of 2008 in U.S. stock markets were the worst start to a calendar year ever. The DAX fell from 8,000 to 6,500 in sympathy with the ever-influential U.S. market. Kerviel lost billions.

The SocGen back-office staff returned to the Baader Bank issue. Kerviel now said the counterparty should be Deutsche Bank. The back-office staff asked the whereabouts of the trade confirmations. On Friday 18 January, Kerviel forwarded two forged e-mails with the subject heading of 'Trade Details' to the back-office staff. He then left Paris by train to spend a weekend in Normandy.

Kerviel reused old emails from other banks and brokers. He later told the police: 'I produced a false e-mail using the possibilities offered to me by our internal messaging service, namely a function which allows me to reuse the header of an email that is sent to me by changing the content of the text that is sent to me. All I had to do was type the text I wanted and the email had all the appearance of an original document.'

By the morning of Saturday 19 January, back-office staff had checked with Deutsche Bank, who did not recognise the trades. SocGen management called Kerviel at the smart seaside resort of Deauville to summon him back to Paris. He texted them back: 'I can't reply. I have no mobile phone coverage.' When he finally spoke to his bosses by telephone, he admitted to inventing a fictitious hedge position but said he had done so to hide the €1.5 billion he made in 2007. He immediately returned to Paris and went directly to the banks head office.

The bank asked a doctor to confirm Kerviel was in a fit mental state to be questioned. Management feared he might be suicidal. His manager spent six hours interrogating his problem trader. Kerviel insisted he had always acted in the best interests of the bank. He said he had discovered a very successful algorithm that led to the 2007 profits of €1.5 billion which he had to disguise using the eight loss-making forward contracts. His manager told him: 'If what you say is true, then you're the best trader I've ever met.'

Throughout Sunday all of Kerviel's transactions were traced in the records of the bank. At 6pm, SocGen convened a board meeting to inform the bank's directors. Kerviel was fired, he was told to stay at home and not to come to the office, and was told not to speak to anyone about the disastrous events. If word leaked out that SocGen had €50 billion of futures to sell, global markets would plunge in fear.

On Wednesday 23 January, the SocGen doctor telephoned Kerviel to tell him there would be a public announcement on the next day and advised him to leave for the countryside. Instead, Kerviel went to stay at his brother's house on the Rue de Rome in Paris.

One week after his return from Normandy, Kerviel was interviewed by the police. He admitted his guilt but said he only ever had good intentions: 'I admit that I fabricated operations, I admit that I cancelled fictitious operations', he told the police. 'I admit having taken large positions that could be qualified, as outside the limits of my mandate, and which I masked by fictitious transactions. I had several motivations in making those orders, but first and foremost I had in mind to make money for the bank.'

Kerviel was placed under formal investigation for three offences of breach of trust, falsifying documents and using falsified documents, and breaching system controls access codes. Kerviel's lawyer claimed a minor victory because the preliminary charges did not include fraud. The judge refused a prosecutor's request for Kerviel to be held for more police questioning and approved bail. His lawyer confirmed: 'He is free and he has been cleared of the charge of fraud, which has been repeatedly emphasised by Société Générale.'

*

In May 2010, and timed for maximum publicity and book sales one month before his trial, Kerviel published his autobiography, in French only, titled L'engrenage: mémoires d'un trader (Downward Spiral: Memoirs of a Trader). In it he made the same claims – he had booked fictitious trades and hid positions, but said his managers were fully aware. Kerviel did exceed his trading limits, he created fictitious trades and fake confirmations, and hid loss-making positions. He knew he was doing wrong. But he went one better than other rogue traders by racking up losses of €4.9 billion on the road to ruin.

As evidence in his book for his belief that his management knew what he was doing, he referenced the many system-generated email alerts which his trading generated which were ignored, the queries from back-office staff which were not followed up, the size of his trading volumes and trade bookings, the lack of holidays which he had taken away from the office and the fact that all of his genuine trades were settled as normal by the banks back-office staff.

He stated some in the bank noted that confirmations from market counterparties were outstanding and that some trades appeared to be suspicious. 'I thought it was incredible that no one came to talk to me about this', he later admitted. 'My positions made money, so, in a way, I told myself that, it legitimatised what I was doing.'

SocGen's many blunders were set out in a damning 69-page report published by a committee of independent bank directors in May 2008. The report found Kerviel's supervisors were 'deficient', his manager lacked trading experience and showed an 'inappropriate degree of tolerance' towards Kerviel taking intra-day positions. He and his own manager in turn failed to react to the 74 email alerts that would have allowed them to identify the concealed futures positions. Both were promptly fired from SocGen.

All major banks use some sort of alert system to monitor and control traders. If a trader's position exceeds his limit, if a trader incurs a large loss, if a trade is not confirmed in a timely manner, if a trade fails to settle on time, then the banks computer system can send an email alert to key management about the issue. The problem with alerts is that if they are sent to too many people, everyone thinks someone else will action them and no one does, or if too many alerts are sent, people lose all interest in them. The key to success is not having the alert system – the key to success is to take action.

SocGen blundered by failing to monitor the level of amendments made to trades. Traders book trades on trade date and expect to settle the trade on settlement date two days later, when one party receives cash and the other party receives stocks, bonds or some other instrument. It is rare for the terms of a trade to change between trade date and settlement date, and only then if the trader made an error, such as recording the wrong price or the wrong dates or the wrong counterparty name. Any amendments made later to trades carry a degree of suspicion and are always worth monitoring closely.

Banks with good internal control processes run daily reports from their systems showing the trade amendments made on the prior day, which are called 'cancel and correct' reports. These reports show trade amendments by product, trading desk or office location but the most useful is a report by trader name. No trader should have more than one or two amendments per day. Anything more is an immediate red flag. If SocGen used such reports they would have identified Kerviel's thousands of automated trade amendments.

SocGen also blundered when it failed to ensure traders followed its vacation rules, which required employees to take regular vacations in order to detect any ongoing frauds. Kerviel explained his reluctance to take holidays on the recent death of his father, that he was still in mourning and that taking a vacation would be inappropriate, and this was an explanation his superiors all too readily accepted.

A SocGen doctor had suggested that Kerviel take a holiday but he refused. Kerviel told the police: 'The simple fact of not taking days off in 2007 should have alerted my management. This is one of the primary rules of internal control. A trader who does not does not take vacations is a trader who does not want to leave his book to another.'

*

Kerviel's trial began on 8 June 2010. In court, Kerviel again admitted exceeding his trading limits, faking documents, and entering false data into bank computers but in his defence said his bosses must have known what he was doing, and that he was 'merely a small cog in the machine.' Le Figaro described Kerviel in the Paris courtroom as: 'A lonely man who takes deep breaths, sitting groggily with a hanging head.'

Kerviel told the court psychologist who was asked to monitor his mental health: 'I accept my share of responsibility, which I don't deny. When you're used to making five hundred thousand euros every day, at some point it becomes normal. The results, the numbers, become banal. You're happy, but it makes less of an effect on you. It's not an ego thing. There are people in the company who are far more brilliant than I am.'

On 5 October, Kerviel was found guilty and sentenced to five years in prison, with two years of the sentence suspended. He was required to make restitution to the bank of the €4.9 billion he had lost. The press named Kerviel as 'the world's poorest man' due to the giant personal debt hanging around his neck.

Kerviel was not happy with the court verdict. 'I would like everyone to shoulder their responsibility and, at the moment, I am the only one paying', he told a French radio station. 'I really get the feeling that they wanted to make me pay for everyone else, that the Générale had to be saved and that the soldier Kerviel had to be killed.'

He objected to the adverse publicity: 'People have been digging around in my life. It was announced that police had found a Koran while searching through my apartment. So, then, people thought I was working for al-Qaida. Ridiculous.'

German magazine Der Spiegel asked him how he felt being the person who had lost the most money trading for a bank? 'To invest €150 million, it only takes a second', Kerviel stated. 'For €1 billion, you need four seconds. Things go so quickly with computers that you lose any sense of the amounts involved. The international market is so big that it absorbs all orders in just a matter of seconds. The wheel continues to spin faster and faster. It's insane.'

Kerviel was realistic about his predicament: 'Think about my position. You have been condemned to pay €4.9 billion, you have jail, you have the justice system against you. You have no life, few friends, no prospects. It's difficult to rebuild any kind of real life with all that hanging over you.'

Kerviel's trials and tribulations dragged on through the French legal system. In March 2014, he received good news when a higher court upheld his prison sentence but ruled he would not have to repay €4.9 billion to SocGen. But Kerviel was not in France.

One month earlier he had met Pope Francis in Rome, and as a lapsed Roman Catholic, had found God again: 'It was incredible to meet the Pope. My mind was closed, and he found the key to open it and let the light in. It is difficult to put words to it', Kerviel admitted.

The trader and God's man on earth discussed what Kerviel called 'the tyranny of financial markets.' A year before the Pope had spoken about capitalism's 'idolatry of money.' The two men seemed to be of a like mind.

Not everyone was convinced at Kerviel's Damascene conversion. Le Figaro described his meeting with the Pope as a 'lovely, desperate media stunt.' The brightly coloured Vatican Guard described the Papal conversation as 'little more than a lapse in security.' Photographs of the meeting show Kerviel tightly gripping the hands of the Pontiff, as if he might never let His Holiness go.

Kerviel decided to walk the Via Francigena, a 1,400-kilometer medieval pilgrims route to Rome from Paris, in reverse. He carried rosary beads blessed by the Pope for his mother and a GPS device to keep him on the straight and narrow path to French justice.

The media found a bearded sun-tanned Kerviel near Modena, Italy. Television images showed him wearing a red jacket, brown cargo pants and hiking boots, carrying a red rucksack, a Winston cigarette in hand, walking swiftly and ignoring journalists trailing behind. He said the aim of his walk by was 'to promote the Pope's message that the system is deeply flawed.' The capitalist was now a repentant pilgrim.

The Paris correspondent of the Financial Times joined Kerviel for part of his walk for an article entitled 'Long Walk to Captivity.' Kerviel knew that prison in France was imminent: 'It could be this afternoon, it could be tomorrow.'

He told of a lighter moment on his protest march. He was stopped by police near Siena for walking on a motorway and was about to be fined until he told the police who he was and mentioned the €4.9 billion in damages he owed in France: 'The policeman totally exploded laughing and said, 'OK, no fine for you, you can just go."

An increasingly serious and morose Kerviel rejected any comparison with Nick Leeson of Barings Bank: 'Rogue trading happens all the time, it's just that, if they lose, they quietly get fired. If they win, no one cares. Do you imagine we would be talking here if I made €4.9 billion? Have you ever heard about any rogue trader that has won?'

Kerviel spent his last days of freedom with his supporters and the media in Ventimiglia, only seven kilometres away from the French border. After a short standoff with justice, he crossed the border and was arrested and taken to prison, but only after a photo opportunity where he paused for the media in front of the French EU border signs.

In September 2014, Kerviel was released from Fleury-Merogis Prison south of Paris having served 150 days of detention, on condition that he was placed under supervision, wore an electronic ankle tag at all times and observed an evening curfew in his home: 'I am super happy to leave today. I want to have a normal life.'

Unbelievably, Kerviel next took a legal action for unfair dismissal against SocGen. And even more unbelievably, and this would only occur in the French legal system, he won his case. In June 2016, after eight long years of legal battles, the Versailles Court of Appeal condemned SocGen for the unlawful firing of Kerviel. The industrial tribunal ruled that the bank dismissed him 'without real or serious cause.'

But in September following an appeal by SocGen, Kerviel was ordered to pay €1 million in damages to the bank. Kerviel was deemed responsible for his criminal actions but the bank was responsible for their civil actions, such as having deficient internal controls and weak systems security. Kerviel was not done yet: 'The fight continues. This gives me the energy to continue this fight. I'm hoping to get it to zero in the end.'

A movie about Kerviel's exploits, L'Outsider, was released in 2006. Kerviel was an outsider growing up in a small village in Brittany when others in SocGen grew up in the big French cities. He was an outsider in University in Nantes and Lyon when others went to the grand universities of France. He was an outsider in the middle-office when others went directly to the front-office. He was an outsider when he hid trades and falsified records. He was an outsider when he walked on a pilgrimage. He was an outsider as he railed against the tyranny of capitalism and markets while others continued to obey the law in their banking jobs.

The France 24 news agency reported Kerviel's views: 'I am ashamed to have been part of this system. I am an ordinary person. I'm not crazy. I didn't earn millions and I didn't drive a Porsche. My daily existence was about making money for the bank. That was my only objective, at any price, regardless of all moral or ethical considerations. I was a jerk at the time and I am going to spend the rest of my life testifying to that.'

*

8 – THE BRIDGE BUM

'When you become roadkill, when you happen to have lost some weight and you're not really healthy, but you know one thing - you know that you have worked your ass off and you're not smart enough to know the answer – that's tough.'

**James Cayne,
The Bear Stearns Companies, Inc.,
New York, March 2008.**

ON Thursday 13 March 2008, the board of directors of The Bear Stearns Companies, Inc. held a crisis meeting by conference call late in the evening. Their Chairman, James Cayne, was hard to reach since he had only recently begun to use a mobile telephone and he did not own a Blackberry to monitor emails. Cayne joined the call late and remotely, because he was playing bridge at the North American Bridge Championships in Detroit. Incredibly, he later left for part of the critical conference call, to return to play cards.

Cayne was the 384th richest person in the U.S. in 2005 according to Forbes magazine, who described him as 'a 71-year-old college dropout' worth $900 million, and 'a colourful leader of tightly run New York investment bank Bear Stearns, after a stint as a scrap iron salesman.' They added regarding his major hobby: 'Bridge aficionados Bill Gates and Warren Buffett are richer, but James Cayne plays better bridge.' He was ranked as one of the best bridge players in the world, and he later became the first Wall Street bank chief to own a company stake worth $1 billion plus.

Cayne attributed his success in banking and bridge to the same principle: 'The best players make the most of the hands they're dealt.' Comparing cards to business, Cayne told a group of interns in July 2006: 'Bridge requires skill and preparation, not luck.'

His company biography when he became CEO of Bear Stearns in 1993 included ten lines about his achievements at Bear Stearns and thirteen lines about his achievements as a bridge player, the latter of which included representing his country at the Bermuda Bowl world championships, winning 13 national U.S. bridge championships and being a Grand Life Master (the highest rank possible) of the American Contract Bridge League.

But now Bear Stearns was in turmoil. The bank owned billions of dollars of almost worthless mortgage-backed securities. Other banks would no longer lend money to the bank. Daily liquidity was close to zero. The bank was only staying alive by borrowing money overnight.

Cayne did not return from Detroit to New York until Saturday night at 6.30pm. Upon arrival, he went to his office at 383 Madison Avenue: 'When I walked in, they said, 'It's $8 to $12 a share. That's the deal with J.P. Morgan." J.P. Morgan Chase, under its CEO Jamie Dimon, was about to consummate a shot-gun takeover of Bear Stearns at a fire sale price. In one week in March 2008, Cayne's life's work of 38 years, was gone. Cayne was Mr. Bear Stearns, the CEO of 'the Bear', as the 14,000 staff referred to their firm.

Cayne, known to friends and foes alike as Jimmy, only garnered his job at Bear Stearns because he played bridge. Bear Stearns was founded in 1923 as an equity trading house by Joseph Bear, Robert Stearns and Harold Mayer. Cayne was a full-time professional bridge player in New York in 1969 when he was interviewed by Harold C. Mayer Jr., the son of one of the founding partners in the firm.

There was no chemistry between the two men and the interview was going nowhere until Mayer asked him to meet Alan 'Ace' Greenberg, who was marked out as the firm's future CEO. Greenberg joined the firm in March 1949, when the Dow Jones Index was at 180 points. Again, there was little chemistry, until Greenberg asked Cayne if he had any hobbies.

Cayne said, 'Yes, I play bridge.'

Greenberg asked, 'How well do you play?'

Cayne replied, 'Mr. Greenberg, if you study bridge the rest of your life, if you play with the best partners and you achieve your potential, you will never play bridge like I play bridge.'

Greenberg offered Cayne a job with the Bear on a

$70,000 salary. Cayne had to get by on $700 per month until he passed his registered representative licence exams.

Cayne was so close to his new boss that he collected Greenberg from his Fifth Avenue apartment each work day and drove him down Manhattan's FDR Drive to the Bear office, then located at 55 Water Street. Both men said the journey was difficult. Cayne spoke all of the time. Greenberg said little or nothing. Cayne said later: 'It was like in the Mafia, where the driver becomes the No. 2, except I insisted he sit in the front. He couldn't sit in the back.'

Cayne and Greenberg became regular bridge partners, and through playing the card game they developed a special trust and an ability to communicate later that set their relationship apart from the usual bonding between a bank's CEO and President. But the lack of easy social interaction signaled the beginnings of acrimony between the rivals. Cayne would later fine staff $100 if they referred to Greenberg by his nickname 'Ace.'

Greenberg coined a name for the best new hires at the time: 'PSDs' for poor, smart, and determined to get rich. Cayne's bridge partner later opined to The New York Times about Cayne: 'He didn't go to Harvard Business School - he was a bridge bum.'

*

James Eliot Cayne was born to a middle-class family on 14 February 1934 in the Chicago suburb of Evanston, Illinois. James was the son of Jean and Maurice Cayne, a patent attorney, and he had one sister,

Merel. His mother was an avid bridge player.

Cayne studied engineering at Purdue University in West Lafayette, Indiana, intending to follow in his father's footsteps, but mostly he played bridge at college. He dropped out after two years when he learned he would have to stay another year to retake a French class he had failed. His parents were incredulous at his decision and they kicked him out of their family home. He later said: 'I don't read and absorb. I hear and I absorb.'

In 1954, he enlisted in the U.S. Army and worked as a court reporter at Camp Zama, a U.S. military garrison town located 40 kilometres southwest of Tokyo. He returned to the U.S. in 1956 and for a while drove a cab in Chicago.

He eloped with the sister of a Purdue fraternity college friend and went with his new wife, Maxine Kaplan, to Salt Lake City to become a travelling photocopier salesman for the American Photocopier Co., in Utah and in the Pacific Midwest. 'I averaged 95 miles per hour', said Cayne. After he fell asleep at the wheel and crashed his Ford motor into a telephone utility pole, a judge restricted him to daytime driving only, cutting short any future career as a traveling salesman.

Cayne returned to Chicago and became a salesman for his brother-in-law's scrap-iron business, a job he managed to hold on to even after divorcing his first wife. 'If you can sell scrap metal', a Bear legend quotes Greenberg telling Cayne, 'you can sell bonds.'

He left an unfulfilling career and a broken marriage in Chicago in 1966 to become a professional bridge player in New York: 'People, for whatever reason, think, if you're a good bridge player you've got a good brain, so I might as well do business with you.'

He drove a cab again and sold adding machines to supplement his meagre income. Later he landed a bond sales job at a small municipal bond brokerage named Lebenthal & Co. 'I earned enough to get by and enjoy a fun bachelor life', he recalled years later.

Cayne was invited to play as a professional bridge player at the Cavendish Club, on East 73rd Street. He was told the club rules for the professionals sitting across the table from some of New York's leading financiers. There was to be no frowning or grimacing, no berating your partners for bad plays, and no soliciting the players for any business.

At a bridge tournament in Manhattan, he met a divorced speech therapist named Patricia Denner, and they began dating: 'It was love at first sight.' She agreed to marry him but only if he got a stable job. 'Get a real job or a new girlfriend', she advised, which led him to the door of Bear Stearns in 1969, age 35, and to a job as retail stockbroker. They married in 1971 and had one child, Alison. Cayne already had one child from his first marriage, Jennice.

Cayne played bridge after work at the Regency Whist Club on Manhattan's East Side with Ace Greenberg and two others. Star billionaire players such as Warren Buffett and Malcolm Forbes occasionally also played on the same team as the four. Together they liked to refer to themselves as Corporate America's Six Honchos. Or 'CASH' for short.

A bridge partner described Cayne to The Washington Post: 'He is tenacious. He gets a bad result and just swallows it and gets on to the next hand. He never gives up. It is a war, it is a battle and he is going to be on your side fighting all the way through.'

Cayne liked the competitive edge of bridge. 'I'm afraid to lose', he once said. 'I hate it. I know how I feel. It is no fun. The agony you suffer is awesome. Defeat is far more painful than victory is pleasurable. In bridge there is pressure on every hand. I play every hand like it's the last hand I'll ever play, even when I'm playing for fun.'

When his mother was close to death in 1989, Cayne took out his cards. 'She passed away two weeks ago', Cayne's wife told The Washington Post. 'The last thing he did was play bridge with her. That was the first time. He knew. I had a feeling this man knew this was the last time he would see his mother. She was so overwhelmed. He had enough insight into what she needed to give it to her. The last week of her life was one happy week.'

His wife also told the newspaper: 'He is like a sponge. If he had five men giving him information and those five men leave, he could give back everything those five men said as if it was him. That is what he does with bridge. He learns a convention and he has to remember it. If a person plays a card that is unusual, he'll remember it the entire hand.'

Cayne played golf. In his later years on a Thursday afternoon, he would leave Manhattan for the East 34th Street Heliport and a 17-minute $1,700 helicopter ride to the Hollywood Golf Club, in Deal, New Jersey. After spending the night at his nearby holiday home, he would play golf on Friday, Saturday and Sunday, with 8am tee off times, and spend the rest of the weekend with his grandchildren or playing online poker.

The Cayne's residence was a 15,743 square foot

home at 60 Lincoln Avenue, Long Branch, New Jersey, set on a 3.5-acre plot. New Jersey property records show the home was valued at $7.6 million in 2022. The couple also owned a holiday home at 1000 South Ocean Boulevard, Boca Raton, Florida, located next to the Boca Raton Beach Club, with its white sands and ocean view. But they spent most of their time at their sixth-floor apartment at 510 Park Avenue, New York, bought in 1981 for $1.1 million.

*

Cayne's first success came in 1975. New York City's finances were in a mess and the city was close to bankruptcy. Clients called Bear looking to sell their distressed New York City municipal bonds. Few banks would touch the bonds but Cayne saw a chance.

Bear bought the bonds, held them and sold them on at a good profit. The bank then made a market for others in municipal bonds. 'It was a great chapter in the history of the firm', boasted Cayne, 'because it changed the brand picture of the company.'

In 1978, Cayne joined the banks Executive Committee and when Bear was floated on the U.S. stock market in 1985, he became the banks sole President. When Greenberg was made Chairman of the bank in July 1993, Cayne filled the vacant CEO role.

Cayne was optimistic when interviewed in 1989: 'This isn't the same firm it used to be. Senior management has had a lot to do with that. We used to be perceived as the gunslingers, let's take a roll. We are risk averse, like me in bridge. We hate to lose.'

Bear prospered in the 1990s. One analyst said of

Bears profits at the time: 'We haven't seen results this good since the miracle of the loaves and fishes.' While equity markets stagnated at the start of the decade, the bond market which Bear dominated, flourished.

Bear was not a work place where the weak survived, where the humble prospered or where anyone rose to the top of the firm by being everybody's best buddy. A large sign hung outside the Bear New York trading room: 'Let's make nothing but money.'

Top executives and traders at Bear were well remunerated under Cayne: 'My father was a patent attorney, and he never made more than $75,000 in his whole life. But if I don't pay my guy $1 million, nine of my competitors are willing to pay him four times that.'

Cayne told The New York Times in 1993, whilst sitting at his desk surveying his screens: 'We are firing on all 99 cylinders. So, you have to ask yourself, What can we do better? And I just can't decide what that might be. We are going to surprise some people this time around. I'll tell you what worries me, that we might be doing something stupid.'

With a card-player's instincts, Cayne avoided risky bets or throwing good money after bad. One example was Long-Term Capital Management L.P, a big hedge fund that almost collapsed in 1998, when it lost about $4.6 billion due to tumbling world markets. When the Federal Reserve asked the top Wall Street bank CEOs to bail out LTCM, Cayne refused to put up any of Bear's own money. A dozen other financial firms pumped $3.65 billion into LTCM to keep it afloat. None of them spoke well about the angry Bear.

Cayne succeeded Greenberg as Chairman in June 2001, and added the title to his existing CEO role. He delegated his day-to-day responsibilities in the bank to two co-presidents; Warren Spector, who ran fixed income and asset management, and Alan Schwartz who ran investment banking and equities.

Bear had begun life as a conservative Wall Street brokerage, buying and selling securities, managing accounts for high-net-worth private clients and providing back-office prime brokerage services to large hedge funds. Now in the first decade of the twenty-first century, one line of their bond business began to truly excel.

Bear had a market niche in issuing securitised bonds, which are debt securities secured on various receivables. At any one-time, large companies such as MasterCard, VISA, Ford, General Motors, MNBA and American Express have billions of receivables due from consumers but these corporations would prefer to receive their cash now, rather than wait. Each individual customer balance may be small, but they can be packaged up into multi-million-dollar bundles and sold to investors. The bonds are secured on the receivables. The same principle applies to all consumer debt or loans, such as mortgages.

The growth in securitisation and the billions of investments were financed with cheap overnight money. Cayne blundered: 'I didn't stop it. I didn't rein in the leverage.'

In 2003, Bear moved to a $500 million 47-storey, octagonal corporate headquarters building located two blocks north of Grand Central Terminal on Manhattan's east side. Cayne described the building as his greatest achievement and as a tangible expression of Bear's success and staying power: 'It's an entire square block in the heart of the city.'

2006 was a stellar year for Bear. Profit surged 40 percent from the prior year to an all-time high of $2.1 billion. Cayne, the longest-serving Chairman and CEO on Wall Street, received $40 million in compensation. Between 2000 and 2008, the top five executives at Bear took home $326 million in compensation and made $1.1 billion from stock sales.

The BSC stock price on the NYSE rose from $16.61 when Cayne took over as CEO in July 1993, to its all-time high of $172.69 in January 2007. Cayne had turned Bear from a conservative private partnership trading and settling securities into the fifth biggest U.S. investment bank, but the bank had an ugly balance sheet stuffed with exotic illiquid securities. Bear had become a veritable house of cards ready to tumble.

*

In June 2007, the U.S. mortgage market hit the first signs of trouble. Bear had formed two large highly-leveraged hedge funds where the investors invested in mortgage securities using mostly borrowed cash. As the value of the mortgage securities fell, so too did the value of the two funds. Bear wrote to their clients in July to confirm that the two hedge funds contained 'very little' or 'effectively no value' for investors.

Bear announced that it would provide a credit line of $3.2 billion to rescue one of the two mortgage-related hedge funds, which reported to Bears joint number two executive Warren Spector. And yes, Spector did play bridge, and rather well too.

But Cayne did not address this vital hedge funds

issue. Throughout the month of July 2007, The Wall Street Journal reported that Cayne spent 10 of the month's 21 working days away from the office, mostly on a golf course or playing bridge.

Cayne expected Spector to deal with the hedge funds mess. From 18 to 29 July 2007, Cayne played bridge at the North American Bridge Championship in Nashville. He was amazed to meet Spector there. Spector was taking his first holiday of the year mid-crisis. Back at the Bear office on 30 July, Cayne fired Spector for being out of the office at the same time as his own absence at the same tournament: 'I didn't trust him anymore.'

Cayne was not happy: 'This is a body blow of massive proportion. When you walk around with the reputation for being the most rigorous risk analyser, assessor, controller and that is trashed, well, you have got to feel bad. This is personal. There is a lot of pain here. I'm angry. I would have bet against this occurring at Bear Stearns. In the last 15 years, I have never walked into a room or been at a dinner party where I did not feel that when people looked at me, they thought I was OK, successful, agile. That might have changed. I feel like people now look at me with a question mark.'

The ratings agency Standard & Poor's placed Bear on a 'negative outlook.' Asked how he felt about this downward move, Cayne said: 'A negative outlook can touch a number of parts of your businesses. It was like having a beautiful child and they have a disease of some sort that you never expect to happen and it did. How did I feel? Lousy.'

Cayne chain-smoked $140 Montecristo cigars. He smoked them in the firm's elevators and in his office which was illegal under New York City health ordinances, and he smoked them in his study in their apartment, which his wife called the 'womb room.' He often spent time there, watching CNBC TV and playing bridge online on his PC.

But in 2007, The Wall Street Journal reported Cayne smoked something stronger. A journalist had spoken to people who played bridge with Cayne at a tournament at the Doubletree hotel in Memphis in 2004. They told her Cayne sometimes smoked marijuana at the end of the day during bridge tournaments. Cayne denied it outright. 'There is no chance that it happened', he said. 'Zero chance.'

Cayne had more pressing problems. Early on 11 September 2007, a black sedan pulled up outside his residence on Park Avenue. Its purpose was to transport the occupant to hospital. Inside, Cayne, then aged 73, lay dangerously ill, probably close to death.

He had woken earlier in the morning complaining of weakness and a loss of appetite. His wife Patricia called their doctor who noted Cayne's rapid deep breathing and low blood pressure. He suspected sepsis, a serious medical condition akin to blood poisoning. He recommended that Cayne be taken to hospital immediately by ambulance.

Cayne disagreed and instead summoned the anonymous town car to take him. Bear had taken such a public hammering that he had no wish to be seen being stretchered into an ambulance, nor to be seen in one outside the New York Presbyterian Hospital.

Doctors located the infection in his prostate. They gave him a 50/50 chance of survival and kept him in hospital for ten days while they gave him 22 gallons of saline infusions and antibiotics. Cayne lost 30 pounds but he survived to battle on.

In November 2007, Bear reported its first ever quarterly loss of $859 million, having written off $1.9 billion worth of mortgage-backed securities. No one wished to purchase the dud securities. The two failed hedge funds had poisoned the entire bank.

In January 2008, Cayne resigned as CEO but remained on as non-executive Chairman of the board. He handed the CEO role his deputy Schwartz. Cayne said that tears were shed on his departure. His rival 'Ace' Greenberg wrote later that these were tears of joy. On his last day at Bear after 38 years working there, Cayne said nothing at all to Greenberg, and Greenberg said nothing at all to Cayne.

In early 2008, liquidity, or the amount of free cash, became critical for Bear. The bank needed about $50 billion in overnight funding and all it could offer in return were mortgage-backed debt securities of an uncertain value. Banks would not lend to Bear.

Bear was forced to issue a public statement: 'There is absolutely no truth to the rumours of liquidity problems that circulated today in the market.' While the firm had $17 billion in cash, Bear was still addicted to leverage, with $11 billion in equity capital supporting $395 billion in assets, an astronomically high leverage ratio of 36 to 1. Bear still owned nearly $40 billion in mortgage bonds that were now considered worthless.

The new CEO Schwartz went on CNBC TV to counter the escalating market rumours: 'We're not being made aware of anybody who is not taking our credit as a counterparty. We don't see any pressure on our liquidity, let alone a liquidity crisis.'

On Friday 14 March, with a guarantee from the

Federal Reserve, J.P. Morgan Chase provided $30 billion of funding to Bear. The rating agencies downgraded Bear and the BSC stock price plunged to $32. Confidence in Bear as a going concern was over.

By Saturday evening, Cayne was back in New York from his bridge tournament in Detroit. The directors of Bear and J.P Morgan worked on the takeover price, which fell from $12 to $2 per share. Greenberg stated that Cayne said to him: 'I am not taking $2.' Greenberg told him bluntly: 'Jimmy, if we don't take $2, we'll get zero. If they're only offering fifty cents, we should take it because it means we're still alive. When you're dead nothing can happen to you except, you'll go to heaven, or hell maybe.'

Cayne and the Bear board approved the deal on the Sunday evening. There were irate and vocal public protests by staff and shareholders at the bargain basement price of $2, so the J.P. Morgan offer was revised upwards. Cayne voted for the improved final $10-a-share deal one week later: 'I've got six million shares, I just got my butt kicked.'

After the watershed demise, t-shirts were sold outside the Bear head office with the slogan: 'I worked for Bear Stearns for 20 years and all I got was a Cayne-ing.' The t-shirt portrayed a cartoon of Cayne standing on a golf putting green, playing a fiddle.

Cayne was left with a few hundred million bucks: 'When you lose a billion but you still have several hundred million left, then it's your heirs that get hurt, not you. Because when you have $1.6 billion and you lose $1 billion, you're not exactly, like, crippled, right?' On 25 March, he sold all his 5.66 million shares at a market price of $10.84. The one billion dollars' worth of shares were now worth a mere $61 million.

Cayne sold his shares via Bear's brokerage unit. Greenberg could have charged him the discounted staff commission of $2,500 but he charged Cayne the full client commission of $77,000. 'If he doesn't like it, he should do his future business elsewhere', Greenberg said.

As a lifelong salesman, trader and card player, Cayne was never equipped for a credit crisis: 'The options were limited. When you become roadkill, when you happen to have lost some weight and you're not really healthy, but you know one thing - you know that you have worked your ass off and you're not smart enough to know the answer – that's tough.'

*

Cayne blundered in building a bank that lacked strategic diversification. It was the smallest of the big Wall Street investment banks. It didn't have the geographical reach of a universal bank like a Citibank or a Deutsche Bank and it was weak in Europe and Asia. It didn't have the top-tier client list of a Goldman Sachs or a Morgan Stanley. It didn't have the national retail deposit base of a Bank of America or a J.P. Morgan Chase with its source of cheap sticky funding. It was too dependent on its prime broker, fixed income and mortgage-backed securities businesses. One employee told New York magazine: 'We were the smallest of the major firms. In a famine, the skinny guy always dies.'

The decision not to join the bailout of LTCM in 1998 came back to haunt Cayne, since his refusal to help greatly annoyed peers on Wall Street, including Henry

Paulson, then the chief operating officer of Goldman Sachs. When Bear needed a rescue, Paulson was the U.S. Treasury Secretary, and he refused to lead a government bailout of Bear.

Cayne's other big blunder was to become the lender to the two failed hedge funds which were riddled with dud mortgage securities. With the liquidation of the funds, Bear took the worthless securities on to its otherwise clean balance sheet, leading to the first quarterly loss in the bank's history and badly damaging Cayne's reputation.

The saddest aspect is that Cayne didn't retire from Bear when he was still winning away from the card table. When the bank crashed, he was 73 years old, easily the oldest senior executive on Wall Street. He stated that there were aspects of the job that wore him down. Being Bear's public face, which meant dealing with shareholders, regulators and media, brought stress. He said he took business setbacks personally. 'There is an awful lot of gratification that comes with this job', he explained. 'There is also heartache.'

A reporter from CNBC asked Cayne why he still came to work when he could sell his shares and retire? He replied: 'If I'm going down, I'm going down like a samurai.'

Cayne was named in TIME magazine's list of '25 People to Blame for the Financial Crisis': 'Plenty of CEOs screwed up on Wall Street. But none seemed more asleep at the switch than Bear Stearns' Cayne. He left the banks office by helicopter for 3½-day golf weekends. He was regularly out of town at bridge tournaments.'

Cayne was not asleep at the switch. He was out of

state and not even near the switch. It is an indisputable fact that at the two most critical points in the survival of Bear, when the two hedge funds collapsed in July 2007, and in the run on the bank in March 2008, Cayne was out of town, out of contact and out of touch, playing cards like a shark.

The New York Post printed a joke about Cayne after the crash of Bear. 'Question - Why was Jimmy Cayne playing bridge last week as his company, Bear Stearns, was heading toward a meltdown? Answer - Probably because it was too cold to golf.'

The author William Cohan wrote a book about the fall of Bear, and had extensive access to Cayne, so implicitly he had the support of Cayne. Yet Cohan described Cayne as the 'Nero of the credit crisis.' But instead of fiddling as Bear burned, he was golfing at the Hollywood Golf Club and playing bridge in Nashville, San Francisco, and Detroit.

In mitigation, Cayne does take some credit in trying to save Bear in its final months. Following the large and unexpected fund losses, Bear needed new capital so Cayne flew to Florida to meet Joe Lewis, a Bahamas-based billionaire commodities investor and Bear brokerage client. Lewis invested in Bear after Cayne convinced him that Bear stock was a bargain. In September 2007, Lewis spent $864 million buying a seven percent stake in the bank. Lewis soon lost his investment. Lewis accepted the huge loss surprisingly well. Cayne said of Lewis: 'He's an adult, not a whiner.'

In mitigation also, when Bear collapsed, Cayne was the non-executive Chairman. He was not an executive Chairman and had no responsibilities for the daily operation, running and management of the bank. But the board selects the CEO, and the Chairman chairs the board. Cayne must accept his responsibilities, like the cards he was dealt all his life.

Greenberg soon became Cayne's worst critic and blamed his many blunders for the firm's collapse, describing Cayne as a 'demagogue' and a megalomaniac more interested in playing bridge than in running the firm: 'The way he conducted himself during the crisis? Just horrible.'

Greenberg said of Cayne in an interview with Bloomberg in 2011: 'He didn't study the books, he didn't know what we owned, he didn't call people in and ask.' He told The New York Times. 'He was a one man show. He didn't listen to anyone.'

Greenberg later penned his thoughts about Cayne in his own biographical book about the fall of Bear: 'He preferred to be home in his pyjamas playing bridge on his computer. In a time of crisis, he flatly wasn't up to the task.'

*

Cayne emerged from retirement in May 2010 to appear before the members of the U.S. Financial Crisis Inquiry Commission in Washington D.C. He sat wearing a dark suit, white shirt and purple tie, with spectacles and wispy grey hair, and looked all of his 76 years. He sipped water nervously from a bottle as he fielded questions for two hours.

In answering the first question from the Commission Chairman, Cayne conceded Bear held too little capital for the assets it owned and the bank's almost 40-to-1 ratio of equity to assets was excessive.

'That was the business and that was, really, industry practice. In retrospect, in hindsight, I would say leverage was too high', he admitted.

He paused and said nothing more in answer to the first question. Former CEO Schwartz, well-groomed and sitting alongside at the table, looked at Cayne and smirked, evidently contemptuous of the important federal proceedings. There was an edgy silence until the Commission Chairman stared down at Cayne and said to him: 'Succinct.'

Cayne told Capitol Hill he blamed the Bear collapse on the 'unjustified and irrational' evaporation of confidence. 'Rumour, innuendo. I'm not going to use the word conspiracy, but it's part of it', he said. When asked whether a plot by others could have contributed to the firm's downfall, his response was vague. 'I heard the same rumours that everybody did, that hedge funds had gathered together. It was all part of a picture of a big, bad goose walking down a lane that's about to get eaten up. Regardless of whether there was a conspiracy or not, the bottom line is the firm came under attack.'

When asked by the Commission if he had made mistakes, he said: 'I take responsibility for what happened. I'm not going to walk away from the responsibility.' When asked if he could have done anything to save Bear, he replied: 'That's a question I've asked myself for close to three years since I retired and I don't have an answer.'

In retirement he continued to play the game that brought him so much criticism during his time at Bear. On the one-year anniversary of Bears collapse, the New York Post tracked him down at a bridge tournament in Houston. 'Bridge is what I do a lot, and when the weather permits, I play a lot of golf', he told the newspaper.

Cayne died on 28 December 2021, at the Monmouth Medical Centre in Long Branch, New Jersey, days after suffering a stroke, at the age of 87. The New York Times reported he was still playing bridge online in the week before his death.

The obituaries credited him with building Bear, but also allowing it to fail. Bloomberg described him as a 'cigar-puffing college dropout.' The Wall Street Journal described him as 'a blunt, competitive, cigar-smoking executive.' The Financial Times described him as 'irascible and iconoclastic.' William Cohan posthumously described the subject of his book as 'cunning, canny, garrulous, gruff, feisty, sneaky and often generous.'

Before his passing the Cayne's had sold their apartment at 510 Park Avenue in 2019 for $15 million, since the Cayne's had not lived in it since 2013. The 5,000 square foot apartment had five bedrooms, a private elevator, his and hers bathrooms, a TV room and a library. The interiors on the property listing were badly dated, with 1990s fittings and furniture, leather sofas, metallic surround fireplaces and oval glass tables.

The master bedroom boasted a telephone built into the bedside locker, further proof that Cayne was not an early adopter of the mobile telephone, to be used in times of corporate crisis. He preferred to take an urgent out of hours telephone call on his home land line, unless he was out of town, perhaps playing in a tournament for bridge bums.

*

9 – THE GORILLA OF WALL STREET

'You do not know what you do not know. Chew on that. Understand the difference between reality and perception. Take smart risks without being reckless. Whatever it is, enjoy the ride. No regrets.'

**Richard Fuld,
Lehman Brothers Holdings Inc.,
New York, September 2008.**

ON Saturday 13 September 2008, Richard Fuld, CEO and Chairman of Lehman Brothers made a critical telephone call to Ken Lewis, CEO of Bank of America. Fuld was desperate. Lehman Brothers was in dire trouble, it was rapidly running out of liquidity, the stock was in free-fall, there was no bail-out on offer from the U.S. government and the U.S.'s oldest and fourth largest investment bank faced certain and total collapse within days. Bank of America had deep pockets and Fuld hoped Lewis would buy his bank and rescue the historic trading house of Lehman.

Fuld thought he already had the basic elements of a deal. The two men had spoken during the week. Some of Bank of America's top executives had been granted an insider look at Lehman's books and assets. But now Fuld was growing uncertain. His recent telephone calls to Lewis at his office had so far gone unreturned. This time Fuld dialed Lewis at his home in Charlotte, North Carolina. Lewis's wife, Donna, picked up the telephone. She told Fuld: 'If Mr. Lewis wanted to call back, he would call back.'

Fuld apologised for bothering her: 'I am so sorry.' Unbeknownst to Fuld, Lewis was in negotiations to buy Merrill Lynch & Co. that weekend. He had lost interest in Lehman since he believed that Lehman's assets were overvalued by $60 billion to $70 billion. Some speculated that Lewis stood beside his wife, prompting her to tell Fuld he wasn't available. 'I can't believe that son of a bitch won't return my calls', Fuld said to his advisers.

Twenty-four hours later on Sunday evening, it was Fuld's turn to receive an unwanted telephone call. Christopher Cox, the Chairman of the Securities & Exchange Commission, addressed Lehman's board of directors by speakerphone at their offices. 'This is serious', said Cox. 'The board has a grave matter before it. You have a grave responsibility and you need to act accordingly.'

The board asked Cox if he was directing them to file for bankruptcy. Cox answered that the decision was the board's to make. The Lehman board did not inspire much confidence. Nine of the external directors were retired. Four of them were over 75 years old. One was a theatre producer, another was a former Navy admiral. Only two directors had direct experience of the financial-services industry. Fuld leaned back in his chair at the end of the telephone call with Cox and said to the others: 'I guess this is goodbye.'

On Monday 15 September, Lehman filed for Chapter 11 protection at 1.45am in the Bankruptcy Court for the Southern District of New York. The year long struggle by Wall Street's longest-serving CEO to save his 158-year-old firm was over.

Lehman's bankruptcy filing listed debts of $613 billion. It was the largest bankruptcy in American history, the largest investment bank failure since Michael Milken's firm, Drexel Burnham Lambert, and it was ten times the size of Enron's collapse when it filed for bankruptcy protection in 2001. 'I feel like I want to throw up', Fuld admitted.

The next Sunday, 21 September, Fuld reportedly left what his employees called 'Club 31', his 31st floor office with a library, a shower and views of the Hudson River, at 745 Seventh Avenue in Midtown Manhattan, for the Lehman company gymnasium. He began his exercise routine. Nearby another Lehman employee was using weights.

Lehman staff at the time were enraged at the collapse of the bank and the loss of their jobs. A CNBC and Vanity Fair contributor reported: 'I have this from two very senior sources - one incredibly senior source, that Fuld went to the gym after Lehman was announced as going under. He was on a treadmill with a heart monitor on. Someone was in the corner, pumping iron and he walked over and he knocked Fuld out cold.'

The pugilistic tale was reported in The New York Daily News, The Daily Telegraph and TIME, but opinion was divided on whether the incident happened or not. The doubters noted that Fuld bore no facial damage when he appeared in the office on the next day. A bank spokesman said: 'It's absolutely untrue. It never happened.' The general manager of the Lehman gymnasium supported his view: 'The statement that he was punched is not true. It's a matter of fact that Fuld has not visited the club since the bankruptcy. We're not even open on Sundays.' The believers recalled it was not the first time Fuld was involved in a punch-up, although this time he was on the receiving end.

Fuld's was in the United States Air Force in 1964, aged 18, when his career in uniform came to an abrupt end. He was on morning parade with other cadets when an officer told Fuld his shoes were not sufficiently polished. Fuld said he disagreed. The officer stamped his boot on one of Fuld's shoes to dirty it and told Fuld to go inside and polish the shoe. Fuld did so without objection. When he returned the officer did the same to his other shoe and told him again to go inside to polish it also. Fuld quietly complied.

When he returned the officer was bullying a smaller cadet. Fuld objected and asked the officer: 'Hey, asshole, why don't you pick on someone your own size?' The officer stepped to within inches of Fuld's face and asked him if he was speaking to him. Fuld said he was. They had a fist fight which left both of them bloodied on the ground.

Fuld was hauled before the commanding officer where he tried to explain his side of the story. He was reminded that the armed forces didn't have two sides and the only side to the story was that Fuld had fought with an officer and therefore he would be expelled. 'This is not going to work out, is it?' Fuld responded. Later he explained: 'I stuck up for another underclass man. Let's just say, I was politely asked to leave the programme.'

*

Richard Severin Fuld Jr. was born in April 1946 in New York into an upper-class Jewish family, the son of Richard Severin Fuld Snr. and Elizabeth Schwab. He grew up in the suburb of Harrison in Westchester County. His family owned a textile company named United Merchants & Manufacturers, which was founded in 1912 by his grandfather.

The same grandfather secured his grandson a summer internship at his long-time bank, Lehman Brothers, in their Denver office. The job was basic but Fuld was immediately hooked. He said later: 'I truly stumbled into investment banking. Once I got exposed to it, I discovered that I actually understood it, and all the pieces fit.'

Fuld attended Wilbraham & Monson Academy, a college-preparatory school in Wilbraham, Massachusetts. He graduated from the University of Colorado with a Bachelor's degree in international business in 1969, but he struggled academically.

Fuld delivered an address at the college's Graduate School of Business, where he explained his career choice. He had first enrolled in aeronautical engineering but he quickly discovered a problem. 'I couldn't do graphics. I was one of those kids with no spatial relationship capabilities. I stumbled into international business.'

Fuld re-joined Lehman Brothers in 1969 on Wall Street where he traded commercial paper; short term debt issued by larger corporations and routinely bought and sold by investors. Lehman Brothers began life in 1850 as a Montgomery, Alabama cotton trader, founded by the three brothers Lehman; German Jewish émigrés Henry, Emanuel, and Meyer. The trio did business for the Confederacy before founding the New York Cotton Exchange. The Lehman corporate motto was: 'Where visions get built.'

Fuld earned his MBA from New York University at night classes in 1973. He rose quickly through the firms ranks. In the early 1980s at the age of 37, Fuld became the head of both the fixed income and the equities divisions, overseeing all trading at Lehman.

No one pushed Fuld around at Lehman. Once he had to visit the office of his then boss, to ask him to sign a large trade ticket which Fuld had executed. His boss was on the telephone and he made Fuld stand and wait, who was waving his ticket in the air impatiently. He didn't end the call but told Fuld he would sign the ticket when every other paper was cleared from his desk. Fuld stepped forward and swept everything on his boss's desk to the floor with his open hand and then said firmly: 'Will you sign it now?'

Fuld's interactions with co-workers were limited, and he grunted in monosyllables. He was described as 'the digital mind trader, someone who spent so much time in front of his green trading screens that he was no longer human.' Fuld was viewed within the firm as a trader's trader, with an athletic physique, intense focus and a liking for profanity.

With dark hair, dark eyes, a wide forehead and despite being five foot ten inches tall, others referred to him by his trading nickname; 'The Gorilla'; one of the scariest men in the market. 'Through little physical cues, he made it seem like a situation will lead to physical violence if you didn't relent', said one executive. Fuld once put a life-size stuffed gorilla in his office off the Lehman's trading floor.

A former head of Lehman's equities syndicate team told ABC News: 'You weren't easy-going around Dick Fuld. You took a couple of extra breaths of air before you started talking to him just so you had some extra oxygen in your brain. He is electric.'

Fuld dressed immaculately for work, in a navy-blue suit from the Richards department store in Greenwich, Connecticut, along with a white shirt, black lace-ups polished to a high sheen, and a Hermès tie. He was not a fan of casual dress at work. 'Sloppy dress, sloppy thinking', he believed. Fuld once asked an over-casual Lehman employee: 'Are you off to the country club?' He did not like beards at work.

Fuld was known for his family-first philosophy. His marriage to Kathleen Ann Bailey, a statuesque blonde, the youngest of eight siblings from a Catholic family on Long Island, was famously happy. Fuld had met Kathy when, against his will, she joined the Lehman's trading desk. 'We can't hire her - she's too pretty', he complained after her interview. 'She'll distract someone and marry them and will be no use to the firm.'

That person turned out to be him. Kathy converted to Judaism, and they married in September 1978, on the day after he was made a partner at Lehman. They had three children: twins, Jacqueline and Chrissie, and a son, Richie. Colleagues noted he would interrupt meetings to take a call from his wife. To their amusement, he called her 'Fuld.'

But life was tough for the wives of Lehman's executives. Vanity Fair reported Fuld expected his top executives to get married, and to stay married. For their wives, the firm could be both a goldfish bowl and a shark tank, with unwritten rules about the clothes they wore, which charities to support and how much to give to each charity. It was not uncommon for Fuld to pull one of his employees aside and ask him questions about their personal or home life. Executives at Lehman's were supposed to be happy with their wives. If they were not happy, they were expected to pretend they were happy.

Fuld hosted summer retreats for top executives and wives at his 71-acre Big Wood River Estate, in Sun Valley, Idaho. The couples arrived on two planes owned by Lehman, known as 'Lehman Air' and were met at the airport by a line of tinted black SUVs. Photographs of the mandatory afternoon golf are of eleven middle-aged white males dressed identically in baseball caps, polo t-shirts, Bermuda shorts and golf gloves.

Fuld resided with his family in their Greenwich, Connecticut home, which had 20 rooms, eight bedrooms, a pool house, a squash court and a tennis court. Within his own family, Fuld told his children, 'Disagree with me all you want in private. Call me an asshole at home all you want. But never air your domestic grievances in public.'

In 2004, Fuld and his wife bought a Spanish

Colonial-style 15,000 square foot holiday home on a 3.3 acre estate on Florida's Jupiter Island, north of Miami, for $13.75 million. They later acquired a $21 million, four-bedroom, four-bathroom apartment at 640 Park Avenue NYC in 2007. And they kept a winter place in Cornwall, Vermont.

Fuld and his wife liked art. In 2005 and 2006 Artnews Magazine featured the Fuld's on its list of Top 200 Art Collectors in the World, as defined by their spending. Fuld was on the board of Trustees at New York's Museum of Modern Art. Kathy was known in the art world for her passion for buying works on paper. The couple attended black-tie fund-raising bashes at the MoMA, where they were photographed for the social diary pages, with Mrs. Fuld in her heels towering over a smaller and grimacing Mr. Fuld.

Fuld plays squash and is a one-time international U.S. squash player. A squash opponent said of Fuld: 'He hates to lose. He is the rare person who simultaneously wants to beat your brains in but also takes a good deal of joy in the things that his opponent does well.'

*

Fuld was running the fixed income division in 1984 when American Express acquired Lehman. The firm almost lost its identity. In 1994, Lehman was spun off as a separate company and Fuld became the CEO. 'I was the only one left standing', he said.

The night he was selected as CEO, Fuld had a panic attack, and he stopped breathing for 45 seconds: 'I realised I was it. I didn't want the job, and I wasn't looking for the job.' But it was also a time of rebirth: 'I came in the next day with terrific resolve.'

In 2000, there was talk about some Wall Street firms merging. Fuld convened his people at an offsite and told them: 'Look, we can do a deal, and you can work for some jerk at a big institution. Or you can work for me.' That was the end of the discussion.

Fuld's greatest test came on 11 September 2001. Lehman's headquarters at Three World Financial Centre suffered substantial damage. Its lobby was used as a morgue facility. One Lehman employee died and 6,400 staff were displaced from their offices. Lehman employees watched bodies falling and the twin towers collapsing right outside their windows. In a moving speech to his employees, Fuld broke into tears after he was asked when the firm would resume trading. 'We don't even know who is alive', he lamented. Fuld led the recovery from offices in New Jersey. Within days the firm's bankers had moved into the Sheraton Hotel in midtown and they were trading again.

Fuld liked to celebrate success. In 2003, when accepting a 'Bank of the Year' honour at an awards gala in London, his voice cracked as he gave an emotion-laden speech, according to the Financial Times. 'This is for my people. Lehman stand! Troops, be recognised. Everyone at Lehman in this room, stand and be recognised', he ordered.

So intense was his passion for the firm that employees were told that they should learn to bleed green, the Lehman's corporate colour. Fuld once complained to a friend: 'In the 28 years you've known me, do you know anyone who bleeds more for Lehman's shareholders, clients and employees? I'm a Lehman lifer.' He worked there for 42 years.

Fuld explained to Wharton Business School how he had changed the culture at Lehman from competition to one of teamwork: 'The early Lehman Brothers was a great example of how not to do it. It was all about me. My job. My people. Pay me. Today, a stellar performance by one person is not enough to make a difference on Wall Street. No one individual can deliver the whole firm to any given client.' He spoke of his views on leadership: 'First, leaders must understand their business. Know how the pieces fit. Read. Network. Connect the dots. Anticipate. Try to limit the surprises; surprises kill you.'

In 2005, when speaking at the Lehman annual shareholder meeting, Fuld foresaw his downfall: 'There's a huge amount of liquidity, which I think has been covering up a number of ills in the market. Higher interest rates will cause more turmoil than I think we've seen.' By 2006, Lehman was the number one underwriter of securities backed by subprime mortgages. Lehman bought California-based BNC Mortgage, which made home loans to the least creditworthy borrowers, since Lehman needed a steady flow of new mortgages to package into bonds and sell on to investors. Lehman bought Aurora Loan Services which in 2007 originated $3 billion of subprime loans per month.

2006 was a stellar earnings year for Lehman, and Fuld was fighting on all fronts. He had t-shirts printed that said 'Lehman to $150' on the front and 'Get out of my way' on the back. When the LEH stock price surpassed $150, he focused the firm on $200.

He hosted a dinner at the New York Museum of Modern Art for the senior executives of the firm: 'We are at war.' But later he told The New York Times: 'I don't like the war comment, to tell you the truth. Every day is a battle, and 'war', well, 'war' connotes that we are trying to kill our enemies. That's not the view that I want them to have. Every day is a grind, every day we're in it, really trying to trudge through the stuff, and don't think this is a walk through the park. Every day is a battle: think about the firm, do the right thing, protect your client, protect the firm, be in it, be a good team member.'

Fuld transformed a small domestic loss-making bond trading company into a top-tier global investment bank with 26,000 staff located in 28 countries. When he took over in 1994, Lehman made a profit of $75 million. In 2007, Lehman's profit was $4.2 billion. In that period the stock price of Lehman increased 20 times over and the staff felt rich.

Fuld attended the World Economic Forum in Davos in January 2007. 'This could be the year when the markets crack', he said. Soon U.S. house prices faltered. For a while Lehman fared better than its peers: 'My first view is, how do I protect the mothership?' Lehman shut BNC Mortgage, fired staff and closed branches of Aurora. In December, Fuld wrote to shareholders: 'Our global franchise and brand have never been stronger, and our record results for the year reflect the continued diversified growth of our businesses.'

In mid-2007, the Financial Times interviewed Fuld and asked him whether the credit crunch would take a significant bite out of Lehman Brothers? 'Do we have some stuff on the books that would be tough to get rid of? Yes', he said, referring to Lehman's mortgage assets. 'Am I worried about it? No. If you have some repricing of these things will we lose some money? Yes. Is it going to kill us? Of course not.'

*

Lehman did not rein back on issuing mortgage securities. In 2007, it underwrote more mortgage-backed securities than any other firm, accumulating an $85 billion portfolio, almost four times the $22.5 billion of shareholder equity Lehman held as a buffer against losses. Fuld and Lehman gambled four times the firm's shareholder equity on mortgage-backed securities. 'Smart risk management is never putting yourself in a position where you can't live to fight another day', Fuld told The Economist magazine.

June 2008 was a watershed. Lehman announced a second quarter loss of $2.8 billion due to $4.1 billion of write downs of mortgage assets. Fuld had 600 staff reviewing the firms mortgage asset valuations to ensure that they were accurate: 'Our goal is simple: It's to create value for our shareholders and for our debt holders, for our clients and for our employees. On many fronts in this cycle, we did not achieve this goal. This is my responsibility.'

In the following months, Lehman stock price headed south. Investors feared a Bear Stearns Mark Two company fire sale scenario. Fuld tried to sell commercial real estate and the investment management division but he failed. He held discussions with a consortium led by the Korea Development Bank to invest in Lehman but he failed also.

On 9 September, it was announced that there would be no deal with KDB and the Lehman stock price fell

45 percent. Dire rumours were instantly communicated, emailed and blogged globally by analysts. Lehman clients panicked. Counter-parties cut credit lines.

Large short sellers of Lehman stock emerged, selling Lehman stock they did not own, anticipating further calamitous stock price falls. 'When I find a short-seller, I want to tear his heart out and eat it before his eyes while he's still alive', Fuld declared. 'Bear Stearns went down on rumours and a liquidity crisis of confidence. Immediately thereafter, the rumours and the naked short sellers came after us.'

Also on 9 September, J.P. Morgan Chase contacted Fuld. J.P. Morgan were bankers to Lehman and they cleared funds through to other banks. They advised that they wished Lehman to put up an additional $5 billion of cash collateral in order to continue to operate their bank accounts at J.P. Morgan. 'They drained us of cash', Fuld lamented.

On 10 September, Lehman announced a third quarter loss of $3.9 billion. In its last week of existence on Wall Street, the Lehman stock price fell 77 percent. Fuld's t-shirts for staff with a stock price of $150 were not wearing so well as the stock closed at $3.65.

The government could bail out Lehman but Treasury Secretary Hank Paulson had other ideas: 'I never once considered that it was appropriate to put taxpayer money on the line in resolving Lehman Brothers. I feel like Butch Cassidy and the Sundance Kid. Who are these guys that just keep coming? If someone thinks Hank Paulson could have made the Fed save Lehman Brothers, the answer is, 'No way.''

Barclays tried to buy most of Lehman but were unable to secure financial commitments from the U.S.

government, and UK regulatory and shareholder approval would have taken weeks to obtain. 'We went down the road with Barclays', said Fuld. 'That transaction, although I believe we were very close, never got consummated.' When Ken Lewis of Bank of America failed to return his telephone calls, Fuld knew it was over.

Just twenty-four hours before Lehman filed for bankruptcy, J.P. Morgan CEO Jamie Dimon had dinner at an upscale Manhattan restaurant with his management team and told them: 'We just hit the iceberg. The boat is filling and the music is still playing. There are not enough lifeboats. Someone is going to die.' That someone was Lehman.

On Monday 15 September, Lehman filed for bankruptcy. Later that day staff arrived at 745 Seventh Avenue to remove their personal effects in bankers boxes. One employee placed the firm up for sale on eBay but the advertisement was removed by eBay. Another wise guy advertised for sale a piece of burnt toast with the initials 'LB.'

Over the years Fuld encouraged his staff to buy stock in the firm, a move designed to spread the wealth. Lehman employees owned 30 percent of the shares of Lehman but now their life's savings and IRA pension funds were suddenly worthless.

Barclays did purchase Lehman's North American investment banking and capital markets businesses for about $1.75 billion. When Manhattan bankruptcy court judge approved the sale to Barclays he stated. 'I have to approve this transaction because it is the only available transaction. This is the most momentous bankruptcy hearing I've ever sat through.' Nomura bought the operations in Europe and Asia Pacific. The sale price of the French investment banking unit, Banque Lehman Brothers, was a mere €1.

Mr. and Mrs. Fuld fell on hard times. Fuld had held on to ten million shares of Lehman until the end and lost almost $1 billion. He sold Lehman shares, that were worth $247 million a year and a half prior, for less than $500,000 after the stock price collapse.

Mrs. Fuld sent a set of rare abstract expressionist drawings for auction at Christies in New York. Among the drawings slated for sale was a 1946-47 Arshile Gorky drawing, estimated to be worth $2.8 million, appropriately titled 'Study for Agony I.'

*

It is not immediately clear if Fuld committed enough blunders to sink Lehman alone or whether he was the victim of external market events. But in the court of public opinion there is good evidence to say that his blunders were several and they were fatal.

Firstly, he steered Lehman deep into the business of subprime mortgages and he bankrolled the lenders in the U.S. that were making loans to home borrowers of very poor credit standing. Lehman took all those loans, commingled them into mortgage bonds to become the number one underwriter of mortgage bonds in the U.S. and passed them on to investors as billions of dollars of what later became worthless debt.

Fuld bought two mortgage companies at the height of the U.S. property market bubble. Aurora Loan Services was an 'Alt-A lender', one which lends to borrowers with less than full loan documentation. No person in their right mind would buy such loans. It was a giant game of musical chairs as Lehman continuously packaged loans and sold the bonds to others but then the music stopped and no one wished to buy the bonds, Lehman was left without a chair and with the largest warehouse of unsellable dud bonds.

Secondly, Fuld failed to recognise the problems, to act quickly enough or to raise enough additional capital. A year of his various efforts proved fruitless. Fuld countered the argument that he had failed to act when he spoke to the House Oversight Committee. 'We strengthened our balance sheet, reduced leverage, improved liquidity, closed our mortgage origination businesses and reduced our exposure to troubled assets. We also raised over $10 billion in new capital. We looked at a wide range of strategic alternatives, including spinning off our commercial-real estate assets to our shareholders.' But it was all too little, too late.

Thirdly, Fuld failed to sell a stake in Lehman to a suitable strategic partner. He spent months in discussions with KDB and Barclays but was unable to complete a deal because it was either too commercially disadvantageous or too unpalatable personally. He even turned down an offer of fresh capital from the billionaire investor Warren Buffet because the latter was trying to extract a ten percent guaranteed return on his investment.

This was at the same time as James Cayne sold Bear Stearns to J.P. Morgan Chase (albeit at $10 per share) and CEO John Thain sold a troubled Merrill Lynch & Co. to Bank of America (albeit with a profitable wealth management division). Where his industry peers Cayne and Thain had executed, Fuld blundered along. Fuld said in December 2007: 'As long as I am alive this firm will never be sold. And if it is sold after I die, I will reach back from the grave and prevent it.'

He had a different view of events when speaking to the House Oversight Committee: 'We also considered selling part or all of the company. We approached many potential investors, but in a market paralysed by a crisis in confidence, none of these discussions came to fruition. Indeed, contrary to what you may have read, I never turned down an offer to buy Lehman Brothers.' In the end Fuld blamed everyone but himself.

Fourthly, the fall of Lehman owes much to Fuld's leadership style, or lack thereof. He ruled with an iron fist, and ultimately his poor leadership and management led to one of the largest bankruptcy filings in history and the financial ruin of tens of thousands of employees and shareholders. He was a man who told his 'troops' what to wear, when to take a shave and when to get married. He did not tolerate dissent or a contrary view. He demolished people with his intensity, his physical presence and his profane language.

Fuld's Wall Street was a war between banks, where winning was everything and losing was nothing. He despised the Big 3 – Morgan Stanley, Merrill Lynch, and especially Goldman Sachs. When he sought government help from the U.S. Treasury Department, the Secretary of the Treasury, Hank Paulson, formerly the CEO of Goldman Sachs, did him no favours. When Fuld sought help from the Bank of America CEO, Ken Lewis ignored his telephone calls, which says much about their personal relationship.

Fuld would have served Lehman better by cultivating friendships, not hostilities, with peers. His arrogance meant that he did too little too late to sell Lehman. Whether it was to a U.S. Air Force officer or others on Wall Street, Fuld acquiesced to no one.

*

Fuld testified before the United States House Committee on Oversight & Government Reform on 6 October 2008 in the matter of 'The Causes and the Effects of the Lehman Brothers Bankruptcy.' Outside on Capitol Hill, Fuld was heckled by onlookers who held up placards with words such as: 'Crook', 'Shame', 'Cap Greed' and 'Jail not Bail.' Fuld said to his advisors: 'I am the ugliest man in America right now.'

Photographers captured an uncomfortable Fuld giving them a long cold gorilla stare. On his way in, Fuld was ambushed by a CNN TV reporter. She asked him if it was fair that he had made so much money when his company was now bankrupt?

'I'm sorry, I'm on my way inside', he replied, as close as he came to an apology.

Inside, Fuld rubbed his eyes, played with his glasses and explained in his slow grating voice: 'As the crisis in confidence spread throughout the capital markets, naked short sellers targeted financial institutions and spread rumours and false information. The impact of this market manipulation became self-fulfilling as short sellers drove down the stock prices of financial firms, the rating agencies lowered their ratings because lower stock prices made it harder to raise capital and reduced financial flexibility. At Lehman Brothers, the crisis in confidence that permeated the markets led to an extraordinary run on the bank. In the end, despite all of our efforts, we were overwhelmed.'

Committee Chairman Henry Waxman questioned Fuld: 'In 2000, you received over $52 million. In 2001, that increased to $98 million. And in 2005, you took home $89 million. In 2006, you made a huge stock sale, and you received over $100 million in that year alone. Are these figures basically accurate?'

Fuld replied: 'Sir, if those are the documents that we provided to you, I would assume they are. I think for the years you're talking about here I believe my cash compensation was closer to $60 million and the amount I took out of the company over and above that was closer to $250 million. Still a large number, though.'

During the proceedings, one Committee member told Fuld: 'If you haven't discovered your role, you are the villain today. So, you have got to act like the villain here.'

During the testimony, Fuld was asked if he wondered why Lehman Brothers was the only investment firm that was allowed to fail, to which he responded: 'Until the day they put me in the ground, I will wonder.'

Fuld continued to answer the Committees questions on the collapse: 'I feel horrible about what has happened to the company. I never sold the vast majority of my Lehman Brothers stock and still owned ten million shares when we filed for bankruptcy. But when the firm did not do well, I was probably the single largest individual shareholder. I don't expect you to feel sorry for me.' They didn't.

'I take full responsibility for the decisions that I made and for the actions that I took. Based on the information that we had at the time, I believe that these decisions and actions were both prudent and appropriate', said the man who brought down the house of Lehman. 'None of us ever gets the opportunity to turn back the clock but with the benefit of hindsight, would I have done things differently? Yes, I would have.'

Fuld almost broke down at the conclusion: 'Not that anyone on this Committee cares about this but I wake up every single night wondering what I could have done differently. I have searched myself every single night. Having said all of that, I can look right at you and say this is a pain that will stay with me for the rest of my life.'

After the collapse, Fuld sold his seaside mansion on Jupiter Island in Florida, bought for more than $13 million five years prior, for a mere $100. The buyer was none other than his wife Kathy. In 2021, the couple sold the same mansion to a genuine buyer for $32.5 million. In 2009, they sold their apartment in Manhattan for $25 million and some works of art for $13.5 million. In 2015, Fuld sold his Sun Valley, Idaho estate.

Fuld founded the Matrix Private Capital Group in 2016, an asset management firm providing investment advice to high-net-worth individuals, family offices and institutions. In the New York City lobby of the firm, the Wall Street Journal reported that a framed print greets visitors with a stark message: 'That Was Then, This Is Now.'

Fuld remained silent until May 2015, when he appeared at a stock conference at the Grand Hyatt hotel in Manhattan. 'I thought it was time for me to raise my ugly head. Wow, I haven't done this in a while', he said to a crowd of 1,300 financial professionals. 'There's nothing graceful about me. This is my first public event since 2008. I don't include my wonderful time with Congress as a public event', he joked.

Fuld continued: 'Hindsight is 20-20. There is no if we, woulda, coulda, shoulda. Please understand, not a day goes by when I don't think about Lehman Brothers. I'd love to tell you I'm over it, it's behind me. It doesn't happen. But having said that, I do have to move on.'

He became philosophical: 'What did Sigmund Freud say? 'You can say whatever you want about me. I'm OK, because I know my mother loves me', he said. 'And my mother still loves me. She's 96.'

He offered a boxing analogy: 'What did Rocky say? 'It's not how hard you hit but whether you get up after you've been knocked down.' I love Rocky.'

Before the Q&A began, Fuld stood up, took off his suit jacket, flexed his arms and puffed out his chest. After being told there would be easy questions at the start of the session, Fuld adopted an exaggerated, deep, movie-announcer voice, replying: 'There is no easy one. We don't have time to hear all the things I would have done differently.'

Fuld was asked why he was still working and why he didn't 'just ride off into the sunset?' 'Why don't you bite me? I didn't think I had a choice', he replied.

The New York Times reported Fuld advised the attendees: 'You do not know what you do not know. Chew on that. Understand the difference between reality and perception. Take smart risks without being reckless. Whatever it is, enjoy the ride. No regrets.'

*

10 – FRED THE SHRED

'A good long rest is the first order of priority, a period of rest and reflection before getting round to what to do next. If you've got any ideas let me know.'

Sir Fred Goodwin,
Royal Bank of Scotland,
Edinburgh, October 2008.

ON 14 September 2005, Her Majesty Queen Elizabeth II, accompanied by HRH the Duke of Edinburgh, travelled by helicopter from Balmoral Castle to Edinburgh to perform an opening ceremony at a bank. Her host for the momentous day was Sir Fred Goodwin, the Chief Executive Officer of The Royal Bank of Scotland Group. The Queen was happy to attend – she banked with Coutts & Co., part of RBS. And this was no ordinary bank office.

The venue was the new 350,000-square-foot three-storey RBS global headquarters set on 78 acres at Gogarburn, on the western outskirts of the Scottish capital, built at a cost of £350 million. The campus was so vast that it had its own shopping mall, including a Tesco supermarket, Starbucks outlet, dry cleaners, pharmacy, dentist and hair salon set along a winding indoor paved street. And an RBS branch for discounted staff banking.

A royal salute was delivered by a regimental Highland pipe band, wearing beefeaters and kilts, before Her Majesty cut the blue ribbon at 11am. Goodwin arranged a simultaneous fly-past as four 111 Squadron Tornado F3 fighter jets, from RAF Leuchars near St. Andrews in Fife, sped overhead. Goodwin arranged the jets through his contacts, since fly-pasts were usually reserved for state occasions rather than for banks.

Friend of Goodwin, RBS ambassador and Scottish hero Sir Jackie Stewart next flew past in an RBS branded Formula One racing car. Goodwin gave Her Majesty a short tour of the interior and handed over a gift of a silver bowl, before HRH signed page one of the visitors book. The guests dined on canapes and quaffed champagne before being given a gift of a commemorative £50 RBS bank note featuring the Gogarburn building. Some marveled at the grand location and wonderful facilities and called it 'Fredtown.' Others would soon refer to the giant building as 'Fred's Folly.'

The overly-generous head office was appropriate for the RBS group at the time. Goodwin had single-handedly transformed a small dull Scottish bank into the fifth largest banking group in the world, with a stock market capitalisation at its peak of more than $70 billion and a diverse range of banking activities from China to the American Mid-West. The bank employed 140,000 staff in 30 countries, with 15,000 of them in Scotland.

The success of RBS was a source of great national pride for the Scots. In 2007, Forbes magazine named RBS as the largest public company in the world ranked by assets, with assets of $3,800 billion, $1,500 billion ahead of banking peers like Citigroup and HSBC. RBS's corporate slogan was 'Make It Happen.' Goodwin did that as CEO.

Her Majesty spoke to the invited guests: 'Scotland has had an enviable reputation for efficient financial management in a highly competitive international market. This building is a fine tribute to the many generations of 'canny' Scottish bankers, who have made, and are still making, such a valuable contribution to the national economy. Even a prudent bank needs to build a new headquarters once in a while.'

But within a few years, the UK government would stump up £45 billion to bail out RBS. Sir Fred would be stripped of his knighthood. It is wrong to say that Goodwin is solely responsible for the collapse of RBS, but he certainly helped to make it happen.

He once said: 'You have a long time to regret it if you don't get it right.' He built an expensive, self-indulgent headquarters just in time for the global financial collapse. The RBS HQ was built on the site of a former psychiatric institution and it was sited close to some pig farms. From some directions, there was a waft of swine in the air.

The Sunday Times Prufrock diary column ran a story that alleged Goodwin had ordered the construction of a 'scallop kitchen' for preparing scallops close to his new personal office, that he had his own special on-site Portakabin built to track progress of the new building and that he wanted a private road built between the headquarters and the airport in order to avoid any delays on the A8. 'It seems that travelling 10 minutes on the A8 is too bourgeois', the newspaper wrote in a piece entitled 'Fred's Bridge Too Far.'

The newspaper said he was seeking membership of Bruntsfield Links Golfing Society but he was told he must join a ten-year waiting list. Goodwin said all these allegations had 'seriously damaged him.' He took high court libel proceedings against the newspaper.

In court it was confirmed that Goodwin's office had an adjacent food preparation area for the purpose of keeping food hot close to his office so the newspaper retracted this part of its story, and that because of his passion for detail he did have his own on-site Portakabin during construction, and he even involved himself down to the choice of the wallpaper for the executive floor, which the Daily Mail reported cost £1,300 per roll.

But the important golfing matter went the way of the Sunday Times when the club secretary at Bruntsfield Links stated in court that Goodwin's personal assistant had contacted him. He said he told the PA: 'We bank with RBS but that makes no difference to becoming a member.' The waiting list was ten years for full membership and three to five years for weekday membership, he said he told the PA. 'I was then asked if I knew who Sir Fred Goodwin was and I said: 'Yes.' He said the conversation ended with the PA telling the club secretary: 'Sir Fred will be disappointed.''

*

Frederick Anderson Goodwin was born in 1958 in Paisley, near Glasgow. His father Fred senior was an electrical engineer with what later became Balfour Beatty and his mother Mary was a homemaker. Paisley was a rough area but the middle-class family lived in the nicer parts, and they later moved to better house built by his father.

Goodwin attended Paisley Grammar School where he was in the top class but he was otherwise unremarkable. He studied law at Glasgow University, becoming the first member of his family to go to university. He played golf and rugby and liked cars. Afterwards he joined the accounting firm of Touche Ross (now Deloitte) and qualified as a Chartered Accountant in 1983. In the early years of his career, he showed promise.

His greatest success at Touche Ross came in 1990 when he coordinated the liquidation of the Bank of Credit & Commercial International, known to other bankers as the Bank of Crooks & Criminals International. BCCI was a bank which included Saddam Hussein and the Medellin drug cartel of Colombia amongst its customers. Goodwin and 500 accounting staff did very well to recover half of the money owed to BCCI depositors.

Goodwin also readied the troubled Rosyth Royal Dockyards for its privatisation in the Thatcher era. He became a partner in Touche Ross at the age of 30 and his local profile was such that in 1995, he was headhunted to lead the Clydesdale Bank. When he left Clydesdale Bank, it was reported that management there partied for several days.

Goodwin joined The Royal Bank of Scotland Group in 1998 as Deputy Chief Executive at the invitation of CEO Sir George Mathewson, who planned soon to become Chairman, having selected Goodwin as his successor in waiting. Mathewson infamously commented that his £759,000 annual bonus in 2001 post the NatWest deal 'would not give you bragging power in a Soho wine bar.' Goodwin assumed the CEO role at RBS in 2001. When he took the helm, RBS was ranked as the 391st largest bank in the world.

The Royal Bank of Scotland was founded in 1727 by a Royal Charter of King George I and was formed because some considered that the only other big Scottish bank, the Bank of Scotland, was too pro-Jacobite. The two banks, the Royal and not so Royal, had remained bitter enemies since the 1700s.

The £21 billion acquisition of NatWest in 2000 was RBS's greatest coup. NatWest was three times larger than RBS and RBS would not have dared to mount a hostile takeover, had it not been for the even smaller Bank of Scotland making the first cheeky move to acquire NatWest. RBS and BOS knew they were too small to prosper and they needed to become bigger. They feared that failure in the contest for NatWest would lead to one of them being the next bank takeover target to be devoured. The NatWest Chairman rejected both Scottish bids, saying: 'there is a difference between running a corner shop and running Tesco.'

Goodwin worked closely with top RBS management on their NatWest bid and his work proved to be of high quality and to be decisive. The BOS bid for NatWest focused on cutting costs but Goodwin devised an RBS plan to grow NatWest revenue and profits. He worked for weeks on the numbers for staffing, technology systems, revenues, budgets and synergies. RBS eventually won the day and claimed the giant English bank. Goodwin's work in the bid was pivotal and he was soon confirmed as RBS CEO. In five years, aged 42, Goodwin had gone from accountant to CEO of the third biggest UK bank.

Goodwin's strategy was to grow by acquisition. In his seven years as CEO of RBS he presided over the acquisition of 26 other banks and financial services companies. RBS bought Irish mortgage provider First Active, it spent £1 billion on the UK car insurer Churchill and it took a five percent stake in the Bank of China for £900 million. RBS added Greenwich Capital Inc., which had large U.S. bond securitisation activities. One City of London analyst opined that Goodwin was 'a megalomaniac who cares more about size than shareholder value.'

In 2004, RBS acquired Charter One in the U.S. for $5.9 billion – a bank which came with many residential mortgages. Some thought RBS paid too much for Charter One. 'You will not be surprised to hear that I do not think we have overpaid', Goodwin stated. He liked to make acquisitions in the USA. 'The U.S. is large, it's well-ordered, and there's prosperity. And we speak the same language - or almost.'

'Fred the Shred' earned his nickname from bank analysts who admired the way he had reduced costs at banks such as the Clydesdale and NatWest. As Goodwin said of himself: 'My name doesn't rhyme with charming or considerate.' Usually, shredding was achieved by cutting staff numbers, such as the 18,000 employees who lost their jobs at NatWest. Goodwin remarked of smaller banks in the UK: 'We see scope for tactical mercy killings of organisations that no longer have a long-term future in the UK.'

*

Despite the public lauding of his achievements and his awards, Goodwin rarely gave interviews, nor did he make many public speeches. He did grant Forbes magazine a rare interview in 2003, in which he was described as being brisk and brusque. 'I always work on the five-second rule. How a job offer makes you feel in the first five seconds when you hear the idea, before you spend ages agonizing, is what you should do.'

His gangling frame and baby face belied a fearsome and arrogant reputation. He stated that he had no time for 'cynics, spectators or dead wood.' He garnered his cruel nickname because he was equally happy to shred his management. His Monday 9.30am executive meetings were known as 'morning beatings.' He would typically single out one direct report for a failing and then castigate him in front of his peers.

Other colleagues said: 'His favourite phrase was: 'I think you're asleep at the wheel.' He would sometimes finish publicly humiliating someone by saying: 'That's life in the big city.' 'It was all about humiliation', said one executive. 'It seemed that Fred was never happy until he'd found someone to belittle.'

One RBS executive said of Goodwin: 'You sense that he could tear you limb from limb, and you are ever so grateful when he doesn't.' He terrified some staff in his office and then told them: 'Fill in the complaints book on your way out of the door.'

Another colleague said Goodwin kept a little black book for the names of those executives who had displeased him: 'If your name was written in pencil then you were on the borderline. If your name was written in ink, you were well and truly fucked.'

An executive said of his life in RBS: 'If there was an issue or a problem Fred was more interested in finding a victim and having them crucified. The bollockings were pretty much daily.' His former head of communications said he once had a 30-minute meeting with Goodwin: 'If it had been a boxing match, it would have been stopped after ten minutes.' Others simply said that Goodwin was a classic bully.

The bank's top executives were treated to quarterly 'mess dinners', at which a karaoke machine was installed. Each of the team was expected to perform a song of their choice in front of colleagues as part of the entertainment. Goodwin liked to deliver his version of Don McLean's 'American Pie.' At midnight, meat pies were delivered and all would drink until 3am. Everyone was still expected to be at work on time next day.

His obsession with cleanliness was evident when at the Clydesdale Bank. One Sunday, Fred drove to a nearby branch of the bank since he had heard the area around the bank ATM was scruffy. He was taking photographs of the offending branch on the street when a police officer came by, spoke to him, took him to the local station and only allowed Goodwin to go on his way when he had convinced police that he was the CEO.

Goodwin hated mess of any kind anywhere. Noticing that staff often piled files and papers on the flat tops of filing cabinets in the RBS offices, he ordered thousands of new filing cabinets with rounded tops in order to discourage the practice. He disliked the use of Sellotape in public areas of the bank and banned it.

Goodwin's lowest point in his time at RBS might have come in 1998. It was reported in the media that he was mugged at one of his own tidy RBS cash machines after his chauffeur stopped so that he could extract some cash. Various newspapers reported that the assailant snatched his bank card while Goodwin's chauffeur waited nearby.

Rugby was one of Goodwin's passions, so RBS sponsored the Six Nations rugby championship. He attended the bank's marquee at Murrayfield where pre-match corporate lunches with champagne were the order of the day, but he was reported not to mingle widely with the invited guests. Some of the bank's staff said that their boss was a little shy. RBS also sponsored tennis star Andy Murray and a Formula 1 motor racing team.

Goodwin's love of playing golf ('golf is a sport that gives enormous pleasure to millions of people world-wide') allowed him to count Jack Nicklaus amongst his friends. RBS issued a commemorative £5 note to celebrate the 250th anniversary of The Royal and Ancient Golf Club of St Andrews in 2004, and Nicklaus and Goodwin were there for the photo opportunity. Nicklaus was paid £1 million per year to be an RBS brand ambassador, as was another of Goodwin's boyhood heroes – Sir Jackie Stewart, which is why he turned up at the opening of the Gogarburn campus to perform a few obligatory wheel spins.

There were early warning signs of corporate hubris.

RBS ran a fleet of 12 chauffeur-driven Mercedes S-class limo cars, which Goodwin ordered to be painted all in the same specific shade, Pantone 281, so they matched the RBS corporate shade of blue. The vehicles were stamped throughout, down to the gear stick, with the RBS logo, making the fleet virtually unsellable when they came to be sold.

Two years after the landmark acquisition of NatWest Bank, RBS made another sizeable acquisition - a £17.5 million private jet. The Dassault Falcon 900 EX aircraft cost £9,000 an hour to operate, it could fly 5,000 miles or for up to 10 hours, and it sat a mere 21 passengers. The aircraft carried the registration G-RBSG which reflected its UK registration and the international banking groups corporate initials. Those inside the bank joked that the aircraft registration stood for Royal Bank of Scotland Goodwin. Soon the Dassault Falcon jet would be up for sale, with one not so careful previous owner.

PM Tony Blair knighted Goodwin, aged 45, in 2004 for his 'services to banking.' Goodwin was Chairman of The Princes Trust, which helps young people get their first job or start their own business. Goodwin sat beside Prince Charles at their VIP functions.

Goodwin met his wife Joyce through his work with Touche Ross. She was a banker with an MBA who had worked for Citibank and BNP Paribas. The romance with Joyce grew after he experienced what he called 'the rough edge of her tongue' during their business encounter. He resided with Joyce and their two children at a £3 million sandstone mansion in Edinburgh's exclusive Grange district.

Goodwin divided his time between the head offices

in Edinburgh and London. When working in London he would stay in a suite at the Savoy Hotel, where a valet would attend to his clothes and laundry. He attended the Oyster Club, whose members dine on pints of Guinness and oysters once a month. His hobbies include shooting and vintage cars. He owned a 1972 Triumph Stag 4-seater convertible and two Ferraris.

In June 2005, Goodwin drove a £195,000 Lamborghini Murcielago at the Goodwood Festival of Speed in West Sussex, but he misjudged a corner and hit a barrier. The Lamborghini ended up on its roof, causing £60,000 of damage. Lamborghini and RBS staff were told to keep the crash quiet. Goodwin would soon cause a bigger crash.

*

2006 remains RBS's finest year of financial performance, with a profit of £9.4 billion. Goodwin wrote to his shareholders: 'We are building a group whose diversity, scale, distribution capacity and operational excellence can deliver superior, sustainable income growth, controlled risk and strong returns.' He added prophetically: 'Central to this is our longstanding aversion to subprime lending, wherever we do business.'

In December 2006, Goodwin promised City of London analysts that RBS would no longer grow by acquisition but it would do so organically. 'We don't need to make any big acquisitions now. We are generating results ahead of expectations on a purely organic basis.' He said that there were no bank deals that were 'desirable, do-able or affordable.'

But in early 2007, Barclays bid big to acquire Dutch bank ABN Amro. RBS then joined a consortium with Banco Santander of Spain and Fortis of the Netherlands to mount a competing bid. The deal suited the consortium since RBS would acquire the desirable U.S. assets of ABN Amro. Goodwin commented when launching the bid, 'The key to good deal-making is being prepared to walk away.' He didn't.

The bidding war lasted throughout the summer until their consortium prevailed. RBS stumped up a contribution of £10 billion as the deal closed in November. Many point to this mega-deal as the absolute peak of the European banking euphoria. To cap a great year, Goodwin was paid £4.2 million in 2007, including a £2.86 million bonus.

Goodwin said at a press conference in February 2008 that there is a moment after you buy something when you think: 'Heavens, what have we got here?' But he said: 'It's important to point out that we are happy with what we bought, and what we bought was exactly what we thought we were buying. There was no Eureka moment, no silver bullet, it was all particularly mundane, but I found that very reassuring.'

He strongly refuted claims that RBS had paid too much: 'We're very pleased to have won that business.' He added RBS had only paid £10 billion. 'That's not to say it's a small acquisition but it's a lot smaller than people think it is.'

By September, the subprime lending crisis was decimating the U.S. The global credit markets tightened and RBS was exposed. The crash of Lehman Brothers reverberated, and the credit markets froze at the thought of which bank would be next.

Goodwin said at the time: 'U.S. house prices are not going to fall by 30 percent. They just aren't.' But they did. Greenwich Capital in Connecticut was still owned by RBS. It was a mini-investment bank which securitised U.S. mortgages into collateralised debt obligations. It was the worst possible business to be in at the worst possible time.

An RBS executive stated that Greenwich did not have a large CDO exposure and he compared packaging CDOs to the manufacture of sausages when he said; 'We package the sausages, but we don't keep the sausages.' This was untrue. In late 2007 and early 2008, Greenwich reported large realised CDO losses and larger loss provisions.

Soon RBS suffered a first-ever half-year financial loss: 'It has been a chastening experience and reporting a pre-tax loss of £691 million is something I and my colleagues regret very much.' Reports said that Goodwin offered to resign but that the RBS board declined his offer. CNN's website said that Goodwin had got off 'Scot-free.'

RBS relied for funding on borrowing short term funds from other banks, beginning with loans of three months tenure. The loans soon became overnight borrowings. The treasury department of RBS had to find tens of billions to keep going each day, repay the loans next day and do the same work again. It was unsustainable.

Now other banks would no longer lend at all to RBS, which was hemorrhaging billions as corporate deposits were withdrawn by scared large depositors. RBS could no longer fund its most basic day-to-day banking operations or settle its obligations in the daily UK bank clearing system. The Governor of the Bank of England Mervyn King later told the BBC: 'RBS couldn't get to the end of the day. The bank was finished.'

On Tuesday 7 October 2008, Goodwin left his London Ritz Hotel suite (the Savoy was undergoing renovations) and took his RBS-blue S-Class Mercedes to the nearby Landmark Hotel. Merrill Lynch was holding a banking industry conference and Goodwin was the keynote speaker. Goodwin gave his presentation. All went well until the Q&A session. One attendee asked Goodwin if the opportunities available to RBS were so exciting and everything was going so well, why had the RBS share price fallen 25 percent while he was speaking? Goodwin left the event right away and headed to his City office.

Goodwin and other UK bank CEO's were summoned to Her Majesty's Treasury where they met the Chancellor of the Exchequer Alistair Darling. It was explained that the UK government would provide a rescue package for the banks in order to prevent the collapse of the UK banking system. There was no room for negotiation and no other alternatives on offer. Goodwin was one of the last bankers to agree to the package at 2am.

Wednesday 8 October 2008 remains the most extraordinary and terrifying day in British banking history. The UK government provided £20 billion to RBS. Within a few short months, the government stumped up a total of £45 billion for RBS, and RBS was nationalised.

On the same day, RBS announced that Goodwin would resign as CEO. The Daily Telegraph ran an article accompanied by a photograph of Goodwin being put through an office shredding machine. The article was entitled 'Shredded Fred.'

Goodwin had been paid about £30 million in his decade at RBS. The government left him with no choice but to go, since his position was untenable. 'This would not have been the manner or circumstances I would have chosen. You know, it's more like a drive-by shooting than a negotiation.'

Goodwin told waiting journalists: 'A good long rest is the first order of priority, a period of rest and reflection before getting round to what to do next. If you've got any ideas let me know.' Goodwin sent an email to RBS staff saying: 'I should step aside at this point to enable a new leader to take the group forward into this next phase of its development', but there was no apology, nor regrets.

In December 2008, Newsweek magazine christened Goodwin as the 'Worst Banker in the World.' The proof was the plunge in RBS's share price in two years from £8 to ten pence. Goodwin was voted the world's worst banker in a Financial Times poll in 2008. Goodwin was so hated by some that his effigy were put up on London Bridge.

RBS unveiled a loss for 2008 of £24 billion, which remains the largest annual loss in British corporate history. It was also RBS's first annual loss in its 281-year history. Some said that the loss was so huge that their ex-CEO should be called 'Fred the Red.'

The fall of Goodwin was officially complete when he was sacked by Prince Charles. Buckingham Palace stated: 'The bank is in such straits Prince Charles had no option but to part company with him. It is out of the question for a business charity to have as its figurehead and role model a man who caused such economic damage.'

In February 2012, the final Royal ignominy was delivered when Goodwin's knighthood was annulled by the Queen on the advice of Her Majesty's Government and the Honours Forfeiture Committee. The last prior person to be stripped of a knighthood by the UK government was Robert Mugabe, the despot of Zimbabwe.

*

Goodwin committed many fatal corporate blunders. He completed a series of giant bank mergers and acquisitions and called them growth. Growth can either occur organically or by acquisition. Organic growth costs a lot less and you know what you are growing. Growth by acquisition can be very expensive and you can end up with a horror story. Goodwin paid top dollar for U.S. assets which soon became a liability for RBS.

RBS became a huge monolithic organisation. It was spread globally across 30 countries with a bewildering array of different siloed businesses. By 2007, RBS became the largest bank in the world, with a balance sheet worth £2 trillion. Reporting lines in the organisation were complicated and blurred. And atop all of this activity was Goodwin with his brusque management style of pillorying those who delivered bad news or who failed. RBS might not have been too big to fail, but it was likely too big to manage.

Senior management and the board of directors of RBS take some of the blame for the decade of blunders. There is no evidence that any of them faced down the dominant personality of Goodwin and told him to stop buying banks, to consolidate what they had, to divest non-core or less profitable businesses, and to accumulate their retained profits in the good times, so as to have more capital as a safety buffer in the bad times.

In particular, former CEO and Chairman Mathewson shoulders personal blame. One of the key tasks of any CEO is succession planning, to identify and recruit the next CEO and to steer their nomination past the board of directors. Mathewson hand-picked Goodwin as his replacement and anointed him, as Mathewson moved up to Chairman.

The ill-advised, history-making and massive ABN Amro deal was executed at the very top of the economic cycle. Goodwin said in 2006 that he would not acquire any more banks, but in 2007, he did precisely that. Bloomberg noted that by 2008, RBS had become Europe's largest lender. ABN Amro proved to be the one acquisition too far as RBS's liquidity was stretched as never before. 'They stayed too long at the party', said one fund manager. 'Sir Fred should have left at midnight and not stayed until 3am.'

Every credible CEO has to keep promises made to the shareholders. In February 2008, Goodwin said: 'There are no plans for any inorganic capital raisings or anything of the sort.' But in April 2008, RBS announced a £12 billion rights issue, which at the time was the largest ever offering of new shares in UK corporate history, offering shares to existing shareholders at £2. He had told his shareholders RBS didn't need more capital, then changed his mind, asked for more capital and depleted that additional capital rapidly.

And finally, he dumped the problems of his bank on his fellow UK citizens by losing so much the bank had to be nationalised. His was not the only bank needing help – HBOS, Northern Rock, the Bradford & Bingley Building Society received assistance too – but RBS was the biggest and worst blunder inherited by the UK government in 2008.

Regulators in the Bank of the England and the Financial Services Authority shoulder some blame. At the time it was an era of light touch regulation of banks, rather the present intrusive supervision. At one point in 2008, RBS's reserves of Tier 1 capital, a measure of financial strength and the vital reserves set aside to cover potential losses, was the lowest among its UK rivals. No one in a regulatory authority ever told Goodwin and RBS not to do a deal, and in particular they waved the ABM Amro deal through blindly at a time when there were alarm bells ringing and red flags waving in global banking.

*

Goodwin disappeared, other than sightings of him in his garden or on trips to stay with friends in France and Spain, until February 2009 when he was hauled before the UK Treasury Select Committee in the Houses of Parliament. He sat squeezed between the former RBS Chairman Sir Tom McKillop and the former Chairman and CEO of Halifax Bank of Scotland. Goodwin displayed a mixture of polite disinterest and vague menace.

John McFall MP began his essential public humiliation. 'Sir Fred, one of the members of the public said to me this morning, 'Do the institutions know what they have done to ordinary people's lives, families and jobs? Everyone in the room pays some form of tax to the UK Government, and the UK Government has forwarded shed-loads, lots of money, to your institutions. What are we getting? In terms of your approach, some people say you have been hesitant to say 'sorry', so I am giving you your opportunity now.'

Goodwin replied. 'I apologised in full, and am happy to do so again, at the public meeting of our shareholders back in November. I too would echo the others comments that there is a profound and unqualified apology for all of the distress that has been caused and I would not wish there to be any doubt about that whatsoever.'

The MP continued: 'When the authorities came before us - the Bank of England and the FSA - they said they had sent warnings out to the banks and they cited January 2007 and April 2007. Sir Fred, why do you think that those warnings were not heeded?'

Goodwin replied: 'I am not sure that they were not heeded. As you can imagine, I have gone over this time and time and time again in my own mind as to what was the point at which we should have seen this differently, and I keep coming back to, at the time there was a view, not that things would continue forever, there was a definite mood that the economy in this country and generally was going to slow down, that financial markets were going to slow down; but at no point did anyone get the scale or the speed at which.'

Another MP put matters more succinctly. 'Sir Fred, how much worse could it have been at RBS if you had not been in charge?'

Goodwin concluded: 'I fully accept my responsibility in the matter we are talking about. I would imagine that there are others out there who think, 'There but for the grace of God.' It was a fact, and all the more numbing, that after a rights issue, right through until the middle of September, we were moving forward positively. It was post-Lehman's that the collapse in confidence, the collapse in markets, just came round and hit us and we were caught at that point. It was very sudden and very sharp. It could have happened to others. I am not aware of a basis for questioning my integrity as a result of it all. I could not be more sorry about what has happened. I am not going to go back through all of that again, but I have invested a lot in RBS, and I do not mean financially, over a very long period of time and it is of great distress to me to see what particularly my colleagues are going through and I do not diminish customers and shareholders as well.'

Following the RBS rescue with public money, it was revealed that Goodwin had a personal pension fund at RBS worth £17 million, which entitled him to an index-linked annual pension of £693,000 for the rest of his life. When questioned about this largesse, he told MPs his pension was a defined benefit scheme: 'My pension is the same as everyone else in the bank.' He later agreed to waive one third of his annual pension.

At the height of Goodwin's infamy, his home was attacked, with the windows broken, and his Mercedes car was vandalised. His children were taunted by others at school. His wife dreaded going outside. He spent time at his £4 million villa in the south of France, where The News of the World hunted him down and called him 'Fred the Fled.' He spent some of his premature enforced retirement tending to his collection of vintage cars, he took to shooting game birds and to the golf course.

Goodwin spends his days at the Archerfield golf club near North Berwick, East Lothian. 'Fred spends a lot of his time down at Archerfield', said one neighbour. 'A couple of my former colleagues saw him sitting in the hot tub dispensing knowledge.'

Mr. and Mrs. Goodwin moved to a £3.5 million mansion in upmarket Colinton in Edinburgh set in 2.3 acres, built originally for footballer Graeme Souness, complete with a floodlit tennis court, a Japanese garden and a fountain in the driveway. The Daily Mail sent a reporter to the house who spoke to the gardener, and who advised: 'Fred does live here, but you won't find him because he's never in.' He has never been charged with any offence following the crash of RBS. Goodwin remains Scot-free.

The Gogarburn head office became partly excess to requirements due to the huge downsizing of the bank. Sixteen thousand RBS staff lost their jobs in the first year after the collapse. But shortly after the UK went into the first coronavirus lockdown in 2020, RBS turned part of the building into a charity distribution hub supplying food and clothing to people in need in the pandemic. Local shops donated their excess stock, including 150,000 chocolate bars and 80,000 tubs of Pot Noodles. Local farmers donated pallets of vegetables for free onward distribution. Goodwin's global bank, scene of a grand Royal opening ceremony only fifteen years earlier, had become a food bank.

*

11 – A GIANT OF A MAN

'The cause of our problems was global, so I can't say sorry with any type of sincerity and decency. But I do say a very genuine thank you.'

**Sean FitzPatrick,
Anglo Irish Bank Corporation,
Dublin, January 2009.**

THE St. Patrick's Day Massacre occurred in Dublin on 17 March 2008. It should have been a quiet morning in Ireland's financial community since it was a bank holiday and there were few bankers and brokers at their desks. But those who had made it in to work were horrified to read their Financial Times. Not only had U.S. investment bank Bear Stearns been sold in a fire sale to rival J.P. Morgan Chase on the previous day, but the well-respected and influential Lex column in the FT noted that certain banks were overly exposed to the UK commercial property sector. The FT named the guilty banks – Halifax Bank of Scotland, the Bradford & Bingley Building Society and Ireland's Anglo Irish Bank Corporation.

The stock market reaction in Dublin was instant as investors took flight. A credit-fueled property boom meant Anglo Irish Bank was correctly identified as being highly vulnerable. The Anglo share price fell 20 percent but recovered later to close down 15 percent at €7. Allied Irish Bank and Bank of Ireland fell in sympathy. By days end €3.5 billion was wiped off the value of Irish stocks and Anglo was firmly in the crosshairs of nervous international investors.

That evening, Anglo Irish Bank Chairman Sean FitzPatrick and CEO David Drumm readied an emergency plan in case customers turned up at Anglo's branches looking for their deposits back. Staff were told to be at work at 6am, they were advised to set up roped-off areas inside the branches for optimal queue management, and above all not to allow queues of customers to build up outside on the street in public view. Anglo saw the Northern Rock Building Society crash in this manner and wished to avoid the same fate. There were some withdrawals of deposits on the next day but there was no panic.

A crisis had been averted by FitzPatrick, the public face of Anglo for three decades. He was a pillar of the Irish banking and business community. Yet in the next few months, his unprecedented banking blunders would sink the bank.

Anglo would soon write off billions in bad property loans, an illicit Anglo share support operation would prove futile, FitzPatrick's hidden personal loans from the bank would be revealed, and a €7.2 billion year end window dressing of the bank's balance sheet would be exposed.

Anglo would report the biggest annual loss, and become the biggest bankruptcy, in Irish corporate history. FitzPatrick would be arrested three times by police, endure two high-profile court cases and be declared bankrupt. He would become the most vilified, derided and blamed man in Irish public life.

*

Sean FitzPatrick was born in Bray, County Wicklow, south of Dublin, in 1948. His father Michael was a dairy farmer and his mother Johanna was a civil servant turned homemaker. He had one older sister, Joyce. He went to school in Loreto Convent Bray and Presentation College Bray, where he only managed to achieve a Pass in Leaving Certificate Mathematics and an Honour in Leaving Certificate French. FitzPatrick was never an academic but he was good at rugby. He played as a centre and captained the junior and senior rugby teams at Presentation College Bray, showing some early signs of leadership.

He spent the school holidays working at the amusement arcades in Bray and on the family farm, and spent the summer after leaving school on building sites in London. He returned to attend University College Dublin where he graduated with a Bachelor of Commerce Degree. He attributed some of his success at UCD to the nuns in his class: 'The nuns at UCD were great at taking notes in class. I was the only one who'd have a cup of coffee with them and I ended up with the best set of notes in college.'

He saw that accountants had good jobs and made good money. In 1969, he joined Reynolds McCarron & O'Connor, (later to become part of Ernst & Young, or EY) where he qualified as a Chartered Accountant, but when he finished his apprenticeship (known as Articles) he was the only one of his student intake not to be offered a permanent job in the firm. He joined Craig Gardner (later to become part of Price Waterhouse Coopers). He always wore a good suit to work and always carried a briefcase, to look important.

FitzPatrick by nature was outgoing and gregarious, and was a small, slight, dapper man. He was known to his friends and colleagues simply as Seanie. A colleague once said: 'He suffered from the 'small man' syndrome. And like a lot of small men, he drives a big Mercedes.' In 1974, he married Caitriona O'Toole, a former secretary in a consultancy company, and they had three children - David, Jonathan and Sarah. He suffered from diabetes and took insulin injections to maintain his blood sugar levels.

A banking career was never his intention. It happened accidentally. In 1974, he joined the Irish Bank of Commerce, a publicly quoted investment bank with a small deposit base and only four employees. He started work as their accountant and took the job because it came with a low interest rate staff mortgage, allowing him to buy his first home. He was a little man in a little job in a little bank in a little capital of a little country.

FitzPatrick's first official job title at the Irish Bank of Commerce was General Manager. Later the Irish Bank of Commerce was taken over by City of Dublin Bank and the combined entity then bought Anglo Irish Bank. When FitzPatrick was told to ask the recruitment firm Hays to make a list of candidates to head the fledgling Anglo Irish Bank, he seized the moment and began a successful campaign to persuade his bosses to give him the job. FitzPatrick became CEO of the combined bank, now renamed Anglo Irish Bank Corporation Ltd, a position he would hold from 1986 until 2005. He liked the grand name because it implied the bank could be big in Ireland, the UK, and further afield.

FitzPatrick was faced with the problem of many small bankers in small banks – how to take on larger established banks. In this case, Anglo was dwarfed by Allied Irish Bank, Bank of Ireland and Ulster Bank. So FitzPatrick had to innovate. He opened his branches to customers at lunchtime. He provided faster turnarounds on lending decisions due to the small size of his bank. A big customer could breakfast with an Anglo banker at the Shelbourne Hotel, next to the St. Stephens Green head office, on Monday, and hear back that his multi-million-euro loan application was approved by the end of the week.

He chose to grow his bank primarily by making larger sized loans to wealthy business people and professionals, and he shunned offering less profitable current accounts, savings accounts and credit cards to retail customers. He found a niche in the medium-sized business market by offering loans which were too big for the hire purchase and finance companies and too small for either AIB or Bank of Ireland to consider. Other banks were unionised but he never allowed a staff trade union to operate in Anglo.

He reduced the amount of red tape and bureaucracy in his bank. He grew the banks commercial property loan portfolio. His favourite type of early loan was said to be to a doctor buying his medical surgery or to a solicitor buying his practice office. Soon his favourite type of loan was a big loan to a big property developer whom he knew well.

FitzPatrick made some selective acquisitions overseas to boost his share of the high-net-worth market. In 1995, Anglo bought a small Austrian bank, Royal Trust Bank. In 1996, Anglo acquired Ansbacher & Co., an exclusive Irish private bank. In 2001, Anglo bought a small Swiss bank in Geneva, Banque Marcuard Cook & Cie. Soon Anglo had a network of offices in Ireland, the UK, Europe, the Isle of Man and the U.S.

FitzPatrick was a networker and knew it was good for business. He continued to play rugby with Bective Rugby Football Club. He was sitting on the substitutes bench one day when Bective scored a spectacular try. A reporter turned to the substitute and asked him the name of the scorer. 'Sean FitzPatrick' was his response. He was a member of Fitzwilliam Lawn Tennis Club and he joined up-market clubs like the Hibernian United Services Club. He was appointed a council member of Chartered Accountants Ireland.

Golf was his favourite sport and it was great for business too. FitzPatrick played in Druid's Glen in County Wicklow, and could often be seen in Michael Smurfit's K Club in Kildare. He had a golf handicap ranging between 10 and 12. One opponent said that his golf style betrayed his character: 'He hated losing. He wanted to bet on every game. If he was losing, he would introduce bets on every hole to compensate. At the end of a game of golf with Sean, there could be 20 bets. He had a low boredom threshold, as much in golf as he had in business. He needed the adrenaline rush, the thrill of the holes.' When asked about the best place to get good business or personal information, FitzPatrick said: 'For the real McCoy, you can't beat the nineteenth hole on the golf course.'

*

Anglo's lending growth in the 2000s was spectacular. They lent to former bricklayers and plasterers who mortgaged their homes to build houses. They lent to publicans to buy more pubs which they demolished to build hotels on city centre sites. They lent big ticket amounts to developers of shopping centres such as the Jervis Centre and The Square in Tallaght in Dublin. They lent millions to developers building giant housing estates in the expanding Dublin suburbs, and to the 5-star Enniskerry Ritz Carlton Hotel, where celebrity chef Gordon Ramsey came to cook and yell at staff.

They lent €468 million to Quinlan Private so that Derek Quinlan and his investors could outbid a Saudi Royal Prince and purchase the flagship Savoy Hotel in London for £750 million. They lent to an Irishman who planned to build the Chicago Spire, which would be the tallest building in the U.S., designed by starchitect Santiago Calatrava, at a cost of $1 billion. They lent over €1 billion to Quinlan Private again in 2007 to finance his purchase of the Jurys Inn hotel group, when they delivered a €1 billion plus bank draft to the deal negotiators in a Dublin solicitors office at 2am one morning.

For a decade, Anglo and its property developing customers rode the Irish property boom. It was fueled by a rising population, a small housing stock, easy 100 percent mortgages and cheap European Central Bank money. While the Germans saved hard, the Irish (and the Greeks) spent like never before. By 2006, more than a fifth of the Irish workforce was employed in building houses. Everyone knew the bubble would burst eventually. The Irish economist David McWilliams foresaw the crash: 'When are we ever going to learn that buying and selling over-priced houses to each other is not going to make us rich?'

All the while, Anglo lavished generous corporate hospitality on its best customers. The bank paid for 25 top customers plus their wives to take a trip on the Orient Express from Paris to Venice. They paid for Ryder Cup golf packages and Six Nations rugby weekends. They flew the top U.S. customers for a trip to play Ireland's best golf courses. They spent tens of thousands of euros on gifts, dining, polo t-shirts, cuff-links, pens and golf balls. They showered customers with tickets to Old Trafford and Anfield, although one bank executive doubted the value of paying for a customer to see a Premier League soccer match from a corporate box complete with prawn sandwiches, when the same Anglo customer could have likely acquired the entire football club if they so wished.

In January 2005, FitzPatrick, aged 55, stepped down as Anglo CEO after 26 years. There were four internal candidates for the job of CEO and after much internal wrangling and dirty politics, David Drumm, aged 37, who formerly ran Anglo's U.S. operations and was the head of Ireland lending, replaced his boss as CEO.

FitzPatrick however did not go far from his bank – he moved upstairs to become the bank Chairman and retained an office in the head office. His new part-time job paid him €350,000 per year.

In June 2007, Anglo was still lending avariciously and the bank share price was at an all-time high despite the signs of a subprime crisis in the U.S. and the likely spill over to the rest of the world. Fitzpatrick and Drumm learnt that the Anglo share price may be rising because Ireland's richest businessman was buying the banks shares. They drove to a hotel in Navan in September 2007 to hold a covert meeting with Sean Quinn, who made his fortune in cement manufacture, hotels, glass and insurance, and who was worth €4.5 billion. He was known as 'The Sandman', beginning by digging aggregates from a quarry and rising to become number 164 on a Forbes magazine list of the wealthiest people on the planet.

The two startled bankers learnt that Quinn owned 24 percent of the share capital of Anglo. Quinn had acquired his shares using a financial instrument called a Contract for Difference. This allowed him to bet on the share price without having to fully pay for his shares. He had entered into the CFDs with stockbrokers who were the parties buying the shares. FitzPatrick and Drumm were horrified. If word leaked out that one investor owned 24 percent of the bank, and if that shareholder ever got into financial trouble, they might unload their huge holding on the stock market and the Anglo share price would plunge.

Soon Quinn owned 29 percent of Anglo. As the share price had fallen in recent months, Quinn had bought more shares to reduce his average purchase price - a classic sign of trying to make a bad investment look better. Quinn had to pay huge margin calls to his brokers. But he was short of cash and asked Anglo for what was called a 'working capital loan' to pay the margin. Anglo obliged and lent hundreds of millions of euros to Quinn.

It was agreed Quinn would convert half of his CFD's into shares and ask his five children to own the shares – their individual three percent holding would not need to be disclosed publicly. The balance of his CFDs would be sold as shares to other new investors. Anglo agreed to find a suitable buyer and asked U.S. investment bank Morgan Stanley to help. This project was given a code name of 'Project Maple', but all efforts were unsuccessful.

The global banking system was in turmoil, liquidity for banks was drying up, property markets were frozen, bank borrowers were missing loan and interest payments, and shares in a small Irish banking property play like Anglo were totally unappealing. The Anglo share price trended down yet still the requests came from Quinn for Anglo to lend more cash to pay margin calls. By mid-2008, Quinn's total borrowing from Anglo was approximately €2.8 billion – the largest single-name credit exposure for the bank.

FitzPatrick and Drumm tried to sell Quinn's shares to a group of investors. They rounded up ten of the largest customers of Anglo, paid them personal visits to seek their help and succeeded in getting them to buy €45 million of shares each. The deal was sweetened for them since Anglo would lend them money to buy the shares. These loans to buy Anglo shares were not illegal under Irish company law, since a company can lend money to another company to buy its own shares once the lending is in the ordinary course of business, and lending is an ordinary activity of any bank. The ten investors in this 'golden circle' were known as the 'Maple 10' after the banks earlier project name.

FitzPatrick and Drumm next planned to make the banks funding appear better to investors. An act of subterfuge was performed in September 2008. Anglo management decided to window dress their balance sheet at the financial year end and make the bank's deposits look better than the reality. Investors place a higher rating on corporate deposits which are considered 'sticky' and less volatile and they place a lower rating on interbank deposits which can move out overnight.

Anglo agreed a plan with management at Irish Life & Permanent whereby Anglo gave €7.2 billion to Irish Life & Permanent (a bank) and received back €7.2 billion from another part of Irish Life called Irish Life Assurance (a corporate entity). This allowed Anglo to increase corporate deposits by €7.2 billion and reduce interbank deposits by €7.2 billion, making Anglo look less sick.

*

By September 2008, the Irish banking system was in full retreat. The smaller Irish Nationwide Building Society had run out of cash, cash deposits were flowing out of all the banks, and the befuddled host of the RTE Liveline radio programme was advising listeners to take their money out of the banks and to put the cash under their mattress or bury it in the garden. Anglo only had days left before it too ran out of cash. Amid this local and international banking turmoil, the Irish government announced a €400 billion bank guarantee scheme covering the deposits, loans and bonds of the six Irish banks – AIB, Bank of Ireland, Anglo, Irish Life & Permanent, EBS and Irish Nationwide.

Initially the bank guarantee was a great success. Next day deposits started flowing back into the Irish banking system. Suddenly and bizarrely, Irish banks had a competitive advantage over other banks which were not government guaranteed. Ulster Bank in Ireland, part of RBS in the UK, was not part of the guarantee. There were unpleasant cases of Anglo staff ringing up customers who had deposits with Ulster Bank to tell them to move their funds to Anglo for the greater safety it offered. Times had now changed.

But for FitzPatrick, his corporate and public life were now unravelling. Few people other than some Anglo administration staff knew that for eight years FitzPatrick had hidden directors loans he had received from Anglo so that they would not be reported in the bank's annual accounts at the end of September. In the last week of September, he would receive an amount of money equal to his directors' loans from executives at Irish Nationwide and this money was used to repay the loans to Anglo before their year-end. Then in the first week of October, he repaid the money to Irish Nationwide using new funds coming from Anglo and the loans were reinstated in the books of Anglo, avoiding any disclosure to both auditors and shareholders. He used the hidden loans to invest in Anglo shares, property funds, wealth management products, investment property, film finance and pension products. FitzPatrick owed Anglo €122 million by September 2007. He referred to the loan process as 'refinancing', others have called it 'warehousing.'

But in the crisis month of September 2008, FitzPatrick omitted to process his usual loans transaction. The loans would be reported as a note to the bank's accounts and the figure for directors loan would soar once the hidden loans were included. FitzPatrick therefore resigned as chairman of Anglo in December 2008. Drumm also resigned in the belief that his continued presence would make it more difficult for Anglo to raise funds. FitzPatrick stated that he broke no laws by hiding his personal loans: 'However, it is clear to me, on reflection, that it was inappropriate and unacceptable from a transparency point of view.'

Anglo reported a pre-tax loss in March 2010 of €12.7 billion for the 15 months to end of December 2009 after writing off €15 billion in bad loans. The losses were the largest in Irish corporate history. Anglo was out of capital. There was too much bad news about window dressed balance sheets and directors loans. The Irish Government had no choice but to fully nationalise the bank and inject extra capital into the rotten bank.

Ireland has a long unsuccessful history in prosecuting alleged white-collar crime and FitzPatrick's case was no different. One Irish newspaper ran a headline at the time: 'If FitzPatrick Lived In New York, He'd Have Been Arrested By Now.' In February 2009, the Garda Bureau of Fraud Investigations, working with the Office of the Director of Corporate Enforcement, raided Anglo's offices. It remains unclear why it took them months to execute the raids, or what had been destroyed in the intervening time.

In the next decade, FitzPatrick was arrested at his home on three occasions by the Gardai Bureau of Fraud Investigations and bailed on all three occasions, and a computer and documents were taken from his home. The Irish Independent reported that when he was arrested FitzPatrick was 'tanned', which in itself is still not a crime in Ireland.

In the Dublin Circuit Criminal Court in April 2014, FitzPatrick was cleared on all counts by a jury of having any involvement in the bank's extension of the €450 million of loans to the group of developers to buy Quinn's shares in Anglo. The jury returned a majority verdict after 13 hours of deliberation. Evidence was produced in court that the regulators, including the Central Bank of Ireland, had been aware of the proposed transaction and had implicitly given their approval. There was a wider 'green jersey' agenda, whereby Irish banks were encouraged to help each other. Two other directors of Anglo were found guilty of providing unlawful financial assistance to the ten individuals but they were spared jail by the judge who said it would be unjust given 'an Irish State agency had led them into error and illegality.'

In May 2017, on day 127 of the longest running criminal trial in the history of the Irish state, the judge ordered that FitzPatrick be found not guilty of hiding millions of euros in personal bank loans from auditors. The judge criticised the investigation by the Officer of the Director of Corporate Enforcement into the matter, including the 'extraordinary' shredding of documents by the ODCE investigator, and the coaching of witnesses from Ernst & Young, meaning there was a risk to FitzPatrick of an unfair trial.

FitzPatrick spoke outside the court: 'It was a very long and tiring and difficult time for myself and my family. So, as you can appreciate it is a wonderful day for me and my family. Thank you very much for everything.' The Director of Public Prosecutions took nine years to bring the unsuccessful case, which says much about the Irish legal system.

FitzPatrick was declared bankrupt by the High Court in July 2010 with debts of €147 million. His lawyers told the court he was 'bowing to the inevitable' after Anglo blocked a proposed settlement deal which would have left him with his family home and half of his pension.

On 29 September 2010, a bizarre incident occurred in Dublin when 41-year-old Joe McNamara was arrested after a concrete mixer truck was driven into the iron gates of the parliamentary Leinster House building. The slogans 'Toxic Bank Anglo', '€1,000,000 on golf balls' and '€500k for golf' were written on the side of the truck and the vehicle registration number was changed to the word 'Bankrupt.' The driver parked at the gates to the parliament, blocking the entrance, and he locked his cabin before climbing onto the roof of the truck. Upon his arrest, the driver from Mayo said: 'My name does not matter. The truck belongs to Anglo Irish Bank. I am returning it to them. Take away the keys.'

The death of Anglo was confirmed in April 2011 when contractors removed the name of Anglo Irish Bank from their offices in Dublin's city centre. The new bank CEO named the removal as 'Operation Baghdad', a comparison to the day the U.S. forces arrived in Baghdad and tore down the big statue to the much-hated Saddam Hussein. Passers-by on St. Stephen's Green blared their car horns, others roared 'Praise

Jesus' and many clapped as they walked in front of the landmark to such a banking disaster.

*

The standards of corporate governance at Anglo during FitzPatrick's tenure were grossly deficient and the blame for that rests firmly with the board of directors of the bank. They allowed one man to be their CEO for almost thirty years, which is a sure-fire recipe for disaster, since that one person will dominate the organisation. No well-run bank or company in today's corporate world allows a CEO to rule for three decades.

When FitzPatrick relinquished the CEO role, the board allowed him to become the Chairman of the bank, which does not represent a sufficient changing of the guard. The Chairman would likely cramp and inhibit the style and authority of the new CEO. FitzPatrick and Goodwin have much in common – their banks became personal fiefdoms.

Like RBS and Northern Rock, Anglo's funding model was inherently flawed. They made long term loans of ten to twenty years to their customers but because they had no retail deposits of size, they were forced to fund this by issuing bonds and by bank borrowings. Interbank borrowing is always short term and may require repayment at short notice. Anglo faced a liquidity crunch when banks would no longer lend to them.

The loan portfolio of the bank remains the primary reason for Anglo's downfall. Good banks ensure there is a diversification of their loan book. They lend to different industry types in different sectors of the economy and then lend to diverse geographies, thereby ensuring they are not exposed to any one part of the economy. Good banks produce detailed information on the mix of their loans and avoid concentration risk. On the other hand, Anglo at the very end simply lent to big property developers in Ireland. Anglo attributed much of its success to its model of strong relationship banking. It lent to the same customers over and over again on successive property projects. But this left its loan book dangerously concentrated in a small number of very large customers.

Unfortunately, prudence, risk management and moderation were not part of the lending strategy. Credit Committee meetings at the bank to approve new loans were said to be ugly and brutal and credit committee meetings were not even minuted until 2004. On occasion loans were secured on the personal guarantees of builders which, when the property crash came, proved to be as worthless as the properties they owned. Lending was unduly concentrated on acquiring building land, and the development of property.

Under Drumm's leadership the bank took a policy decision which might have later saved the bank but they failed to implement their new policy. Management had grown concerned at the rocketing price for land and development property and decided to cap their property development lending at 20 percent of total lending and then to reduce it further to 15 percent of total lending. The bank was also not supposed to lend more than one percent of its total loan book to any one customer but in December 2005 it had ten top customers to whom it had lent more than one percent of its total loan book. The planned changes proved impossible to implement because the bank was too addicted to property lending. It rarely declined loans. One London broker described Anglo as 'a building society on crack.'

Like Goodwin at RBS, FitzPatrick decided to build an impressive new head office for his growing bank. A greenfield site was selected in Docklands overlooking the north side of the river Liffey, close to major accounting and law firms. Naturally the contract to build the head office was awarded to one of Anglo's best customers. At the time of the collapse the building was a skeleton of exposed concrete floors, pilings and pillars, and it stayed that way for several years as a public reminder of the hubris of Anglo. Later in a move not without irony, the building was bought by the Central Bank of Ireland as its new head office, where it stands as a monument to good regulation rather that profligate banking. Not for the first time, a bank built a new head office just in time for its collapse.

The regulation of Ireland's banks by the Central Bank of Ireland and the Financial Services Regulator was light touch and non-intrusive. The country's top banking regulator, Patrick Neary, spoke at a chartered accountants conference in November 2007: 'Irish banks are solidly profitable and well-capitalised.' The Irish regulators were asleep at the wheel and were under resourced and amateurish.

FitzPatrick was no fan of bank regulation. He once told RTE TV news: 'The danger of having too much regulation is that you are just going to stifle business and we are not going to have any success or growth. So, what are we going to have? A situation where we have everything totally regulated and nothing happening? Is that what we want? You need regulation but you don't need over-regulation. What we need is appropriate regulation.'

In June 2007, FitzPatrick told a Dublin corporate dinner that business people had created the Celtic Tiger boom and that Ireland's regulatory regime had gone far enough. 'It is time to shout stop', he said. 'We should be proud of our success, not suspicious of it. Our wealth creators should be rewarded and admired not subjected to levels of scrutiny which convicted criminals would rightly find intrusive. This is corporate McCarthyism.'

Greed played a major part in FitzPatrick's blunders. He didn't resign as CEO because of the banks poor results or funding difficulties – he resigned because his hidden personal loans became public knowledge. He had already earned millions in salary, bonuses and pension contributions over his thirty years in Anglo. He was not a poor man, yet he saw it necessary to borrow €122 million for his own personal investments, just to make more money. He had no ethical or moral compass in his time at Anglo.

Sean Quinn and family made their own monumental blunder in investing in Anglo – they put all their eggs in one rotten basket. Quinn lost more than €3 billion investing in Anglo and he later went bankrupt and lost his entire business empire.

The final cost to the Irish tax payer of FitzPatrick's blunders and Anglo's downfall was €34 billion plus, which is proof that a small man in a small bank in a small country can still do big damage to a small economy. The impact was so severe that a Troika of senior officials from the European Central Bank, the European Commission and the International Monetary Fund arrived in Ireland to dictate future fiscal policy to the government, leading to years of harsh budgets and financial austerity for the citizens.

At the time of its implosion Anglo had a balance sheet size of €70 billion, meaning that exactly half of its lending ultimately turned out to be bad. A London hedge fund manager said at the time that Anglo was simply 'the world's worst bank.'

*

FitzPatrick retired behind the hedges of his Whitshed Road, Greystones, County Wicklow home. Occasionally he was seen playing golf on the adjacent course or taking walks along the sea front and marina. He was photographed at the Euro 2012 soccer finals in Poland, where he stayed at a €550-a night Poznan hotel, and he visited Spain on golfing trips.

Along the way, FitzPatrick had laid a pension nest egg when he sold two million shares in Anglo, half his holding, to net himself €27.6 million for his retirement. He bought a Spanish holiday home in San Pedro, Marbella for €438,000 in June 2005 and bought an investment apartment at Station Road in Killiney, County Dublin for €2.6 million. As he once said about his personal wealth: 'There are a lot of millionaires in this bank.'

He was interviewed on RTE radio, where he was asked if he would apologise to the Irish people for the damage he and his bank had caused to the small island nation. He said: 'Well, you know it would be very easy for me to answer a call like that and say sorry. What I have got to say is that the cause of our problems was global, so I can't say sorry with any type of sincerity and decency. But I do say a very genuine thank you.'

Later than same day, FitzPatrick spoke at a business event in Greystones golf club in County Wicklow. The Minster for Finance was preparing the budget and FitzPatrick had some advice for him. He said the government should abandon the 'sacred cows', and should abolish state pensions for all, end child benefit payments and stop giving elderly people free medical cards for the health service. His comments were reported in the media. The public were outraged at his views. He was not making any new friends.

In another interview with RTE before the crash of Anglo, FitzPatrick was asked this question about the risk profile at Anglo: 'This is what the other guys are running around saying about you guys: 'They're nothing but buccaneers, nothing but pirates. You know they take far too many risks and it's all going to come and topple down one day."

FitzPatrick retorted: 'Will they last? Will they, they're a fine bank but will they last? That has been said about us in the Seventies, the Eighties, the Nineties, and indeed even in recent years, but we have arrived, and we ain't going anywhere.'

FitzPatrick recalled feeling the disdain of his counterparts at the bigger, better-established Irish banks: 'I remember going to dinner parties in Dublin 4 and introducing myself as Sean FitzPatrick from Anglo Irish Bank and they'd look at me, and someone from AIB or Bank of Ireland would sort of snigger, and I would say to my own staff coming back to work, the day will come when you are at a dinner party and you say you work in Anglo Irish Bank. There will be silence around the table.' He was proven right.

FitzPatrick died on 8 November 2021, aged 73, due to cardiac arrest. His sudden death was the lead news story on RTE TV that evening, and the report featured vintage era shots of a boyish FitzPatrick with a mop of tousled woolly hair and a then fashionable double-breasted suit, sitting in a small banking hall with an Anglo logo, beside treasury dealers on their telephones trying to look busy in front of the camera.

He was described in the report as being synonymous with the rise and fall of the Celtic Tiger Irish economy, as a visionary who built the third largest bank in Ireland, which later became a 'ball of smoke.' But later he was 'a lightning rod for public anger.' On the deadly Irish website rip.ie, the public condolences comments page was disabled on FitzPatrick's death notice, presumably to stop any hateful comments upon his passing.

In a defiant and loving funeral eulogy, his daughter Sarah said: 'Sean FitzPatrick was our dad. And that is who I'm going to talk about today. Dad had a lot of professional highs and lows in his life. When we were down, he would pick us up. He would constantly remind us that the road in life is long and winding, but the measure of a person is not their successes but, in fact, how they could find a way to move forward when they have been knocked down off the horse. In that regard, our dad was a giant of a man.'

*

12 – THE PLAYBOY OF TEMA

'We were told to push the boundaries, so we pushed the boundaries. We were told you wouldn't know where the limit of the boundary was until you got a slap on the back of the wrist. We found that boundary, we found the edge, we fell off and I got arrested.'

Kweku Adoboli,
Union Bank of Switzerland AG,
London, September 2011.

ON the morning of 14 September 2011, Kweku Adoboli, a 31-year-old trader with Union Bank of Switzerland, London, received a telephone call from William Steward, an accountant working in the back-office, who challenged Adoboli about his trading activity. Fears about his trading first arose in August when an investigation by Steward was launched. Their telephone call lasted two minutes and thirteen seconds and was recorded on the bank's tapes:

'Steward: We need to clarify these exposures, because it seems a bit strange, because we're seeing a debit and, like, an asset exposure with iShares and with Société Générale. Which seems a bit strange because if one, you know, if they're two sides of the same trade, I can't understand why we would have an asset on both sides?

Adoboli: Erm … This is what … if you could explain to me as what you understand an asset to be?

Steward: Well, this is the net value of the unsettled trade, so if you bought an equity and it's gone up in value, you've got a net asset, and if you've sold an equity and it's gone down in value, you've got a net asset.

Adoboli: Ok understood, cash P and L basically.

Steward: I would expect if you bought from Blackrock and sold to SocGen, effectively, then one should be an asset and one a liability.

Adoboli: Yep.

Steward: Erm, now we don't have the full sort of trade level granularity in the ledger so you know it's possible we're looking at a mixture of these trades and other trades, but we just need to understand, you know, whether these exposures are correct.

Adoboli: I'll come back to you in a few minutes.'

Adoboli had already stalled Steward, telling him he was 'really, really busy' and 'we had an annoying client who was taking up half my day plus we had all these client meetings and the market was going crazy, plus I was a man or two down pretty much every day.' In an earlier telephone call to Adoboli, Steward queried a trade which was due to be settled by another bank and said: 'If they didn't settle it, we'd be in the shit.'

At 1.30pm, Adoboli left the UBS office at 45 Finsbury Avenue, near Liverpool Street Station, on the northern fringes of the City of London, telling others he was going to his doctor. He stopped at St Mary Moorfields Catholic Church to pray. One hour later, Adoboli sent the following email to Steward, titled 'An explanation of my trades':

'Hello Will,

It is with great stress and disappointment that I write this mail.

First of all, the ETF trades that you see on the ledger are not trades that have been done with a counterparty as I have previously described. I used the bookings as a way to suppress the P and L losses that I accrued through off book trades that I made. Those trades which were previously profit making, became loss making as the market sold off aggressively through the aggressive sell-off days of July and early August.

There are still live trades on the book that will need to be unwound. Namely a short position in DAX futures (which have been rolled to December expiry) and a short position in S&P 500 futures that are due to expire on Friday.

I have now left the office for the sake of discretion. I will need to come back in to discuss the positions and explain face to face, but for reasons that are obvious, I did not think it wise to stay on the desk this afternoon.

I fully expect that questions will be asked as to why nobody else was aware of these trades. I take full responsibility for my actions and the shit storm that will now ensue. I am deeply sorry to have left this mess for everyone and to have put my bank, and my colleagues, at risk.

Thanks,

Kweku.'

Despite the email being loaded with trader jargon and acronyms, the shocking contents announced a clear and present danger for UBS London. Something was seriously rotten in the trading books of the giant Swiss investment bank and the trader who was responsible for the mess had left the building.

Adoboli sent his email from his personal email account from the relative safety of home. Following receipt of his email, his manager telephoned Adoboli and told him to return to the office. When Adoboli arrived, the manager and a compliance officer met him and they attempted to quantify UBS's exposure to his trades. Adoboli said he owned $5 billion of U.S. S&P 500 futures and $3.75 billion of German DAX futures. His manager had no idea how he could amass a position of that size without alarm bells going off.

Adoboli faced hours of late-night interviews with UBS management on the executive sixth floor. They offered him Domino's pizza as midnight came. On that same evening, Adoboli changed his Facebook profile status to an insightful: 'Need a miracle.'

Adoboli later told the Financial Times: 'By now I'm texting my girlfriend, it's midnight, half past midnight. She's like, what's happening? When are you coming home? And then my phone battery died and then at one they came in, at half one, they came in and said, really sorry Kweku, we know we said you could go home but we've had to call the police and they're coming to arrest you. I was like, OK. You're just girding yourself, right.'

Police officers arrested Adoboli at 3.35am. He had

taken massive, speculative bets on S&P 500, DAX, and EuroStoxx index futures over the prior three months. 'He wasn't very good at it', said one UBS executive later. 'He went long when the markets were at their peak, and short when they were at their bottom.'

But all the time Adoboli was also recording fake, forward-settling exchange traded fund trades in the UBS computer systems, to make it appear as if his positions were hedged and were risk free. He had traded away £1.4 billion, the largest unauthorised trading loss in British banking history.

*

Kweku Adoboli was born on 21 May 1980 in Ghana into a life of relative privilege. His father described himself as a 'self-made man' having worked at the United Nations as a personnel officer in UN peace-keeping forces until his retirement in June 2007. Thus, the Adoboli family travelled extensively as he served with the UN in places such as Israel, Cambodia, Iraq, Afghanistan, South Lebanon, East Timor and Kosovo.

His son Kweku lived from the age of four in Jerusalem, Damascus and Baghdad, and attended the international schools favoured by diplomats. Adoboli later wrote: 'Because we moved around so much, I was blessed with the joy of making friends quickly.'

The media soon tracked down Adoboli's father in Ghana. He lived in the neighbourhood of Community 12 in Tema, an industrial city on the Atlantic coast, located about 25 kilometres east of the capital, Accra, with a population of 160,000. It is known as the Harbour City since it is Ghana's largest sea port. The trading centre is home to an oil refinery and many factories but also contains suburbs for commuters who work in Accra. The Adoboli family home was a large cream detached two-storey house, with a double garage, stone pillars, upstairs balconies and metal grilles on the lower windows. A black Mercedes saloon was parked out front.

Adoboli's father John told the London media his son had made 'a mistake or wrongful judgment. We are all here reading all the things being said about him. The family is heartbroken because fraud is not our way of life. I brought them up to be God-fearing and to appreciate decency. Growing up and through to school days they were very brilliant and respectful. I also gave them the best education as I can. I want the world to have an open mind. He should not be sentenced before the trial begins', he added. 'I feel bad. Our name is now everywhere in the world. I go to the internet. We are devastated.'

He said his son refused to buy a car in London because he didn't want to pay for street parking. 'We are not flamboyant. That is not how we are. We are simple people.'

The family decided to give their son a great education and more stability in his life, so Adoboli, at the age of 12, boarded at the independent Ackworth School from 1992 to 1998, with fees of £19,635 per annum. The prestigious coeducational day and boarding public school lay in quiet countryside near Wakefield, West Yorkshire, and was founded in the eighteenth century by the Quakers, a religious organisation which asks followers to develop a personal approach to religion, and which stresses the importance of honesty.

Pupils were asked to observe periods of reflective silence before meals, to attend regular worship meetings, and to learn the value of living a peaceful, simple lifestyle. The school motto was: 'Non sibi sed omnibus.' – 'Not for oneself but for all.'

Adoboli was a popular and diligent pupil and impressed enough to become the head boy of the school. Former classmates described him as 'fun-loving' and 'hard-working' and recalled him being a skillful hockey player. The head teacher said he had been 'a student who made a very positive contribution to the school community' and described him to the BBC as an 'outstanding student, who was able academically, was a good sportsman and was a natural leader who was widely respected by students and staff.' His father said he received such reports with great pride: 'He was head boy among a lot of white boys.'

Adoboli began studying Chemical Engineering at the University of Nottingham in 2000, but later changed to study a B.Sc. in Computer Science and Management. He was a member of the Students Union committee, where he was the Communications Officer, and he coordinated Freshers Week. 'He was an absolute whizz with computers', said one contemporary. 'He was very well-known around the university because he was very sociable, and he told us his father was a diplomat who worked for the United Nations.'

In the summer of 2002, Adoboli obtained an internship in the operations department of UBS London, which aligned him for a subsequent permanent role. UBS asked the intern Adoboli to deliver an automated tool to calculate the value of assets under management at UBS globally, which he concluded to be

$1.3 trillion.

He only undertook an internship at UBS because he couldn't get a better role in management consulting elsewhere: 'What's ridiculous is by the end of my 10-week internship at UBS, I had become part of the culture. I was told that our values matched. When they offered me a job, I was proud and I thought they had embraced me.'

After graduation, Adoboli started as a trainee analyst in UBS London in September 2003 on a salary of £30,000, which later rose to a salary of £33,000 plus a £7,500 bonus in his second year. He spent the first two years as a back-office trade support analyst, learning how to book and settle trades. He became intimately aware of how the bank's operational and accounting controls worked and saw their strengths and weaknesses in action on a daily basis. He learnt what specific events triggered the alerts to management and how best to avoid this happening.

He landed a role in 2006 on the Global Synthetic Equity Trading Delta One desk. There he became part of a close-knit quartet known as 'the four musketeers.' He began trading exchange traded funds, which are bundles of stocks, commodities or other assets.

In the rough and tumble world of trading, Adoboli was referred to within UBS as 'the good cop of the ETF team.' The Delta One desk undertook big-ticket short-term proprietary speculative trading in global markets. The die of stupidity was already cast. 'People were a little surprised when he turned up on the trading desk because he didn't have a trading background', one former colleague told the Daily Telegraph.

*

In 2007, with 10 months trading experience, Adoboli found himself jointly responsible for the bank's $50 billion ETF, Index Swap, Index Futures and Single Stock Futures trading book. He was promoted to Associate Director in 2008 and to Director in March 2010, which came with a salary plus bonus of almost £200,000. By 2011, Adoboli was earning a salary of £110,000 and bonus of £250,000, ten times his 2003 starting salary. He was identified as a high-potential future leader by UBS's Ascent staff programme. His job included meeting with clients and promoting UBS on University campus visits.

Colleagues knew Adoboli as a dedicated trader who put in long hours at work, although he could be difficult or demanding with colleagues. Another trader on the ETF desk later told his trial that he found Adoboli to be 'unfriendly, emphatic, unpleasant, distant and superior', and he had a rule that he should never be asked the same question twice.

One former colleague told the Financial Times that Adoboli was the go-to guy on the trading floor when there was a trading error which needed to be fixed: 'We didn't know how he did it, but we didn't want to know.'

Four months earlier, he had rented a 3,000 square foot warehouse conversion in Brune Street, Shoreditch, east London, close to fashionable Spitalfields Market, a ten minute walk from the UBS office. The open plan apartment had minimalist interiors, white walls and limestone floors. Other apartments in the same building had sold for £1 million to £2 million. The rent was £1,000 per week. His neighbours spoke of a courteous, charming man, albeit one prone to throwing loud late night parties with lots of girls.

Reporters spoke to his ex-landlord who said the huge Shoreditch apartment was 'a bit like an art gallery' and was 'big enough for ten bedrooms.' He added: 'He moved out about four months ago. He was a very, very nice guy. I have not got a bad word to say about him. He was not the tidiest person but he was a good tenant. He was very well spoken, his references all passed. But I asked him to leave because I like to refresh the tenants in the apartment. There were a couple of times when he was behind on rent but he made it up quickly. I never had any reason to doubt him. He was very polite. He would speak to anyone. He had a girlfriend who was a nurse, and he dressed very smartly. I can't believe what's happening. I can't believe it is him.'

A neighbour who also worked in finance in the City of London commented: 'I knew he worked for UBS. We had a chat recently about how tough the markets were and he said it was a bloody shit fight, and we both agreed how tough it was at the moment.' The same neighbour said Adoboli would often bring 'pretty girls' back to the apartment. 'He had lots of attractive girls coming by. He lived alone. He had friends around all the time. I know a pretty girl when I see one and he had pretty girls over all the time.'

Another former neighbour told the Daily Mail that Adoboli would hold all-night raves about once a month: 'I would complain about his music. I would sometimes scream out in the middle of the night, turn down your fucking music. But he did seem nice, once when I complained about the music, he sent me a bottle of champagne to apologise.'

Outside of work, Adoboli's interests listed on Facebook included expensive wine (collecting Argentinian boutique wines), photography, mountain biking, football and the tough U.S. crime drama 'The Wire.' He also disclosed online that he had been dating a nurse for a year. His bank job took him away from London on trips to France and the United States, and he took holidays home to Ghana to see family and friends.

His Facebook profile had photographs of a usually well-dressed man, short in height and stocky around the midriff. He had once updated his Facebook status to: 'Can we shut down global markets for a week so everyone can just chill out?' He also posted online: 'Will they? Won't they? Reduced to watching Fox TV News for guidance, it's a grim affair.'

*

Adoboli's first problems arose in late 2008, when he began to engage in unauthorised trading, placing bets on the future direction of the stock markets. His initial trading deception was insignificant. He made a $400,000 loss on a trade in October 2008, and decided to hide the loss rather than to tell his manager.

He later testified in court that this was when he formulated a mechanism, known as the 'umbrella account', whereby some profits were held off the trading books and earmarked to offset rising losses on the ETF desk by being drip-fed back into the desk's profit and loss account. The 'umbrella account' was an internal slush fund to store skimmed profits, a sort of rainy-day fund. By 2009 and 2010, his subterfuge was going well and the umbrella account's $40 million profit gave him confidence to engage in bigger trades. He regularly engaged in trading which exceeded the bank's daily trading exposure per-employee of $100 million.

Adoboli next created fictitious ETF trades, which settle over a longer time cycle than the instruments on which he was actually losing money. He recorded them with European counterparties who were not obliged by market rules to confirm ETF trades, so he avoided the need for trade confirmations and the risk of a dispute with a counterparty.

He entered this false trade information into UBS's computer systems to offset and hide the risky unauthorised trades he was undertaking, effectively inventing false trades as hedges. The latter if real, would have reduced his exposure. He also extended the date on which some trades would settle to a later date, to buy more time to make up the losses.

2011 was not a good year for the markets. First there was the Greek debt crisis, then a tsunami swept Japan and there was a long running debacle about the U.S. debt ceiling. Global stock markets became more volatile and more difficult to trade profitably.

His trial was told of a text message exchange in June 2011 involving Adoboli and another individual in which he spoke about his trading. Adoboli was asked whether he was still at work to which he replied: 'Yeah, still at work, having to explain how we made so much money.' His respondent answered: 'I hope in a good way. Are you being accused of theft? (and he added a smiley emoji face).' Adoboli replied: 'Ha, Ha. No!'

On 23 June, Adoboli was praised by his line manager in New York, for making a $6 million profit in one day, which was a record for the bank. Soon after his boss sent a second email scolding him for not asking him for the permission to exceed risk limits.

His crisis began in mid-2011. Between 23 and 30 June, he created a short position betting markets would fall, and he masked his unhedged short trades with a fictitious long position. Adoboli later testified in court that by late June he was under huge pressure from senior managers to abandon his bearish view of the markets and take a long trading position. As a result of this pressure, he said: 'I broke, I just broke. I should have held on. I absolutely lost control. I was no longer in control of the trades we were doing.'

So, on 1 July, he flipped his short trades to an outright long position. He was now doubling down, a classic sign of desperation for any trader or gambler. In the subsequent market sell-off, Adoboli's losses accelerated in July and peaked at £7.5 billion on 8 August, at a time when the bank believed his exposure was only several million pounds.

He told the Financial Times that he was physically and mentally exhausted by this time: 'There's only so long you can go sleeping three broken hours a night. I probably wouldn't have ended up losing control in the way that I did. I would have recognised at a much earlier point that, OK, we've lost x amount at this point, OK, there's still probably this much downside to go; let me think about it rationally, flip my positions back again. But I couldn't do that; there was no energy left. And you end up going into autopilot when you're that tired, and of course autopilot means that you make mistakes, you don't recognise warning signs when they're all around you, and it snowballs from there.'

In his trial Adoboli described one July evening that year when he was supposed to go out for dinner with his girlfriend. He told the court: 'I went a bit catatonic. I was curled up on my bed. She was asking me what was wrong. I just couldn't explain.'

He said his girlfriend eventually persuaded him to tell his bosses: 'In the end she was the strength. She was the person who said to me: 'Look, Kweku, if you can't do this, if you can't fix this, then look within yourself and maybe go and tell someone. This is going to kill you. You can't keep fighting this battle that you are clearly not winning."

His final trading phase involved taking another short position between 11 August and 13 September using ETFs with more extended settlement dates. He booked trades to settle on 22 September but he knew that his luck would finally run out at this date. His losses remained and his risk exposure remained enormous at about $7 billion. By August, accountant Steward was chasing Adoboli daily about discrepancies with his trades.

On Monday 12 September, Adoboli says he gathered the three other traders on the ETF desk for a crisis meeting at the All Bar One across from the UBS office. He told them he was burnt out and was ready to give up trading and said if he took full responsibility for everything and said no one else knew what he was doing, he figured he'd be fired but the others would stay clear of any blame. But his colleagues told him they were going to disown him. Adoboli sent a text to his girlfriend on the same night which stated: 'I'm a little upset because the boys have sold me down the river.' On Wednesday 14 September, he accepted defeat, left the desk for the last time and sent his guilty email.

*

Adoboli was remanded in HMP Wandsworth from September 2011 to June 2012. On his first New Year's Eve in prison, he heard the banging of cell doors and the inmates chanting his name, after he appeared on ITV as one of the news stories of the year. He was granted conditional bail subject to being electronically tagged and placed under curfew at a friend's house.

His trial opened at Southwark Crown Court on 10 September 2012. Despite the very incriminating email sent to Steward, Adoboli pleaded not guilty 'to get disclosure on everything that happened, so I could contribute to learning and cultural change.' He wore a dark suit, white shirt and bright tie, and a red British Legion poppy to court.

The prosecution told the court Adoboli was only 'a gamble or two away from destroying Switzerland's largest bank.' They said his motive was to increase his bonus, his status, his job prospects and his ego. The usual trader insults were thrown at him during his trial; 'an adrenaline junkie, driven by money, a massive show-off, a gambler.'

Adoboli claimed in court he had lost control of his trades under pressure from his bosses to generate even bigger profits by taking greater risks: 'There were no secrets, there was no hiding, there was no holding back. We were told to go for it, we went for it. We were told to push the boundaries, so we pushed the boundaries. We were told you wouldn't know where the limit of the boundary was until you got a slap on the back of the wrist. We found that boundary, we found the edge, we fell off and I got arrested.'

He testified during the nine-week trial: 'The pressures were huge.' He said that in 2007, he and a co-worker aged 24, were left struggling to manage a $50 billion portfolio of investments. He told the court: 'Our book was massive; a tiny mistake could lead to huge losses. We were losing so much money it was mental. We were two kids trying to figure how this could work. We had 30 months of experience between us. That's like two kids running the economy of Ghana. I had imposter syndrome every day.'

Adoboli seemed confident at the trial and was surrounded by friends. His father had travelled from Tema to offer support. Glowing character references were read to the court from his girlfriend and his ex-headmaster. Positive work appraisals were read out.

Adoboli claimed his co-workers on the ETF desk, his line managers and the back-office staff all knew about his illicit trading activities and had turned a blind eye to his breaching of risk limits as long as he was making good profits. He said that traders at all investment banks viewed compliance policies as being 'aspirational' in nature rather than being fixed, and they had to bend the rules if they were to achieve their profit goals.

His 'umbrella account' featured prominently in the trial. Chat messages were read out between Adoboli and a trader on the ETF desk showing the other trader was grateful for the umbrella's existence. In one message the trader wrote to Adoboli: 'Thank fuck for your umbrella.' In another message the trader said: 'Rest on your umbrella' and in a further message he told Adoboli to 'umbrella the rest.' The umbrella became a verb.

On 20 November 2012, the jury found him guilty of fraud. The judge sentenced Adoboli to seven years in prison and remarked in his sentencing comments: 'The tragedy for you is that you had everything going for you. Your father was in a responsible position which enabled you to be educated at a private school. I am not saying that you come from a privileged background, but you had some advantages that other people do not enjoy. In addition, you had your own natural talents. You are highly intelligent. You are plainly very articulate. And as I told the jury, you appear to have a considerable amount of charm. Your fall from grace as a result of these convictions is spectacular.'

Adoboli served his sentence at HMP The Verne in Dorset, HMP Ford in West Sussex, and HMP Maidstone in Kent. He later told the London Evening Standard about his stay at HMP The Verne where he was considered to be a minor celebrity. 'People were like: 'Mate, it's the billion-dollar banker.' I kept myself to myself at first. I was bullied by security, they searched my cell every Friday for four weeks in a row, no one gets that. They turn it upside down, pull apart your legal paperwork.' Eventually he made friends there, worked as a listener for the Samaritans and became chair of the prison council.

Whilst inside, he began corresponding with a journalist from the Financial Times. 'I'm doing my best to keep my head up but it's not easy', he wrote to her. The two corresponded over four years and the journalist visited him several times in prison.

He told her about prison routine. At 5am, he watched TV news and wrote letters in his cell. At

7.45am he called his girlfriend before she went to work. At 8am he went to the gym for one hour. He worked as an equality representative in the prison's diversity centre. After lunch, he went to the library to read newspapers. He underwent counselling, learnt to play the guitar and sang on Saturdays in the church's Pentecostal fellowship. 'This prison is like a really rubbish boarding school that you can't leave', he wrote.

He was released from HMP Maidstone in June 2015. A friend met him and drove him to Livingston, Scotland where he lived for the next three years. He said he owed much to his friends: 'Two friends from university, who I live with now, were amazing. When I broke up with my partner two-and-a-half years into my sentence I was smoking non-stop, not sleeping, drinking too much coffee. I spoke to them on the telephone and they came down from Scotland to check up on me.' In October 2015, the Financial Conduct Authority banned Adoboli for life from working again in the finance industry in the UK. He was unemployed but getting any job in the UK would soon become legally impossible.

*

Adoboli's blunders are the same as those of other stupid bankers on trading desks. Nothing is gained by hiding losses, booking fictitious trades, manufacturing hedge trades, faking trade confirmations and using error or umbrella accounts. These nefarious acts only serve to delay inevitable discovery. If a trader loses $10 million, they should have the backbone to tell their manager, and accept the consequences. They may be fired quietly but they can walk down the street, hand their CV to another bank, do an interview and start a new job at a new bank without any fears about the sins of the past.

Losing $10 million is bad luck and it becomes the banks problem. But if a trader loses $1 billion, they are named and shamed in public, they are prosecuted, tried, convicted and jailed, they are banned, they will never again work in banking and their life is destroyed. If you lose $1 billion, it's your problem.

UBS takes credit for the fact that its eager accounting staff did identify anomalies in Adoboli's trading and their investigative work led directly to his downfall. But for its blunders, UBS was fined £30 million by the Financial Services Authority for a lack of controls to prevent unauthorised trading in its London investment bank.

Adoboli's biggest blunder came from left field. He had lived in England for 23 years, from the age of 12, but had never applied for British citizenship. Therefore, he was liable for automatic deportation under Section 32 of the UK Borders Act 2007 as a foreign criminal who had been sentenced to at least four years of imprisonment. An immigration tribunal ruled that he should be deported to Ghana. He could not work in the meantime.

He took to doing some unpaid work as an expert in ethics in banking, when most likely the opposite applies. He delivered talks to students, traders and others in banking about how to avoid making the mistakes which he made.

He told the London Evening Standard: 'I fucked up.' He said the pending deportation caused divisions at home: 'My father thinks if this country wants to deport me, I should go back to Ghana. But he has to understand that he sent me here, I built an alternative surrogate family here. If I leave, I'm allowing them to take away a massive part of my identity. I never stopped to think that my passport restricted my freedom.'

Adoboli was arrested and detained at Livingston police station on 12 November 2020. Two days later, four security officers accompanied him from Dungavel detention centre to Harmondsworth Immigration Removal Centre near London, taking turns to drive the mini-bus on the nine-hour journey. He spoke by telephone to the Edinburgh Evening News from Oxford Services on the M40 motorway: 'It all feels surreal. I'm massively stressed. It's like being in a film. It's a bit of an out of body experience.'

He was placed on a Kenya Airways flight at Heathrow and left behind his new partner of four months, Alice Grey, with whom he had been living in Livingston. Five security guards flew with him, one sitting on either side and three sitting in the row in front. His lawyer protested at the flight: 'We are deeply upset about the manner in which he was whisked away, because there was no chance to say goodbye. He supports Leeds United. He's a Yorkshireman. He is being sent to a place where he hasn't lived since he was four.'

His flight via Nairobi touched down at Accra's Kotoka international airport, but Adoboli was not rejoicing at his homecoming: 'This is not about not liking Ghana', he said of his lengthy battle against deportation. 'It is about what has been taken away from me in the UK.' He travelled light, with a backpack, and had to leave behind his clothes: 'I don't have much use for my waxed Barbour coat here. It's hanging in the wardrobe.'

Speaking to The Guardian from his father's house in Tema, he was in two minds: 'It's the first time I have felt free in seven years. The Home Office destroys lives.' He told Bloomberg his first nine months back in Ghana were largely spent indoors as he struggled with depression and that he initially disguised himself during trips outside the house.

Adoboli gave an interview in 2020 on the Zylofon FM radio programme where he asserted the UK government took deliberate steps to break up his three and half year long relationship with his then British-born Iraqi girlfriend. He claimed to have had less opportunities in prison for visits than British inmates, and the pressure of deportation weighed heavily on the couple: 'She had to make a choice of moving to Ghana with me. I suspect that she said no.' On the day his girlfriend called their relationship off, they had been on the verge of a breakup for about four to five months. When she visited him in prison for the last time, she sat across him and said 'she could not do this anymore.'

He concluded by playing the race card: 'Don't let anyone believe that the British are somehow the most tolerant, they are not, they are deeply racist when it comes to how they handle foreign nationals.' When asked why he did not apply for a British passport, he said that due to his job, he did not have the time to go for his British passport, therefore, he used his Ghanaian passport for his work travels. 'I was proud of my 'Ghanaianess' and I had a Ghanaian passport in which there was a 10-year US visa, and a 5-year European visa. Our Ghanaian passport isn't as good as the British passport.'

Adoboli describes himself on LinkedIn as a public speaker, a commentator and a culture and systems advisor but his online work history unsurprisingly fails to mention his time trading at UBS. His Twitter profile header contains this mystic Ewe ethnic language proverb: 'It is only the child who goes to fetch water that breaks the pot.' In his time at UBS, Adoboli didn't fetch much water but he sure broke a lot of pots.

From his roots in Tema in one of the world's poorest countries to a £1,000-a-week loft apartment in the City of London and a £360,000 compensation package at a global investment bank, Adoboli had once embodied the ultimate in personal success and social mobility.

But the international playboy is back home in Tema. He gave a TV interview to Ghana Joy News a few days after being deported to Ghana, where he sat hunched in his chair and held hands with the interviewer as he wiped crocodile tears away: 'It's good to be home.'

*

13 – THE LONDON WHALE

'I was public enemy No. 1. Everyone, every single authority, everyone, I think, reading the press articles, wanted to behead me or destroy me or smash me.'

Bruno Iksil,
J.P. Morgan Chase & Co.,
London, April 2012.

AT 5.58pm on 5 April 2012, Ina Drew, a veteran New York-based banker and head of the Chief Investment Office, or CIO, at J.P. Morgan Chase & Co., sent the following email to the bank's Operating Committee, which included the bank's Chief Executive Officer and Chairman Jamie Dimon, to advise of an increasingly significant problem, about which Bloomberg and The Wall Street Journal were going to print shortly:

'I want to update the Operating Committee on what is going on with the credit derivatives book in CIO especially given a WSJ article which will come out tomorrow. One of the activities in CIO is a credit derivatives book which was built under Achilles in London at the time of the merger. The book has been extremely profitable for the company (circa. $2.5 billion) over the last several years.

Post December 2011, the macro scenario was upgraded and our investment activities turned pro risk, the book was moved into a long position. The specific derivative index that was utilised has not performed for a number of reasons. In addition, the position was not sized or managed very well. Hedge funds that have the other side are actively and aggressively battling and are using the situation as a forum to attack us.

We made mistakes here which I am in the process of working through. The drawdown thus far has been 500 mil dollars but nets to 350 mil since there are other non-derivative positions in the same credit book. I wanted my partners to be aware of the situation and I will answer any specific questions at OC on Monday.'

Her core message was to communicate a loss in the vague round sum amount of $500 million, which had been reduced by a gain of $150 million from other trading products. The Operating Committee was the most senior management committee in the bank but none of the members knew worse news was to follow in the coming weeks.

CEO Dimon, the silver-haired poster boy of American banking replied to Drew: 'Ok. Send me some info. Also how does it relate or not to our wind down credit exotics book?' Dimon read the email, digested it and replied at 6pm, within two minutes, proof that the CEO of the U.S.'s biggest bank was admirably competent in managing emails. His personal motto was 'to return every phone call and every email, every day.'

As Drew feared, on 6 April, The Wall Street Journal printed an article: "London Whale' Rattles Debt Market: In recent weeks, hedge funds and other investors have been puzzled by unusual movements in some credit markets, and have been buzzing about the identity of a deep-pocketed trader dubbed the 'London Whale.' That trader, according to people familiar with the matter, is a low-profile, French-born J.P. Morgan Chase & Co. employee named Bruno Michel Iksil. Mr. Iksil has taken large positions for the bank in insurance-like products called credit-default swaps. Lately, partly in reaction to market movements possibly resulting from Mr. Iksil's trades, some hedge funds and others have made heavy opposing bets, according to people close to the matter. Those investors have been buying default protection on a basket of company bonds using an index of the credit-default swaps. Mr. Iksil has been selling the protection, placing his own bet that the companies won't default. Mr. Iksil, who works primarily out of London, has earned around $100 million a year for the bank's Chief Investment Office, or CIO, in recent years, according to people familiar with the matter. There is no suggestion the bank or the trader acted improperly. Mr. Iksil didn't respond to calls and emails seeking comment.'

The trader, Bruno Iksil, a father of four in his mid-forties, called his wife Karen, who was at their family home near Chartres, 90 kilometres south west of Paris. He was concerned that the 'London Whale' nickname would turn him into a scapegoat. He told her: 'It's bad.' She replied, 'Yes, but it's wrong, so you have nothing to fear.' Iksil said, 'Yes, but it's such bad publicity for the firm. I'm going to be destroyed just for that, just for that. Even if I have nothing to do with that, just because my name is stuck to that.'

Iksil's telephone did not stop ringing for days. His London manager instructed him not to answer: 'If you communicate, they will go after you. They will go after you big time. They will take everything from you. Because you are nothing versus this firm.'

Press articles appeared, including those entitled: 'The Tale of a Whale', 'Making Waves Against the Whale', 'Beached Whale', 'The London Whale's Wake' and 'A Whale of a Story.' Forbes magazine went one better with: 'London Whale Harpooned.'

The Daily Mail spoke to Iksil's sister, Sandrine, who lived in Leicester: 'Bruno rarely talks about his work and if you met him, you would not think he is a trader in the City. He is very quiet and is a family man. He does not own a flash sports car and his main hobby would be cooking. He enjoys being in the kitchen. He certainly has never talked to me about his work. He also insists on getting home each weekend to be with his wife and children. He works from home on Fridays. They are just a normal family.'

Iksil said his ultimate manager Drew telephoned him from New York on 11 April, saying: 'We're all in the same boat, right? We're all in the same boat. Cheer up, man.'

CEO Dimon told analysts on 13 April that the media attention on the big bets taken by one of the bank's traders in London, now known as the 'London Whale', was 'a complete tempest in a teapot.' He boasted of the company's 'fortress balance sheet' but the giant JPM balance sheet would soon suffer an embarrassing breach in its battlements.

On 10 May, JPM revealed a $2 billion trading loss in the London CIO team. The market continued to move. On 11 May, the portfolio suffered a loss of $570 million in a single day. The Federal Bureau of Investigation began a review and the bank received questions from federal prosecutors in New York. JPM began to dismantle the loss-making portfolio. Iksil was fired in July, along with two colleagues in the London CIO team.

Dimon now changed his corporate tune given the calamitous developments: 'The portfolio has proved to be riskier, more volatile and less effective as an economic hedge than we thought. There are many errors, sloppiness and bad judgment. It puts egg on our face and we deserve any criticism we get.'

On Friday 11 May, five weeks after her email to the Operating Committee, Drew resigned, ending her 30-year career at JPM and her $14 million annual compensation.

On the same day, Iksil was safely back home after his usual weekly commute on Eurostar to Paris. The Guardian contacted Iksil by telephone, who refused to say more than: 'I cannot talk about it. You will have to speak to the bank's representatives.'

In June, JPM disclosed CIO losses of $4.4 billion. When the bank released Q2 earnings results on 13 July, the trading loss had climbed to $5.8 billion. By the end of 2012, the final loss was $6.2 billion. But was one fishy trader solely responsible for this loss?

*

Bruno Michel Iksil's family came from Russia before his ancestors settled in France. Iksil was born in 1968 in a middle-class neighbourhood in Paris. His father was an engineering executive and his mother was a chemist. He read Molière, Racine, Sartre and Dostoyevsky. At school, he did well in mathematics, physics and languages.

In 1988, Iksil was among the top 150 students for engineering results in the French higher education exam and he entered the prestigious Ecole Centrale Paris to study Nuclear Chemical Engineering. He graduated in 1992 and then spent one year doing military service. He planned to work in a nuclear chemistry role but then a recession hit.

He took an information technology and risk management role in the Paris office of Transact Control, a hedge fund. He was fascinated by the markets and aspects of trading and progressed quickly. In 1997, he joined French bank Natixis as a bond trader. Three years later, he moved to join asset manager, CDC Ixis, to trade currencies and bonds. Later he re-joined the renamed Natixis Banques Populaires, and traded the more exotic financial products, such as asset-backed securities and credit derivatives.

Iksil lived an hour's train ride from Paris with Karen, who was a teacher, and their children. Iksil grew tired of trading, because of the focus on short-term profits, and he considered leaving banking. 'You have to make money every month, which means you have to follow the crowd, even if the crowd is completely stupid', he said.

In 2005, a friend of a friend at J.P. Morgan Chase in London told him of a role in their equity derivatives proprietary trading desk. Working at a top-tier global investment bank in the financial heart of Europe was an opportunity he could not decline. Leaving France was a difficult decision for the family, but Iksil decided to join JPM.

That summer, he and Karen were married, which would make immigration easier, and they moved to the UK. The Iksil's lived in quiet Kings Langley, 20 miles northwest of central London. His wife did not speak English and she struggled to settle in the UK. In 2007, Karen and their children returned to France. Iksil moved into a rented apartment in unfashionable Earl's Court along with a French friend who worked at Natixis.

Iksil was then considered for an internal role at JPM's Chief Investment Office, a new top-level unit managing risk for the bank as a whole by trading derivatives to hedge against potential losses elsewhere in the bank. The CIO was formerly part of JPM's treasury function but was split out in 2005 to manage the bank's large excess deposits.

Iksil wanted to see the inner workings of a global bank. He told his wife, 'I will be able to say not only was I at J.P. Morgan, but I was working for the guys on the top who were hedging the firm. That was so complementary to my path.' She said: 'OK, fine. Try.'

Ina Drew was the global head of CIO based in New York, and a direct report of Dimon. She was a steely character who exercised a strong grip on her 430 staff, of whom 140 were traders. The London based CIO team was headed by Achilles Macris, a trader with dual

Greek and American citizenship who joined JPM from Dresdner Kleinwort in 2006.

Iksil's direct boss was Javier Martin-Artajo, a Spanish national, who earned $11 million in 2011. The team's junior member was another Frenchman, Julien Grout, who earned $1 million in 2011. Martin-Artajo oversaw Iksil and Grout as they traded. The two other team members were Eric de Sangues and Luis Buraya.

Friends and colleagues described Iksil as 'professorial' and a 'rocket scientist' who obsessed over the minutiae of markets. He liked to do mathematics exercises or play around with Excel spreadsheets in his spare time. Several people described Iksil as naïve and shy and said he was more likely to talk about philosophy than engage in trading-floor banter, and he avoided the party scene often associated with the trader lifestyle.

He rarely wore a suit or a tie to work and preferred black jeans. He was known as a particularly 'discreet' trader, and was 'not a great socialiser', said one colleague, who added: 'His main focus was on work, and seeing his family. He was very single-minded.'

Those who worked with Iksil said he would stress that his role was that of a risk manager, hedging risks in the wider JPM, not a star trader. 'The typical traders, they did not like me', he said. 'They did not like the way I thought. I don't like this Liar's Poker thing, it's totally stupid. But there are guys who love that. And I'm not this kind of guy.'

The Wall Street Journal reported that Iksil was a 'fatherly' character and 'not the sort of trader who drives a Ferrari and wears a Rolex' and he was a family man who takes the train home on the weekends. His Bloomberg profile noted that he was a 'champion of 'kick it", he liked 'walking over water', but he was also 'humble.' He worked in the JPM tower at 25 Bank Street, overlooking Canary Wharf in London's Docklands from Monday to Thursday, before his commute.

The financial markets granted Iksil his nickname. Chatroom messages between brokers and dealers initially referred to 'the big guy' in the market. Later he became known as the 'White Whale' because of the seemingly bottomless pockets of the CIO and his leviathan-sized trades. But the 'London Whale' name stuck, due to his location.

Iksil was well compensated by JPM. A U.S. Senate report stated he earned $6.8 million in 2011. He later confirmed his compensation was indeed in the range of $6 to $7 million a year during his years at the CIO, but he said it consisted mostly of JPM stock awards.

In November 2010, Iksil was promoted to a Managing Director. He was puzzled since his role and responsibilities were unchanged. Iksil was 'directing' no one else and was 'managing' nothing more than when he was a Vice President, when he joined CIO in 2006. He said his boss Martin-Artajo told him: 'At the end of 2011, Eric, Luis and Julien will report to you but get over it. It's a chocolate medal, it doesn't change anything.'

*

CIO's role within JPM was to make investments to balance the risks from other parts of the bank. Theoretically, if a JPM loan to a corporate went bad, CIO's investing would be used to mitigate losses from the bad loan. But as the CIO unit grew over the years, its investment activities became detached from the rest of the bank's operations.

The CIO activities hedged structural risks and it invested to bring the company's asset and liabilities into better alignment. JPM had total deposits of $1.1 trillion and loans of $700 billion, so it had $400 billion of excess cash to invest in a variety of different asset classes. Senior executives stressed to Iksil that the purpose of the CIO was to limit bank losses, not to generate big profits. 'If the trading book makes $500 million because the market rallies and you've not told us, you're fired', Iksil said Macris once told him.

CIO made their bets on a basket of credit-default swaps. They traded in an index of derivatives of 125 companies debt, given the technical name of CDX.NA.IG, short codes for Credit Default Exposure, North America and Investment Grade. This was a derivative that measured the difference in interest rates on investment-grade worthy companies and the benchmark London Interbank Offered Rate (LIBOR) interest rate.

The London CIO team created a special investment portfolio for the index trades called the synthetic credit portfolio, or SCP. Synthetic means that although the portfolio does not contain actual credit exposure, it behaves as if it has credit exposure. The SCP trades were like insurance. Iksil was the trader in charge of the SCP from January 2007.

In 2009, the CIO's synthetic credit portfolio generated $1.05 billion revenue for JPM. Iksil gained a reputation for making contrarian bets that often paid off during market downturns. By 2012, the CIO had a whale of a trading book of $350 billion. 'I was not a typical hedge fund manager that they could squeeze out', Iksil said.

In 2011, Iksil became concerned by mounting losses within the London CIO. In emails and meetings between 2011 and early 2012, he repeatedly tried to alert senior management, including Drew, to the risk that JPM could lose billions of dollars. But he said he was ordered by his senior managers to continue with the oversized trading strategy.

Word began to leak to the market about the activities and huge scale of the CIO. Increasingly, heavy opposing bets to the CIO positions were being made by other traders. By late 2011, Drew finally decided to reduce the CIO's synthetic credit portfolio.

This strategy was not without a large degree of risk. If traders and hedge funds outside JPM learnt of the large unwind and knew that JPM were big sellers, they could bet against the bank, forcing it to take significant losses. Iksil said he advised CIO management that there would be costs to unwind such a large number of trades in such an illiquid market.

The CIO unwound positions in the SCP, but changed tack when that action did lead to losses. Dimon told shareholders this decision to reduce the synthetic credit portfolio in late 2011 was 'flawed, complex, poorly reviewed, poorly executed and poorly monitored.' Drew told traders in the CIO to take a more flexible approach in 2012 and to be more sensitive to the profit-and-loss impact of their trading. The size of the SCP rose exponentially from about $4 billion in notional value at the start of 2011, to $51 billion in notional value at the end of 2011, and up to $157 billion in notional value by early 2012.

CIO's losses grew as Iksil sold and depressed the CDX index price further. The prices CIO received from other market participants were distorted because those with opposing positions (CIO was long where they were short) were engaged in tactical trading. Iksil's warnings gathered pace in early 2012, and he said he was instructed to add to his positions to boost the CDX price to prevent further losses. He told senior managers that the move would 'cost a fortune.'

JPM decided to defend the position they held and to protect their profit and loss. The strategy was so large that it was obvious to investors who saw an opportunity to bet big against JPM, whom they viewed as being exposed and cornered in the market like a rat. Iksil had too much to sell and the hedge funds were not interested in buying. It was like playing a hand of poker but first showing your own cards to the other players.

For four days from 20 January 2012, CIO's portfolio exceeded the bank's value at risk limits. So, JPM temporarily raised its risk limits. On 23 January, the risk management group emailed Dimon to ask for his authority to temporarily raise the bank's overall risk limit. The same email informed Dimon that the CIO 'has developed an improved' risk model that would reduce the CIO's measurement of risk by nearly half. Dimon approved the value at risk model change in a two-word email on 23 January: 'I approve.' The change made the total CIO portfolio, at $375 billion, appear safer than it actually was and gave traders more leeway to make risky bets.

On 27 January, CIO changed its measure of risk, which immediately cut in half the CIO's supposed risk, pushing it back below the bank's limit. This enabled the CIO to triple the size of its portfolio and remain with limits, albeit after some creative and biased risk management changes.

Hedge funds knew that the 'London Whale' was behind the trades and they bet he could not afford to keep protecting his position if they attacked him hard enough. They took larger opposing positions, driving up the SCP's insurance costs, and the SCP's losses ballooned further.

The speculators who likely leaked the original news of the large positions to Bloomberg and The Wall Street Journal in April 2012 had lured the whale out into open waters and were circling the floundering beast with a multitude of harpoons.

*

One of the most important aspects of trading is to price a portfolio of instruments correctly on a daily basis. Pricing financial instruments is known as 'marking to market' and the prices are known as marks. Prices for most traded products are instantly available on trading platforms such as Bloomberg or Reuters. Banks take an end of day feed of the latest prices from these systems and feed the prices into bank systems, thereby delivering fully-automated pricing without the possibility of inappropriate human intervention.

The problems begin when a bank is trading an illiquid instrument, which is one which does not trade very often or when it does so, it trades only in small quantities. So, a market-sourced price may be out of date, perhaps weeks old, or it may not apply if a bank, such as the CIO in JPM, has a large amount to sell where they already have a large share of the market. In these cases, the bank may allow traders to price the instruments.

In the CIO, the junior trader Grout was in charge of marking the portfolio's positions each day. This was a difficult job. Because the market for some instruments was small and illiquid, he generally could not simply look to a single definitive price source. Instead, he collected data from different sources about the value of the positions, such as recently traded prices and current quotes in the market, and after exercising his judgment and often in consultation with another CIO trader, he assigned a value to each position.

Iksil wished to mark the portfolio correctly but his manager did not fully agree with this aspiration. The growing disconnect between Iksil and Martin-Artajo was obvious when Iksil called Grout on 16 March and said on the recorded telephone line: 'I can't keep this going, we do a one-off at the end of the month to remain calm. I don't know where he wants to stop, but it's getting idiotic. Now it's worse than before. There's nothing that can be done, absolutely nothing that can be done, there's no hope. The book continues to grow more and more monstrous.'

On 20 March, Martin-Artajo reacted angrily after he received news that Iksil had reported a single-day loss of $40 million to senior management. Iksil had decided to mark down the prices, which led to the loss. In a recorded telephone call, his boss asked Iksil: 'Why did you do that?' Iksil replied, 'I thought we should, you know, not do like minus five basis points every day but just say okay, boom, you know there is something happening.'

Martin-Artajo said: 'I don't understand your logic, mate, I just don't understand. I told my boss, he told me that he didn't want to show the loss until we know what we are going to do tomorrow. But it doesn't matter I know that you have a problem, you want to be at peace with yourself. I didn't want to show the P&L and my boss told me yesterday not to do it. So okay, we're just going to have to explain that this is getting worse.'

Iksil told his manager he had described the timing lag in profit and loss between the real and marked prices as being $800 million. Martin Artajo responded: 'You're losing your mind here, man, you're sending an email that you would get, what is this 800 million bucks? This is just what we explain tomorrow, you don't need to explain in an email man.'

On 23 March, Iksil told Martin-Artajo that the SCP losses on that day were between $300 million and $600 million. In electronic instant messages which were later retrieved, Iksil asked Grout to ask Martin-Artajo what level of losses to report for the day.

Iksil concluded by saying that he no longer knew what marks to use: 'It is over, it is hopeless now. I tell you; they are going to trash, destroy us. Tonight, you'll have at least 600m, bid ask, mid, bid ask, you have 300m at least. It is everywhere, all over the place. We are dead I tell you.'

The junior trader Grout replied: 'Will you give me the colour please? If there is some.'

Iksil wrote: 'Nothing for now. It will be negotiated with the investment bank at the top and I am going to be hauled over the coals. You don't lose 500m without consequences. Ask Javier what profit and loss we print today, please, go see Javier. I don't know which profit and loss I should send.'

Grout later asked Iksil: 'Did you talk to Javier?'

Iksil replied: 'Yes. We show minus three basis points until month end on this one. All that I am asking you is to tell Javier what you see. That's it and he decides what we show. Because me, I don't know anymore.'

Despite the emails predicting losses of between $300 million and $600 million on 23 March, the CIO reported internally in JPM a daily loss of only $12.5 million.

Iksil messaged a colleague at JPM who was not part of the CIO later that day: 'Btw we take a big hit today, across the board, right where we have a position. Well, it is not the end of the world but the end of what I have done so far, for sure, I cannot fight, I cannot wait, I cannot argue, I may not come back on Monday. I will know this afternoon.'

Iksil messaged that the problem was the CIO positions were too big. He saw that he was no longer part of the market. He had become the market: 'It had to happen. It started back in 2008 you see. I survived pretty well until I was alone to be the target. Yes, I mean the guys know my position because I am too big for the market. But here is the loss and it becomes too large and this is it. We realise that I am too visible.'

Grout became so confused by the conflicting instructions from Martin-Artajo to show no losses, and from Iksil to show the losses, that he did both, with disastrous consequences. He reported the more optimistic numbers in the SCP book but also kept a spreadsheet of the real numbers on the side showing how far apart the two prices were. This spreadsheet was later discovered by the regulators, which did not help

JPM's cause. It was like the mafia keeping one set of books for the tax man and one set of real books.

At the quarter-end in March 2012, Iksil reported to Martin-Artajo a $200 million loss for the day. Martin-Artajo told Iksil that he could leave work for the day and he himself managed to get the loss down to $138 million. The total mis-marking of the portfolio as at 30 March, was $718 million, according to a later JPM investigation.

A full-blown crisis now erupted in the CIO as Drew ordered Martin-Artajo and Iksil to 'put the phones down' and to stop trading credit derivatives in the SCP book. The book was instantly frozen but it continued to incur losses as the prices moved against JPM. When news of the losses went public, Drew penned her 5 April email to management. Heads rolled shortly, Drew resigned and all hell broke loose inside JPM.

*

JPM issued a task force report in January 2013, which focused on what happened, how it happened and what remedial measures were needed. The names of London individuals were excluded to comply with UK data privacy laws. Iksil was not named in the report.

The task force report found five failings. CIO's judgment, execution and escalation of issues in the first quarter of 2012 were poor. The firm did not ensure that the controls and oversight of CIO evolved with the increased complexity and risks of CIO's activities. CIO Risk Management lacked the personnel and structure necessary to manage the risks of the Synthetic Credit Portfolio. The risk limits applicable to the CIO were not sufficiently granular. Approval and implementation of the new CIO value at risk model for the SCP in late January 2012 were flawed.

Later, the U.S. Senate Permanent Subcommittee on Investigations opened its hearing on the events in March 2013. Drew, the former head of the CIO, stared down the committee, with bleached hair and wearing a powder blue suit, and said she believed her oversight of the SCP was 'reasonable and diligent' and that she 'naturally relied heavily' on the views of Macris and Martin-Artajo in her decision-making around the portfolio.

The JPM employees located in London, Macris, Martin-Artajo, Iksil and Grout, all declined the Subcommittee's requests for interviews and because they resided outside of the U.S., they were beyond the Subcommittee's subpoena authority. The Senate 1,317-page summary of the public hearings named Iksil 667 times. Most of the mentions related to transcripts of instant messages and emails which he had sent, warning management of the growing disaster in the CIO, and which did not prove incriminatory on his part.

The U.S. Department of Justice investigated the loss in conjunction with the Financial Fraud Enforcement Task Force and the Federal Bureau of Investigation. The DoJ found Iksil had urged his colleagues to disclose the true size of the CIO losses, but junior trader Grout, at the instruction of their boss Martin-Artajo, continued to hide the losses. Iksil became safe from harm when he signed a non-prosecution deal with the DoJ.

Criminal charges against Martin-Artajo and Grout came to a halt in 2017 when the DoJ said it no longer believed that it could rely on the testimony of Iksil, based on statements he made.

CEO Dimon made mistakes: 'The CIO, particularly the Synthetic Credit Portfolio, should have gotten more scrutiny from both senior management, and I include myself in that, and the firm-wide risk control function. Make sure that people on risk committees are always asking questions, sharing information, and that you have very, very granular limits when you're taking risk. In the rest of the company, we have those disciplines in place. We didn't have it here. These were egregious mistakes. They were self-inflicted, we were accountable and what happened violates our own standards and principles by how we want to operate the company. This is not how we want to run a business.'

Dimon blundered unusually in this instance. He wrote off a tempest too early. 'These problems were our fault, and it is our job to fix them. In fact, I feel terrible that we let our regulators down. The 'London Whale' was the stupidest and most embarrassing situation I have ever been a part of', he wrote in his annual letter to JPM shareholders.

In September 2013, JPM paid a $920 million regulatory settlement, for serious failings, misstating financial results and lacking effective internal controls to detect and prevent its traders from fraudulently overvaluing investments. The fine represented only 13 days of the annual profits of JPM.

Iksil's only blunder was in not leaving JPM sooner. If you work in a bank and see your colleagues, manager and managers manager being unethical and mismarking positions to hide losses which deceive shareholders and regulators, then you must act. Iksil should have walked out of JPM in 2011 and filed a protected disclosure with the regulatory authorities to protect himself but to expose others to the full rigours of the law. But perhaps walking away from a $7 million annual compensation package is not easy.

*

Iksil has publicly presented his version of the events on three occasions. The first was when he resurfaced from the depths in 2016. Frustrated by references to him and the 'London Whale' tag, he penned a 2,100-word undated, unaddressed, densely-written, closely-typed and confusing letter to the media at large.

He wrote he was a scapegoat for decisions taken by superiors and that he was instructed repeatedly by management in the bank's CIO to execute the trading strategy that caused the losses. 'The losses suffered by the CIO were not the actions of one person acting in an unauthorised manner', Iksil concluded.

There was a whiff of conspiracy theory about his letter. He complained that media reporting was defamatory and he requested the media outlets to stop naming him as the 'London Whale.' In truth, he should have asked his lawyer to write a better letter.

The second public occasion was in April 2017, when he was interviewed by the Financial News London website. He declined to be photographed for the interview or to allow the journalist to speak to his wife. Iksil said he had spent the past five years with his family at his rural home in France. He ran, cycled or swam each day, played card games with his children and helped them with their homework.

Iksil had not worked since his dismissal. The bank

clawed back 80 percent of his earnings over the seven years he worked there, but given his compensation in the good years, money was unlikely to be a problem, although the damage to his career was terminal.

In the interview, he spoke about the end of this time at the CIO. 'I was public enemy No. 1. Everyone, every single authority, everyone, I think, reading the press articles, wanted to behead me or destroy me or smash me. I have to retrieve my reputation, my intellectual property and, simply, my life. So far, all of this has been stolen', Iksil complained.

The third public occasion was when Iksil placed the draft manuscript of his book on his personal website: https://londonwhalemarionet.monsite-orange.fr/.

A marionette is a specific kind of puppet, one that is operated with sticks and wires or strings that move its arms, legs, and head in a nearly lifelike way. One sees how Iksil views his CIO role.

His book is titled 'Confidential Impunity.' The manuscript is a gigantic work at 369 pages and 150,000 words, and it is a visual eyesore, with different typefaces and font sizes, much bolding and underlining, brightly coloured text and rhetorical questions.

Despite having a contents page, it is a disorganised random collection of manic thoughts, cut and paste emails, and extracts from the U.S Senate hearings, the JPM task force report and regulatory reports. It is highly repetitive, for example he mentions his 'chocolate medal' promotion no less than nineteen times. If he had more time, he surely could have written a shorter more digestible work of non-fiction.

The manuscript is unreadable. It may be because English is not Iksil's first language and the work has been lost in translation but it is likely the result of the complex thought processes of the always professorial Iksil. Iksil has tried to secure a publishing contract for his book for years without any success. It's not difficult to see why.

Iksil makes no apology: 'Many readers will find the text dense and at times difficult to grasp. I apologise for that. What makes it difficult is not the underlying trading and banking universe that is pictured in the background. The real challenge is that this case is just a series of smoke and mirrors.'

No criminal or civil charges were ever brought against Iksil in the UK or the U.S. He is innocent until anyone proves him guilty of anything. In fact, the U.S. authorities described Iksil in August 2013 as a 'voice of reason who did sound the alarm more than once.' But the 'London Whale' nickname will follow Iksil for the rest of his days.

He said many people have told him to move on with his life, but he said this is impossible. His reason for continuing to seek a publisher for his book is simple: 'I've been waiting now for years. I think it's time to say the things. The truth has to be told. I have to fight. I have no choice. I have to make people aware of what really happened.'

*

THE ROGUES GALLERY

False Profits

'After what has been done to me there is no room for truth. They've depicted me as a despicable character. The words have been twisted, and the truth turned merrily on its head.'

Joseph Jett, Kidder, Peabody & Co. Inc.

The King of SIMEX

'I'm sorry for what I did but I'm not going to walk around with my head hung in shame for the rest of my life and so anybody expecting that will be disappointed.'

Nick Leeson, Baring Futures (Singapore) Pte.

The Confession

'Once you've stepped in to rogue trading, it's like quicksand.'

Toshihide Iguchi, Daiwa Bank Ltd.

Sex in the City

'The investors knew that they were buying risky funds. People believe in gurus. As long as there is success, they don't want to face reality in order not to destroy their illusions.'

Peter Young, Deutsche Morgan Grenfell.

A Pillar of the Community

'Unfortunately, God is still working on me. For me, we're on God's timetable, not mine.'

John Rusnak, Allfirst Financial Inc.

The Subprime Villain

'We have a view that, this time, we can help.'

Howie Hubler, Morgan Stanley.

The Outsider

'I was a jerk at the time and I am going to spend the rest of my life testifying to that.'

Jérôme Kerviel, Société Générale.

The Bridge Bum

'Bridge is what I do a lot, and when the weather permits, I play a lot of golf.'

James Cayne, The Bear Stearns Companies, Inc.

The Gorilla of Wall Street

'I am the ugliest man in America right now.'

Richard Fuld, Lehman Brothers Holdings Inc.

Fred the Shred

'This would not have been the manner or circumstances I would have chosen. You know, it's more like a drive-by shooting than a negotiation.'

Sir Fred Goodwin, Royal Bank of Scotland.

A Giant of a Man

'We have arrived, and we ain't going anywhere.'

Sean FitzPatrick, Anglo Irish Bank Corporation.

The Playboy of Tema

'It's good to be home.'

Kweku Adoboli, Union Bank of Switzerland AG.

The London Whale

'The truth has to be told. I have to fight. I have no choice. I have to make people aware of what really happened.'

Bruno Iksil, J.P. Morgan Chase & Co.

ACKNOWLEDGEMENTS

I must first acknowledge that the idea for the format of this book came when reading 'Military Blunders' by Saul David, where the author recounts the greatest disasters of the battlefield. The tales range from the English cavalry officer in the Crimea War in 1854 pointing vaguely in the direction of the Russians at Balaclava, and saying: 'There are your guns', to the Allied troops speeding northwards in their tanks to Arnhem in 1944, only to find they were heading to a bridge too far. In accessible bite-size chapters, David recalls the events with great characters, plot development, twists and turns and a satisfying, if disastrous, conclusion. I set out to replicate this approach with the greatest banking disasters of all time, and the people who made the blunders.

I wish to acknowledge the different news sources used when writing this book. These include financial websites such as Bloomberg, Reuters, The Financial Times, Fortune, CNBC & Forbes.

For the chapters set on Wall Street, the websites of The Wall Street Journal, The New York Times, the New York Post, The Washington Post, the New Yorker Magazine, TIME, Salon and Vanity Fair were essential.

For the chapters set in other cities, I researched websites such as the Baltimore Sun, the Scotsman, the Irish Independent and the Irish Times.

Other helpful websites were those of the Guardian, the Daily Mail, the BBC & CNN.

A list of the top news sources used for each chapter is included in this book.

I welcome feedback from readers, which can be sent to pwgkpwgk@gmail.com. Or please contact me via LinkedIn.

Paul Kilduff
Dublin
August 2022

References

Chapter 1 – False Profits – Joseph Jett, Kidder, Peabody & Co. Inc.

'Kidder Reports Fraud and Ousts a Top Trader.' The New York Times, 18 April 1994.

'G.E. Shaken by Phantom Trades at Kidder Unit.' The New York Times, 19 April 1994.

'Fallen Bond Trader Sees Himself As an Outsider and a Scapegoat.' The New York Times, 5 June 1994.

'Jett's Supervisor at Kidder Breaks Silence.' The New York Times, 26 July 1994.

'Timeline of Events in the Kidder Trading Scandal.' AP News, 5 August 1994.

'Kidder Scandal Tied to Failure Of Supervision.' The New York Times, 5 August 1994.

'How Profit Was Created on Paper.' The New York Times, 5 August 1994.

'Jack Welch's Nightmare on Wall Street.' CNN, 5 September 1994.

'A Scoundrel or a Scapegoat?' The New York Times, 6 April 1997.

'Former Kidder Trader Fined.' The Washington Post, 22 July 1998.

'The Othello of Kidder Peabody Spins His Side of the Story.' Observer, 5 April 1999.

'Wall Street Lynching.' Salon magazine, 27 May 1999.

'Ex-Street big snared in domestic, SEC battles.' New York Post, 24 February 2010.

'Where is Joseph Jett now?' France News 24, 10 March 2010.

Chapter 2 - The King of SIMEX - Nick Leeson, Baring Futures (Singapore) Pte.

'How account 88888 sank Britain's oldest bank.' The Independent, 16 February 1996.

'The man who broke the Queen's bank.' Irish Times, 24 February 1996.

'Leeson to have cancer operation.' BBC News, 8 August 1998.

'How Leeson broke the bank.' BBC News, 22 June 1999.

'Rogue trader Nick Leeson: 'I wanted to kill myself.'' CNN, 24 April 2013.

'An audience with Nick Leeson.' Financial News London, 27 February 2018.

'Nick Leeson tells of 'bonkers' trip to evade law.' Irish Independent, 20 August 2018.

'Rogue trader Nick Leeson is back in business.' Irish

Times, 6 February 2020.

Chapter 3 - The Confession - Toshihide Iguchi, Daiwa Bank Ltd.

'Japanese bank says bond trader lost $1.1 billion.' The Washington Post, 26 September 1995.

'U.S. holds trader in bank's big loss.' The New York Times, 27 September 1995.

'An unusual path to big-time trading.' The New York Times, 27 September 1995.

'A Blown Billion.' TIME, 9 October 1995.

'Japanese bank is indicted in U.S. and barred.' The New York Times, 3 November 1995.

'Booting out the Bank.' TIME, 13 November 1995.

'Prison Confession: I didn't set out to rob a bank.' TIME, 10 February 1997.

'Rogue traders who went off the rails.' Financial Times, 24 January 2009.

'I'm not a criminal: Daiwa rogue trader who lost $1.1 billion.' CNBC, 29 April 2014.

Chapter 4 - Sex in the City - Peter Young, Deutsche Morgan Grenfell.

'Gents Behaving Oddly.' The Guardian, 12 September 1996.

'We sawed off the bad apple.' Der Spiegel, 15 September 1996.

'Britain expected to open probe of fund manager.' The Wall Street Journal, 27 September 1996.

'UK launches investigation of former DMG fund manager.' The Wall Street Journal, 30 September 1996.

'Former fund manager Peter Young appears in court on fraud charges and wears a dress.' Reuters, 10 November 1998.

'Accused man puts his best dress on for court.' Bucks Free Press, 14 November 1998.

'UK fund manager faces fraud trial.' BBC News, 30 April 1999.

'Ex-Stock Picker, Sued for Fraud, Turns Heads With Lipstick, Heels.' The Wall Street Journal, 24 May 1999.

'Fraud case fund boss unfit to stand trial.' The Guardian, 16 December 2000.

'Crossdresser's wife tells of trauma for her children.' Bucks Free Press, 19 December 2000.

'City high flyer who heard voices urging him to change sex.' The Guardian, 25 January 2002.

'The accidental money manager.' Institutional Investor, 30 April 2002.

Chapter 5 - A Pillar of the Community - John Rusnak, Allfirst Financial Inc.

'Hunt for trader after £500 million goes missing.' Daily Mail, 6 February 2002.

'Trader Is Said to Have Defrauded Irish Bank of $750 Million.' The New York Times, 6 February 2002.

'Bank hunts trader in fraud probe.' CNN, 6 February 2002.

'Rogue trader 'Mr. Middle America." BBC News, 7 February 2002.

'Trader a 'churchgoing family man." CNN, 7 February 2002.

'AIB loss stands at $691 million.' CNN, 20 February 2002.

'In prison, rogue trader pursues humility.' Baltimore Sun, 5 March 2005.

'Seeking Redemption After a $750 Million Mistake.' Inc. Magazine, 10 February 2014.

'Convicted Allfirst trader seeks redemption hiring others.' Baltimore Sun, 12 April 2014.

'Clean living: The man who cost AIB $691 Million.' Irish Times, 12 September 2014.

Chapter 6 - The Subprime Villain - Howie Hubler, Morgan Stanley.

'Morgan Stanley becomes latest victim of subprime meltdown.' ABC News, 20 December 2007.

'Only the Men Survive.' New York Magazine, 25 April 2008.

'Morgan Stanley Tries on a New Psyche.' The New York Times, 16 January 2010.

'Howie Hubler of New Jersey: The Return of a Subprime Villain.' The New York Observer, 24 March 2010.

'Betting on the Blind Side.' Vanity Fair, 1 March 2010.

'After $9 Billion Loss, Trader Revives Career.' The Wall Street Journal, 13 September 2010.

'Top 10 Biggest Trading Losses in History.' TIME, 11 May 2012.

'Notorious 'subprime villain' Howie Hubler unloading Rumson estate for $4.5M.' New Jersey News, 10 May 2016.

Chapter 7 - The Outsider - Jérôme Kerviel, Société Générale.

'Six sleepless nights reveal full impact of scandal.' Financial Times, 24 January 2008.

'Paris neighbours express shock and dismay.' Financial Times, 25 January 2008.

'French Trader Is Remembered as Mr. Average.' The New York Times, 26 January 2008.

'SocGen unravels 'exceptional fraud."' Financial Times, 28 January 2008.

'From rogue trader to Robin Hood: Why Jerome Kerviel is a national hero in France.' Daily Mail, 1 February 2008.

'Kerviel: 'I will not be made a scapegoat."' Financial Times, 5 February 2008.

'The Omen - How an obscure Breton trader gamed oversight weaknesses in the banking system.' The New Yorker, 20 October 2008.

'I was merely a small cog in the machine.' Der Spiegel, 16 November 2010.

'Jérôme Kerviel's long walk to captivity.' Financial Times, 9 May 2014.

'French 'rogue trader' Kerviel released from prison.' France News 24, 8 September 2014.

Chapter 8 - The Bridge Bum - James Cayne, The Bear Stearns Companies, Inc.

'Careful Player Moves Closer to the Top at Bear Stearns.' The Wall Street Journal, 14 July 1993.

'Private Sector; Call Him a Specialist in Bridge Financing.' The New York Times, 24 March 2002.

'Distinct Culture at Bear Stearns Helps It Surmount a Grim Market.' The Wall Street Journal, 28 March 2003.

'The Forbes 400 - The Richest People in America.' Forbes Magazine, 2005.

'Bear CEO's Handling of Crisis Raises Issues.' The Wall Street Journal, 1 November 2007.

'Bringing Down Bear Stearns.' Vanity Fair, 30 June 2008.

'The rise and fall of Jimmy Cayne.' CNN, 25 August 2008.

'25 People to Blame for the Financial Crisis.' TIME, 11 February 2009.

'Former Bear Stearns chief James Cayne dies.' Financial Times, 29 December 2021.

'The Card Shark: Jimmy Cayne and the Wars of Old Wall Street.' Puck, 5 January 2022.

Chapter 9 - The Gorilla of Wall Street - Richard Fuld, Lehman Brothers Holdings Inc.

'The Improbable Power Broker - How Dick Fuld transformed Lehman from Wall Street also-ran to super-hot machine.' Fortune, 13 April 2006.

'The Survivor.' The New York Times, 28 October 2007.

'Bleeding Green: The Fall of Fuld.' ABC News, 3 October 2008.

'Lehman Brothers Boss Defends $484 Million in Salary, Bonus.' ABC News, 6 October 2008.

'Richard Fuld punched in face in Lehman Brothers gym.' Daily Telegraph, 7 October 2008.

'Burning Down His House.' New York Magazine, 30

November 2008.

'Lehman's Desperate Housewives.' Vanity Fair, 1 March 2010.

'Unrepentant Dick Fuld blames Washington for Lehman collapse.' Financial Times, 28 May 2015.

'Inside the Sun Valley estate of ex-Lehman CEO Richard Fuld.' CNN, 9 July 2015.

'Dick Fuld makes quiet comeback on Wall Street.' Financial Times, 6 November 2017.

'Florida seaside mansion of Lehman Brothers' last CEO sells for $32.5 million.' New York Post, 18 May 2021.

Chapter 10 - Fred the Shred - Sir Fred Goodwin, Royal Bank of Scotland.

'Brisk and brusque.' Forbes Magazine, 6 January 2003.

'Prufrock: Aroma at the top for Fred's scallops.' Sunday Times, 14 March 2004.

'Queen opens £350 million bank HQ.' The Scotsman, 14 September 2005.

'Sir Fred Goodwin shredded by ABN takeover.' The Daily Telegraph, 12 October 2008.

'The World's Worst Banker.' Newsweek, 1 December 2008.

'Treasury Select Committee: Bonfire of the Bankers.' The Independent, 11 February 2009.

'Fred 'The Shred' Goodwin returns home, determined to rebuild his fortune.' Daily Mail, 14 November 2009.

'Sir Fred Goodwin: the life and times of a modern capitalist.' The Guardian, 19 January 2012.

'Goodwin Knighthood decision.' UK Cabinet Office, 31 January 2012.

'How Fred the Shred made grown men cry.' Daily Mail, 19 September 2013.

'Meat pies at midnight, a £20 million private jet and top bankers made to pull up weeds. How Fred the Shred lived in the lap of luxury and fostered a culture of fear.' The Scottish Mail on Sunday, 1 June 2014.

'Ex-RBS Chief, a Symbol of British Banking Excess, Retires to Life in Scotland.' Wall Street Journal, 7 July 2018.

Chapter 11 - A Giant of a Man - Sean FitzPatrick, Anglo Irish Bank Corporation Ltd.

'Marian Finucane Show', RTE Radio, 4 October 2008.

'Irish stand united in hatred of banker Sean FitzPatrick.' USA Today, 28 January 2009.

'Implosion of a legend in his own lunchtime.' Irish Independent, 21 March 2010.

'The chancer who ran amok.' Irish Independent, 21 March 2010.

'Bankruptcy hasn't curbed luxury lifestyle of 'outsider' Sean FitzPatrick', Irish Independent, 25 July 2012.

'Former Anglo Irish bank chief Sean FitzPatrick dies.' Irish Times, 9 November 2021.

'Sean FitzPatrick timeline: from a dairy farmer's son to Anglo chief.' Irish Times, 9 November 2021.

'Sean FitzPatrick: The controversial Anglo Irish banker emblematic of Celtic Tiger Ireland has died aged 73.' Irish Independent, 9 November 2021.

'Sean FitzPatrick, banker, 1948-2021.' Financial Times, 12 November 2021.

'Sean FitzPatrick obituary: Poster boy banker who became a toxic figure.' Irish Times, 13 November 2021.

'Sean FitzPatrick funeral: a traditional send-off for a dearly loved family man.' Irish Times, 16 November 2021.

Chapter 12 - The Playboy of Tema - Kweku Adoboli, Union Bank of Switzerland Group AG.

'UBS star trader's arrest brought rapid career rise to a halt.' The Guardian, 15 September 2011.

'Rogue trader's £1,000-a-week apartment - the size of an art gallery.' Daily Mail, 18 September 2011.

'Transcript of UBS trader's 'bombshell email.' Financial Times, 14 September 2012.

'UBS rogue trader Kweku Adoboli jailed over UK's biggest fraud.' The Guardian, 20 November 2012.

'UBS rogue trader Kweku Adoboli's last telephone call with bosses.' The Guardian, 20 November 2012.

'Hi Kweku, we need to clarify these exposures.' Financial Times, 20 November 2012.

'Rise and fall of Adoboli the 'family' man.' Financial Times, 20 November 2012.

'How public school head boy driven by 'lust for wealth' committed UK's biggest-ever banking fraud.' Daily Mail, 20 November 2012.

'Kweku Adoboli: portrait of a gambling addict.' London Evening Standard, 20 November 2012.

'UBS fined £30 million over rogue trader.' The Guardian, 26 November 2012.

'Kweku Adoboli: a rogue trader's tale.' Financial

Times, 22 October 2015.

'UBS rogue trader: 'It could happen again.'' BBC News, 1 August 2016.

'Kweku Adoboli: Banking broke me - but I deserve a second chance.' London Evening Standard, 28 August 2018.

'Former banker transported to London from Edinburgh for deportation.' Edinburgh Evening News, 14 September 2018.

'My time in an immigration detention centre nearly destroyed my humanity.' The Guardian, 11 October 2018.

'Kweku Adoboli deported to Ghana on flight from Heathrow.' The Guardian, 14 November 2018.

'One-On-One With Former UBS Banker, Adoboli.' Ghana Joy News, 20 November 2018.

'Deported rogue trader: 'The Home Office destroys lives.'' The Guardian, 26 November 2018.

Chapter 13 - The London Whale - Bruno Iksil, J.P. Morgan Chase & Co.

''London Whale' Rattles Debt Market.' The Wall Street Journal, 6 April 2012.

'Boss of Voldemort trader who lost $2 billion at J.P. Morgan earns $14 million a year.' Daily Mail, 11 May 2012.

'J.P. Morgan's 'whale' causes a splash.' Financial Times, 11 May 2012.

'The City trader who lost $2 billion.' The Independent, 12 May 2012.

'From 'Caveman' to 'Whale.' The Wall Street Journal, 17 May 2012.

'Will the London Whale Swallow Jamie Dimon?' The New Yorker, 15 March 2013.

'Prosecutors strike unusual deal with 'London Whale.' Financial Times, 14 August 2013.

"London Whale' Breaks Silence.' The Wall Street Journal, 22 February 2016.

'London Whale complains of unfair blame for $6.2 billion J.P. Morgan losses.' Financial Times, 23 February 2016.

'The 'London Whale' trader lost $6.2 billion, but he may walk off scot-free.' The Washington Post, 13 April 2017.

'The London Whale resurfaces: Bruno Iksil speaks out.' Financial News London, 17 April 2017.

*

FURTHER READING

Chapter 1 - False Profits - Joseph Jett, Kidder, Peabody & Co. Inc.

Black and White on Wall Street: The Untold Story of the Man Wrongly Accused of Bringing Down Kidder Peabody, Joseph Jett with Sabra Chartrand (William Morrow & Co., 1999).

Report of Inquiry into False Trading Profits at Kidder, Peabody & Co. Incorporated (Davis Polk & Wardwell, 1994).

U.S. Securities & Exchange Commission – Opinion in the matter of Orlando Joseph Jett, 61 East Eighth St., New York, NY 100035, (5 March 2004).

Chapter 2 - The King of SIMEX - Nick Leeson, Baring Futures (Singapore) Pte.

Stephen Fay, The Collapse of Barings - Panic, Ignorance and Greed (Arrow Books, 1996).

John Gapper and Nicholas Denton, All That Glitters – The Fall of Barings (Penguin, 1996).

Nick Leeson, Rogue Trader (Little, Brown & Company, 1996).

Judith Rawnsley, Going for Broke - Nick Leeson and the Collapse of Barings Bank (Harper Collins, 1995).

Board of Banking Supervision, Report of the Inquiry into the Circumstances of the Collapse of Barings (Her Majesty's Stationery Office, 1995).

Chapter 3 - The Confession - Toshihide Iguchi, Daiwa Bank Ltd.

Toshihide Iguchi, My Billion Dollar Education - Inside the Mind of a Rogue Trader (2014).

United States District Court, Southern District of New York, United States of America v. Daiwa Bank Ltd., Indictment – Conspiracy to Defraud the Federal Reserve Board (1995).

Chapter 4 - Sex in the City - Peter Young, Deutsche Morgan Grenfell.

Werner Plumpe, Alexander Nützenadel, Catherine Schenk, Deutsche Bank: The Global Hausbank, 1870 – 2020 (Bloomsbury Publishing, 2020).

Chapter 5 - A Pillar of the Community - John Rusnak, Allfirst Financial Inc.

Siobhan Creaton & Conor O'Clery, Panic at the Bank (Gill & Macmillan, 2002).

Promontory Financial Group and Wachtell, Lipton, Rosen & Katz, Report to the Boards of Directors of Allied Irish Banks, P.L.C., Allfirst Financial Inc., and Allfirst Bank concerning Currency Trading Losses (2002).

United States District Court, District of Maryland, United States of America v. John M. Rusnak, Indictment (2002).

Chapter 6 - The Subprime Villain - Howie Hubler, Morgan Stanley.

Michael Lewis, The Big Short – Inside the Doomsday Machine (Norton, 2010).

Chapter 7 - The Outsider - Jérôme Kerviel, Société Générale.

Jérôme Kerviel, L'Engrenage - Mémoires d'un trader

(Flammarion, 2010).

Pierre-Antoine Delhommais, Cinq Milliards en fumée. Les dessous du scandale de la Société Générale (Seuil, 2008).

Chapter 8 - The Bridge Bum - James Cayne, The Bear Stearns Companies, Inc.

William D. Cohan, House of Cards: A Tale of Hubris and Wretched Excess on Wall Street (Doubleday, 2009).

Kate Kelly, Street Fighters: The Last 72 Hours of Bear Stearns, the Toughest Firm on Wall Street (Portfolio, 2010).

Alan C. Greenberg, The Rise and Fall of Bear Stearns (Simon & Schuster, 2010).

United States Congress, Final Report of the National Commission on the Causes of the Financial and Economic Crisis in the United States (2011).

Chapter 9 - The Gorilla of Wall Street - Richard Fuld, Lehman Brothers Holdings Inc.

Ken Auletta, Greed and Glory on Wall Street - The Fall of the House of Lehman (Warner Books, 1987).

Lawrence McDonald, A Colossal Failure of Common Sense - The Incredible Inside Story of the Collapse of Lehman Brothers (Ebury Press, 2009).

Andrew Ross Sorkin, Too Big to Fail - Inside the Battle to Save Wall Street (Penguin, 2009).

Chapter 10 - Fred the Shred - Sir Fred Goodwin, Royal Bank of Scotland.

Iain Martin, Making It Happen - Fred Goodwin, RBS and the Men who blew up the British Economy (Simon & Schuster, 2013).

Ian Fraser, Shredded - Inside RBS, the Bank That Broke Britain (Birlinn, 2014).

House of Commons, Minutes of Evidence taken before Treasury Committee - Sir Fred Goodwin, Sir Tom McKillop, Mr. Andy Hornby and Lord Stevenson of Coddenham (2009).

Chapter 11 - A Giant of a Man - Sean FitzPatrick, Anglo Irish Bank Corporation Ltd.

Shane Ross, The Bankers – How the Banks brought Ireland to its knees (Penguin, 2009).

Simon Carswell, Anglo Republic – Inside the Bank that broke Ireland (Penguin, 2013).

Chapter 12 - The Playboy of Tema - Kweku Adoboli, Union Bank of Switzerland Group AG.

Sebastian Borger, Verzockt, Kweku Adoboli und die UBS (Stämpfli Verlag, 2013).

Sentencing remarks of Mr. Justice Keith, R-v Kweku Adoboli. Judiciary of England and Wales (2012).

Chapter 13 - The London Whale - Bruno Iksil, J.P. Morgan Chase & Co.

Hearing before the Permanent Subcommittee on Investigations of the Committee on Homeland Security and Governmental Affairs, United States Senate – J.P. Morgan Chase Whale Trades - A Case History of Derivatives Risks and Abuses (2013).

J.P. Morgan Chase & Co - Report of J.P. Morgan Chase & Co. Management Task Force Regarding 2012 CIO Losses (2013).

*

Coming in 2024 ... from Paul Kilduff

Greedy Bankers

The world's worst banking crooks revealed

Printed in Great Britain
by Amazon